THE POEMS OF
PATRICK BRANWELL BRONTË

The Poems of
Patrick Branwell Brontë

A NEW ANNOTATED AND ENLARGED EDITION
OF THE SHAKESPEARE HEAD BRONTË

Edited by Tom Winnifrith

PUBLISHED FOR THE SHAKESPEARE HEAD PRESS
BY BASIL BLACKWELL

THIS EDITION © TOM WINNIFRITH
AND THE SHAKESPEARE HEAD PRESS 1983

FIRST PUBLISHED 1983
BASIL BLACKWELL PUBLISHER LIMITED
108 COWLEY ROAD, OXFORD OX4 1JF, ENGLAND

All rights reserved. No part of this publication may
be reproduced, stored in a retrieval system, or
transmitted, in any form or by any means, electronic,
mechanical, photocopying, recording or otherwise,
without the prior permission of the publisher.

British Library Cataloguing in Publication Data

Brontë, Branwell
    The poems of Branwell Brontë.
    I. Title   II. Winnifrith, Tom
    821'.8   PR4174.B23
    ISBN 0-631-12553-1

HERTFORDSHIRE
LIBRARY SERVICE

821|BRo

1429128

2 4 OCT 1983

TYPESET BY GLOUCESTER TYPESETTING SERVICES
PRINTED IN GREAT BRITAIN
BY T. J. PRESS LTD, PADSTOW

CONTENTS

ACKNOWLEDGEMENTS

I WOULD like to acknowledge a generous grant from the British Academy which enabled me to examine Brontë manuscripts in America. The University of Warwick gave me a term's sabbatical leave to complete my work. I have to thank the librarians of the Berg Collection in the New York Public Library, the British Library, the Brontë Parsonage Museum, the Brotherton Collection in the University of Leeds, the Houghton Library in Harvard University, the Pierpont Morgan Library, New York, the National Library of Scotland, and the Humanities Research Centre in the University of Texas, for access to and permission to quote from the manuscripts in their collections. I am also indebted for various kinds of help to Dr Christine Alexander, Mr Allan Boiton, Mrs Mary Butterfield, Mr Edward Chitham, Mrs Elizabeth Greenwood, Miss Agnes Hatfield, Miss Nicola Harris, Mr and Mrs Tony Hutton, Professor and Mrs George Hunter, Miss Heather Maclean, Mr David Martin, Mr Andrew Nicholson, Professor Victor Neufeldt, Miss Jill Willder, and Mrs Christine Wyman. I would like to dedicate this book to my students, past and present, at the University of Warwick, who have kept alive by their enthusiasm my interest in the Brontës.

GENERAL INTRODUCTION

THE Shakespeare Head Brontë is in more senses than one a monument to Brontë scholarship. Even after fifty years its nineteen lavishly produced volumes, all collector's pieces, remain as standard and authoritative works of reference for students of the Brontës. The four volumes of letters, although clearly neither complete nor accurate, have recently been reprinted in their original form in the absence of any satisfactory substitute. The novels, published in nine volumes, though a pleasure to read because of their beautiful print, are less in demand as a result of a number of popular and scholarly competitors. The poetry of Emily Brontë was edited more satisfactorily by C. W. Hatfield than in the Shakespeare Head edition, and is likely to be published in a full scholarly edition in the near future. The poetry of Anne Brontë has been well edited recently by Edward Chitham. But for the poetry and the juvenilia of Charlotte and Branwell Brontë we are still dependent upon the three volumes in which T. J. Wise and J. A. Symington endeavoured to collect the considerable bulk of prose and verse which the two eldest surviving Brontës had left behind them.

Both Wise and Symington were apparently well qualified for the post of editor, but had hidden disqualifications. Wise had published a respected if inaccurate bibliography of the Brontës and numerous expensive privately printed editions of their juvenilia. He had at one stage been president of the Brontë Society and for many years vice-president. But by the time that the Shakespeare Head was being produced his exposure as a forger of first editions by Carter and Pollard was already being threatened; worry, ill health, old age and eventually death prevented him from exercising anything but a token editorship.

After his death Wise was definitely convicted of forging manuscripts and further found guilty of purloining valuable material from the British Museum, but it is only recently that his regrettable record in the field of Brontë manuscripts and editions has been exposed. Wise acquired many manuscripts dishonestly, copied them inaccurately, and then edited them in a slovenly fashion.

It is not clear how far Symington was aware of the extent of Wise's dishonesty. There is in the Wrenn collection at the University of Texas an interesting collection of letters between Symington and Wise in which Symington sycophantically addresses Wise as editor in chief, and Wise, pleading ill health, gives curt and uninformative replies. Symington had been curator of the Brontë Museum in Haworth and at the time of publication of the Shakespeare Head edition was closely involved in the setting up of the Brotherton Collection in Leeds. But neither in Leeds nor in Haworth is Symington's name one to conjure with; he seems to have acquired several Brontë manuscripts under suspicious circumstances. When the University of Rutgers acquired Symington's collection, which would appear to have included several items inherited from Wise, it was found that several manuscripts which Rutgers thought they had bought were not included in the sale.

As an editor Symington would appear to have done his best with the intractable material at his disposal. Thanks to Wise the Brontë manuscripts had been separated and scattered. Some of the manuscripts were untraceable, and Symington had to rely on printed editions. Some of these editions were inaccurate, and this is not surprising in view of the indecipherable nature of many of the Brontë's juvenile manuscripts. Symington was living in an age before rapid travel across the Atlantic and improved photographic devices could solve the problems of those wishing to consult manuscripts in many different places. The Brontës' habit of copying out their poems several times and of inserting pieces of poetry in the middle of their prose stories was no help to anyone trying to produce a definitive edition of the Brontës' poetry or to distinguish their poetry from their prose. Finally, the poor quality of much of the Brontës' early writing, understandable in view of their youth, was something of an embarrassment to both editor and publisher.

In his labours Symington was greatly helped by the pioneer work of C. W. Hatfield, a man of very different calibre from the editors of the Shakespeare Head Brontë. Hatfield worked on the Brontë manuscripts for many years, although employed full time as a civil servant. He neither sought nor obtained much financial benefit from his work. His help is acknowledged, though not perhaps as bountifully as it should have been, in introductions to different volumes of the Shakespeare Head edition. Correspondence from Hatfield to J. Davidson Cook in the Special Collections Library, University of Vancouver, to Symington and Wise in the Wrenn Collection, University of Texas, and to the eccentric Brontë scholar, J. Malham Dimbleby in the Bradford Public Library trace the various stages of Hatfield's involvement in the Shakespeare Head project. His unfailing courtesy cannot mask his disillusionment with a number of the volumes produced, although it is comforting for the editor of Branwell's poems to know that in this section of Symington's work Hatfield was pleased that his own endeavours had been fairly faithfully reproduced.

This is one reason why the production of a new edition of Branwell's poems is less formidable than other Brontë projects. In addition most of the manuscripts of Branwell's poetry are in England. In *The Brontës and their Background* (Macmillan, 1973) I raised the possibility that with Wise on the scene much of what Branwell wrote could have been passed off as the work of Charlotte for financial reasons. Symington thought this might be so; the minute handwriting is a source of confusion; and we do find unladylike phrases in what is supposed to be Charlotte's work.

But after examining the relevant manuscripts I am able to revoke my former suspicions. Hatfield, who had no financial axe to grind, was confident in letters to Malham Dimbleby that most confusions of authorship had been cleared up, and that Symington's suspicions were unjustified. The handwriting of Charlotte and Branwell, even in a minute form, is distinct. The differences are well recorded in the preface by Hatfield to the inappropriately named *Complete Poems of Emily Brontë* (Hodder and Stoughton, 1933), edited officially by C. K. Shorter. The initial t, which Branwell does not cross, is the most obvious distinguishing feature. The signatures, either of Charlotte or Branwell, or of their various personae might seem suspicious in their multiplicity, but turn out in practice to be a fairly foolproof method of distinguishing one Brontë from another. There are a few unsigned poems which do raise problems of authorship, although it is Emily rather than Charlotte who is the main possible source of confusion with Branwell. It is of course quite possible that the Brontës were strongly influenced by each other, and even transcribed each other's manuscripts. This is particularly likely to be the case with Branwell, the laziest of the Brontë children who, as the one boy, probably exercised undue influence. The problem of influence and transcription is not, however, one that can be solved with any certainty, and in any case the editor of Branwell's poetry still has more than his fair share of problems. Like his sisters Branwell copied and recopied his poems, but unlike them he published very little in his lifetime, although this was not for want of trying. His latest version may seem the best to print, although like Wordsworth, but for different reasons, Branwell did not necessarily improve as a poet with increasing maturity. For reasons of economy it has been thought desirable to reprint the Shakespeare Head version of poems as they were originally printed in *The Poems of Charlotte and Patrick Branwell Brontë*, making corrections and recording variations in the notes. For poems that were originally published in *The Miscellaneous and Unpublished Writings of Charlotte and Patrick Branwell Brontë*, or were not published in the Shakespeare Head edition, I have usually printed from the latest manuscript, again recording variations in the notes.

The editors of the Shakespeare Head edition faced, as they frankly acknowledged, a difficult problem in deciding which poems to include in which of their volumes. Many of the Brontës' poems form part of an immense cycle of prose and poetry centred round the imaginary realms of Angria and Gondal. Emily and Anne wrote about Gondal in prose and verse, but none of their Gondal prose has survived; this creates problems of interpretation, but simplifies editorial difficulties. With Charlotte and Branwell the reverse is the case. We do have the benefit of the Angrian prose stories as background, but it is hard to know how much weight we should give to this background. In particular it is difficult to know whether to print Angrian poems as part of the Angrian prose cycle or as poetic entities in their own right. If we do the first, we lose sight of the Brontës' poetic development; if the second, we lose sight of the context in which the poems of the Brontës were written.

Branwell solves this particular problem for us. In the year 1837 in a single notebook he copied out with extensive revisions a number of poems, most of which he had originally written as part of the Angrian saga. Symington and Wise published virtually none of the poems in *The Poems of Charlotte and Patrick Branwell Brontë*, although some found their way into one of the *Miscellaneous and Unpublished* volumes, with the text usually established from the earlier versions. In printing the entire contents of Branwell's 1837 notebook, while excluding other Angrian poems which are found in the middle of the prose juvenilia, I feel that I am to a certain extent following Branwell's own distinction between poetry on the one hand and Angria on the other. I have also omitted a number of very juvenile poems which Branwell wrote under the pseudonym Young Soult the

Rhymer, although some of these have never been published: they are almost indecipherable and hardly worth deciphering. Branwell's two blank verse tragedies, *The Revenge* and *Caractacus*, are of more interest, as are his translations of the first book of Horace's Odes, but these are omitted for reasons of space. I have made a preliminary check list of all poems by Branwell Brontë not included in this edition, but am aware that this list may not be complete, and that unpublished poems may yet turn up.

Branwell's punctuation and spelling are idiosyncratic. The manuscripts in minute handwriting are almost unpunctuated, whereas some later poems, some of which were written with a view to publication, have punctuation that is almost regular. Symington and Wise sensibly correct spelling and alter punctuation to conform with modern usage, and I have only corrected their alterations in the notes where the alterations are misleading, or where the misspelling is significant. Some manuscripts have corrections which are legible and others have alternative readings. I have endeavoured to record these corrections and alternatives in the notes.

I am aware that I have left room for some future student of Branwell Brontë to produce a more comprehensive edition. Such an edition would include all the poems Branwell ever wrote and all his errors of spelling and punctuation. It would endeavour to decipher some of Branwell's more cryptic deletions and print variant versions of the same poem in full rather than in niggardly note form. Some of Charlotte's prose juvenilia have been edited in this lavish way, and there is certainly scope for a new edition of Emily's poetry along these lines.

Branwell is, however, not as good a poet as Emily, nor is his juvenile work worth studying in detail as a guide to his mature writing, since unlike his sisters he never produced any mature work. A full scholarly edition of Branwell's poems would hardly seem to justify the labour or the expense incurred in producing it. There is, however, a need to produce an edition that is accurate, available and readable. Branwell was the second best poet in the Brontë family and some of his poems are worth studying in their own right. He was at various times very close to all his three sisters, and many of his poems can provide important insights into their literary development. Finally Branwell's escapades do shed a lurid light across the sombre Brontë scene, and although there are even greater dangers in using poetry as a source of biography than in using fiction, the poems are part of the evidence we use to write the Brontë story, and it is important that this evidence should be as fully and accurately transcribed as possible.

BIOGRAPHICAL NOTE

PATRICK Branwell Brontë was born at Thornton, Yorkshire on 26 June 1817. He was the fourth child, but first son, of the Revd Patrick Brontë and Maria Branwell, and the choice of his Christian names reflects, no doubt, the pride of his parents in his birth. Emily Brontë was born in July 1818 and Anne Brontë in January 1820. In April 1820 the Brontës moved to Haworth, but five months later Mrs Brontë, who had had six children in six years, was dead. In September 1821 her elder sister Miss Elizabeth Branwell came up from her native Cornwall to look after the six orphaned children.

The education of these children clearly posed a problem. Mr Brontë himself had risen from being the son of an Irish crofter to being a clergyman of the Church of England, and this sudden rise had been achieved through his education. We would therefore expect him to devote time, energy and money to the schooling of his children, and as a widower he had special reasons for trying to get the best school he could find. As is well known he sent his four daughters to a charity school at Cowan Bridge with tragic results. Branwell's education is more problematic. His friend Leyland said that he went for a short time to Haworth Grammar School, a decaying establishment some distance away from the village, but there is no record of him having attended classes there. Possibly he stayed there for only a few months, being removed when the two eldest Brontë girls returned home to die in 1825. Unlike his shy sisters Branwell never had difficulty in making friends in all walks of society, and there is no particular reason for assuming that he left school because he was unhappy or unsuccessful there.

By all accounts Maria Brontë, who died on 6 May 1825 at the

age of eleven, was a remarkable girl who had done her best to fill the gap left by her dead mother. Her death when Branwell was eight must have made him wretched, but need not have had the profound effect on his psychological or literary development which some Brontë biographers have imagined. Poems like *Misery, Part II*, which actually mention Maria by name, and the Caroline poems which mention the death of a sister, may have an autobiographical basis.

After the tragedy at Cowan Bridge Mr Brontë decided to educate his children at home. Miss Branwell gave the girls their lessons, while he himself took charge of Branwell. This degree of preference is likely to have caused some resentment among the Brontë sisters, although in some quarters even today it would be considered perfectly natural. In any event it is doubtful whether the education that Mr Brontë provided was of all that much practical benefit to Branwell. It is not clear just how good a scholar Mr Brontë was; he had been educated at the unreformed Cambridge where in spite of Bentley and Porson a mechanical acquaintance with Latin and Greek was considered adequate. Branwell's early poems and stories show an interest in Classical history, his later translations of Horace show some fluency in Latin, and he was able to gain, presumably on the strength of his Classical attainments, posts as a private tutor. But then, as now, a Classical education, unless it is extended to university level, is of little practical benefit, merely giving the student an unfortunate and unjustified sense of his own superiority over those less privileged.

In other respects Mr Brontë's influence was more fortunate. He was keenly interested in politics, and the years of Branwell's boyhood were years of considerable political excitement, culminating in the Reform Bill of 1832. Mr Brontë supported the Tories, whose chief hero was the Duke of Wellington. The Duke's earlier exploits as a commander in the Peninsular War were objects of great interest among the Brontë children, and

Branwell's early prose manuscripts, though devoid of much literary merit, show a precocious knowledge of military and political matters.

Information about current and recent history could be gained from the newspapers which we know were read in the Brontë household and from *Blackwood's Magazine*. Mrs Gaskell records and wonders at this mature literary diet. She is less informative about another source of the young Brontës' reading, the library at Ponden House. The Heatons of Ponden House were an eccentric Yorkshire family, with whom Mr Brontë was bound to have contact, since Mr Heaton was the chief trustee of Haworth church. Their library contained many books which would not normally be read by the average nineteenth-century clergyman's family, and yet it is evident that the Brontës did read these books, since there is evidence of them copying, albeit innocently, some of the licentious stories found in the Ponden House catalogue, and even copying the actual title pages of books in Ponden House.

In June 1824 Mr Brontë bought a box of toy soldiers for Branwell, and in the late 1820s the young Brontës began producing a series of magazines in tiny handwriting in which the imaginary exploits of these soldiers were recorded. Some of the early manuscripts are of a very juvenile nature, and are closely modelled on literary originals, in particular *Blackwood's Magazine*. At some stage before 1834 Emily and Anne, whose involvement with the juvenile writings of Charlotte and Branwell appears to have been fairly limited, broke away and created their own world of Gondal, but Charlotte and Branwell continued writing in some kind of collaboration for a whole decade, although Charlotte was sometimes away at school.

It is difficult to do justice in a brief space to the vast corpus of the Brontë juvenilia, much of which has yet to be published. Right from the start Branwell and Charlotte wrote in a mixture of prose and verse. Both prose and verse dealt usually, but not invariably, with the establishment of the imaginary kingdom of Angria placed somewhere in the West Coast of Africa. Articles in *Blackwood's Magazine* and a copy of Mungo Park's explorations in the library at Ponden supplied the background information for Africa, although the description of the new Angrian kingdom bore very little relation to African reality. Originally the models for the chief characters in the Angrian saga were the toy soldiers, but after a time the Duke of Wellington's two sons, the Marquess of Douro and Lord Charles Wellesley, took a more prominent part, although again there was little relation between the history of these characters in real life and the fantastic adventures which Branwell and Charlotte attributed to them.

In 1831 Charlotte went to school at Miss Wooler's and in her absence Branwell invented the character of Rogue, otherwise known as Alexander Percy, Viscount Elrington and Earl of Northangerland. Similarly Charlotte's hero, the Marquess of Douro, was elevated to the title of Duke of Zamorna and King of Angria. In 1834 Zamorna and Northangerland, whose daughter Mary Zamorna had married, carved out the new kingdom of Angria for themselves, moving away from Verdopolis which had been hitherto the centre of the imaginary realm in which the Brontës' heroes and heroines disported themselves.

There is a harmless if not very attractive streak of snobbery about the young Brontës' writing. The degree of sexual licence permitted to both Zamorna and Northangerland may seem surprising, emanating from the children of a clergyman, although Queen Victoria had yet to come to the throne, and the leading politicians of the day were still allowed the licence of the Regency era. Branwell's preference for the distinctly villainous Percy, as opposed to the vaguely virtuous if amorous Zamorna, reflects a rebellious nature; earlier on he had made the French Marshal Soult as opposed to the Duke of Wellington his hero.

The literary aspects of the juvenilia are harder to assess. They have been compared to epics, and although it seems a travesty of the term epic to apply it to the frankly fustian juvenilia, it is true that as in primary epic the juvenilia draw on a shifting body of background material, knowledge of which by the audience is assumed by the author of a particular tale. Thus it is a mistake to look for any wholly consistent pattern of events linking one poem or story with another. A character may be killed off in one story, only to emerge again in a later tale.

Charlotte was worried by the power she had over her characters and also by the way in which she was able to lose herself in the fantastic world she had built up. There is no evidence of Branwell being similarly affected, and he went on writing poems under the pseudonym Northangerland until almost the end of his life. But it is a mistake to make Angria the sole clue to Branwell's poetry, since he revised Angrian poems out of their prose context. For this reason and for the reason that the Angrian background is a shifting rather than a fixed one, notes on the Angrian context have been kept in this edition to the minimum necessary for understanding.

All the Brontës' writing, mature as well as juvenile, shows an interest in painting, and all four children drew and painted almost as enthusiastically as they wrote. But it was Branwell for whom a career as a professional painter was envisaged. This was a mistake. His existing portraits do not show any particular merit. The Brontë family did not have any real knowledge of the artistic world, although Branwell's teacher, William Robinson, had been a student at the Royal Academy. Nor would Branwell seem to have had the necessary application or commitment.

The story of Branwell's visit to London, probably in the autumn of 1835, is difficult to narrate. We have a fictional account by Branwell, in the adventures of Charles Wentworth, of a journey to the metropolis in which the hero dissipates his time, energy and money with little squibs of rum. Long after Branwell's death villagers in Haworth remembered or professed to remember how he had returned, claiming that he had been robbed. His family passed over the incident in absolute silence. There was presumably some rather sordid explanation of Branwell's failure, but we are unlikely to be able to discover this.

When Branwell returned home he found only Emily there, as Charlotte and Anne were away at Miss Wooler's. Emily had made an unsuccessful attempt to be a pupil at this school, and brother and sister may have been drawn together by their common failure. After his visit to London Branwell worked very hard at his poetry, copying out several Angrian pieces with revisions, and writing new poems. He wrote several letters to *Blackwood's Magazine* between 1835 and 1837, offering them his services as an editor and contributor, and he also wrote to Wordsworth on 19 January 1837.

No doubt both Blackwood's and Wordsworth were besieged with letters from aspiring poets, although their failure to reply to Branwell seems a little harsh. The poems Branwell dispatched ('Misery' to Blackwood's and 'Still and bright, in twilight shining' to Wordsworth) are not without merit, and there is something to commend in many of the poems written by Branwell during this period. They are of course imbued with Romanticism, to which Branwell had come by various routes. He was later to become the friend of Hartley Coleridge. Southey had been an early hero of the Brontës, and Charlotte wrote to him and to Hartley Coleridge for advice. The decline of both Southey and Wordsworth into Tory churchmen would not seem a decline to the Brontës. Branwell's experiences in London must have made him more enthusiastic about the Lake poets, although there is also a Byronic note about his heroes, more sinned against than sinning, but sinning all the same. This too may spring from his disillusionment in London. The influence of Keats and Shelley is found more in Emily's poetry, although some kind of collaboration with Emily is not impossible in this period.

Emily, it is now thought, tried to become a schoolteacher at Law Hill in 1838. In 1837 Charlotte, who had shown an enthusiastic interest in Branwell's prose Angrian stories, confided in her Roe Head journal that she was worried by the hold Angria had over her, although she did continue writing, albeit in a more realistic vein. Branwell's literary output both in verse and prose during the year 1837 was certainly impressive in quantity, but it did not bring in any money, and in May 1838 he returned to art, taking up residence in Bradford to earn his living as a portrait painter.

Branwell stayed in Bradford for a year, and, though he did not complete many portraits, he made many friends including Hartley Coleridge, Joseph Leyland the sculptor, and his brother Francis, Branwell's first biographer. Conviviality had its dangers and may have contributed to the departure from Bradford with some portraits uncompleted. He did however complete in 1838 and revise in 1839 an important narrative poem, alternatively known as *Sir Henry Tunstall* and *The Wanderer*. In June 1839 we find Mr Brontë rather pathetically reading the Classics with Branwell, and, though they did not get very far in their prescribed course of study, this return to the Classics may have earned Branwell his first regular job as a tutor to the family of Mr Posthlethwaite of Broughton-in-Furness. It also certainly led to Branwell's translation of the first book of Horace's odes, completed in June 1840.

It is however around this time that drunkenness can be definitely proved against Branwell. Hitherto this can only be guessed from references in the juvenilia, but a letter to John Brown, the sexton at Haworth, describes a drunken carousal in Kendal in fairly graphic detail, and it is usually assumed that Mr Posthlethwaite dismissed Branwell for drunkenness in June 1840. In August of that year he gained employment as a railway clerk at Sowerby Bridge, moving on 1 April 1841 to the post of head clerk at the more remote station of Luddenden Foot. From this post he was dismissed a year later for carelessness in his accounts.

During his time at Luddenden Foot Branwell wrote several poems, these being written out in a notebook which contained notes on the railway and other jottings. The contrast between Branwell's romantic aspirations and humble reality is well shown in this notebook, which also reveals Branwell's temperamental inability to hold down his menial post. On his return home he found Charlotte and Emily away in Brussels and Anne away with the Robinsons of Thorp Green. His wounded pride received some solace with the publication of a few poems in the *Leeds Intelligencer* and *Halifax Guardian* in the summer of 1842. In October 1842, both the Revd William Weightman, Mr Brontë's curate and by all accounts a good influence on Branwell, and Miss Branwell died, and in January 1843 Branwell joined Anne as tutor at the house of the Robinsons.

Branwell's period of employment at Thorp Green was the longest and most disastrous of his efforts to earn his living. Very little poetry written by Branwell between 1843 and 1845 has survived, if indeed he wrote any. At first sight he seemed to be doing well, earning more than Anne, and according to Charlotte being equally valued. In her 1845 diary paper Anne said that she had had some unpleasant and undreamt-of experiences of human nature, and on 17 June 1845 Mr Robinson dismissed Branwell for behaviour bad beyond expression.

We shall probably never know what this behaviour was. Branwell spread the story that he had fallen in love with Mrs Robinson, and she with him. His poetry and a last prose fragment 'And the weary are at rest' reflect this story. It seems rather unromantic to suggest that neither Mrs Robinson, aged forty-five, nor Branwell, an eccentric and undersized twenty-eight, seem to have had the right character for this star-crossed idyll. Human passion works in extraordinary ways, and it is possible that Branwell imagined there was a love affair, and that Mrs

Robinson amused herself by feeding his imagination. Mr Robinson did not appear to think there was any guilt on the part of his wife, as his accounts show that he showered presents on her after dismissing Branwell. His death in May 1846 caused further confusion, as Branwell appeared to think that Mrs Robinson would marry him, and that she was only prevented from doing so by a codicil in Mr Robinson's will. No such codicil existed.

By this time Branwell's condition had badly deteriorated, and it becomes hard for us to distinguish fact from fancy. His poetry, though full of a maudlin self pity, is not entirely without merit even in the last years of his life, but in all other respects he must have been a burden and a worry to his family. His repeated failures in employment and the disgraceful circumstances of his final dismissal were rapidly overshadowed by drunkenness, drugs and debts. Soon a darker shadow loomed. Branwell frequently threatened suicide, and it became obvious that he had not much longer to live. His atheism, always a source of worry to the orthodox members of his family, now became a terrible anxiety, as they must have feared eternal punishment for the unbeliever, although Branwell's sisters were to repudiate this doctrine. Fortunately, although it is hard to distinguish truth from pious legend, Branwell would have seemed to have died on 24 September 1848 with merciful suddenness and with some kind of return to Christian beliefs.

Branwell's story is a tragic one, and it is made more tragic by the fact that his sisters achieved just the literary recognition and fame that he so desperately sought. They did have greater self-discipline, but more was expected of Branwell, and he was exposed to greater temptations. It was not that Branwell lacked literary talent, as a study of his poetry will reveal; it was merely that he dissipated this talent.

TEXTUAL INTRODUCTION

I HAVE divided Branwell's poems into four sections, three of which are printed in full and the fourth listed as an Appendix. In the first section I have reproduced the text of the Shakespeare Head *Poems of Charlotte and Patrick Branwell Brontë*. The editors of this edition printed about half of the poetry that Branwell wrote. They were influenced, as I have explained in my general introduction, and they explain in theirs, by the availability of readily accessible printed versions and manuscripts, and by largely subjective considerations about which poems were part of Angria, and which poems were too bad or too scrappy or too juvenile to be included. Some omissions such as those of the poem entitled 'Thorp Green' and those beginning 'Behold a waste of waving sea' and 'Side by side at twilight sitting' seem inexplicable. Thanks to the labours of C. W. Hatfield, who had prepared, in a typewritten volume now in the Brontë Parsonage Museum, a much fuller text of Branwell's poems, the text of the Shakespeare Head version is in a reasonably satisfactory state. Certain American manuscripts were not available to Hatfield or to the editors of the Shakespeare Head, who relied instead on inaccurate transcripts supplied by Wise or inaccurate printed editions. I have had here to record extensive corrections in the notes. The problem is much more severe in the case of Charlotte Brontë's poems. Most of the manuscripts sent to Leyland have been lost, and in the case of these poems all we can do is check the Shakespeare Head text against the Leyland text, with which it usually agrees.

The Shakespeare Head rarely, and Hatfield only sometimes, acknowledged that Branwell copied and recopied his poems and that it is helpful to record earlier and later variants. I have endeavoured to do this in the notes. Occasionally it is difficult to distinguish between poems that are variants, and poems that are poems in their own right. Neither Hatfield nor the Shakespeare Head were very interested in corrections or alternative readings; I have tried to record these wherever possible, although not all the corrected readings in Branwell's minuscule handwriting are legible.

Section 2 is a reproduction in full of Branwell's fair copy notebook which he made in 1837. This notebook I have entitled Notebook B. In it he copied with alterations poems that he previously included in his Angrian stories, carefully recording the number of lines, the date of composition and the date of transcription. He added a number of poems to his original list, but most of these can be accurately dated. Some of these poems were printed in their original, i.e. pre-1837, version in the Shakespeare Head edition of the *Miscellaneous and Unpublished Writings of Charlotte and Patrick Branwell Brontë*, but many of them have not been published. Most of them have an Angrian context, and were Branwell's prose stories more readily accessible or decipherable, it might have been worthwhile to compare them with the original poems in the Angrian stories. I have not done this even in the case of five poems which have been brought to my notice in the Brotherton collection or the previously printed versions in the Shakespeare Head *Miscellaneous and Unpublished Writings*. Branwell was twenty when he transcribed the poems in the 1837 notebook; it does not really seem worth examining his more juvenile variants in any great detail.

I have included the third variant of the poem on Lord Nelson in Section 2, although it would not really seem to belong to Notebook B, since it is not dated, nor has the number of lines been attached to it. The same is true of *Azrael*, but this I have not included in Section 2, as the version we have in Notebook B is our only source for the poem in Section 1. The variant of *The End of All* can be fitted into Notebook B, although it is separately catalogued in the Bonnell Collection, Haworth, having presumably fallen out or been torn out from the notebook. I have included this poem in Section 2 and a few other poems which are early variants of poems in Section 1.

In Section 3 I have printed a number of Branwell's other poems which the Shakespeare Head overlooked. I am aware that this section may seem scrappy, consisting of some good poems which the Shakespeare Head unaccountably missed, some fragments and some poems which might properly count as variants. Most of these poems have been published before, and I have not included some unpublished poetry which is either Angrian or juvenile or inaccessible, or all three. I have endeavoured to list such poems in an Appendix, although well aware that the list is not complete. Branwell's *Translations from Horace* are neither Angrian nor immature nor inaccessible, but really deserve a separate volume to themselves.

Branwell's handwriting takes many forms. He wrote *Thermopylae* and a few other notes on his poems in a faultless copperplate with his right hand. Notebook B is written in a fairly small upright hand which I have called small normal. Most of his poems before 1840 were written in a very small print-like script which I have called minuscule. In the fair copy book now in fragments in which he wrote a number of poems of 1836 and 1837, which I have called Notebook A, this script is very regular. Later, especially in the notebook he used at Luddenden Foot, which I have entitled Notebook C, the minuscule print becomes much more straggling, approaching and in one poem actually changing to the rather sprawling hand in which Branwell wrote a number of his later poems. I have tried to divide Branwell's hand into these four categories, aware that the dividing line is not hard and fast.

It is likewise difficult to draw a hard and fast line in matters of punctuation and corrections. None of the Brontës was good at punctuation and spelling, and I have followed the editors of the

Shakespeare Head in silently correcting Branwell's errors. Branwell's eccentric indentation has likewise been made more regular. The amount of punctuation and correction provides some insight into whether Branwell intended a version to be a final one, although there are errors of punctuation (and spelling) even in versions which the poet intended for publication. Apart from manuscripts which we know Branwell wished to publish it is difficult and dangerous to draw any conclusions about Branwell's supposed lapses into degeneracy, drunkenness and despair from his orthography, since the most sober and optimistic of us are entitled to write our rough notes and private poems in an illegible scrawl.

ABBREVIATIONS

Notebook A $6\frac{1}{4}'' \times 3\frac{3}{4}''$. Lined paper. Originally 60 pp. Much scattered. Described in BC, p. 95.

Notebook B $9\frac{1}{2}'' \times 7\frac{3}{4}''$. Stiff brown covers. Originally 82 pp. Mainly in BPM. Described in BC, p. 100.

Notebook C $6'' \times 4''$. Red cover. Originally 28 pp. The Ludden-den Foot Notebook. Mainly in BPM, some pages in BCL. Described in BC, p. 100 and BST¹, p. 72.

BC   The Catalogue of the Brontë Parsonage Museum (Haworth, 1927)

BCH   The Bonnell Collection, Haworth

BCL   The Brotherton Collection, Leeds University Library

BCNY   The Berg Collection, New York Public Library

BCPML   The Bonnell Collection, Pierpont Morgan Library, New York

BL   The British Library

BPM   The Brontë Parsonage Museum, Haworth

BST¹   The *Brontë Society Transactions*, 37 (1927)

BST²   The *Brontë Society Transactions*, 43 (1933)

EBP   *The Complete Poems of Emily Jane Brontë*, edited by C. K. Shorter (London, 1923)

G   W. Gerin, *Branwell Brontë* (London, 1961). My debt to Miss Gerin is, I hope, obvious, although I disagree with her on some of her biographical speculations

GCB   E. C. Gaskell, *The Life of Charlotte Brontë* (London, 1857)

H   Unpublished typewritten notes of C. W. Hatfield in the Brontë Parsonage Museum. I am grateful to the family of Mr Hatfield for allowing me to use these notes, which I hope I have acknowledged

HG   The *Halifax Guardian*

HLH   The Houghton Library, Harvard University

HRT   The Humanities Research Centre, University of Texas

L   F. Leyland, *The Brontë Family, with Special Reference to Patrick Branwell Brontë*, 2 vols. (London, 1886). Valuable both as a source for and commentary on Branwell's poems

LI   The *Leeds Intelligencer*

M   D. du Maurier, *The Infernal World of Branwell Brontë* (London, 1960)

NLS   The National Library of Scotland

O   M. Oliphant, *Annals of a Publishing House: William Blackwood and his Sons*, 3 vols. (Edinburgh, 1897)

Q   T. de Quincey, *Memorials*, edited by A. H. Japp, 2 vols. (London, 1891)

R   F. Ratchford, *The Brontës' Web of Childhood* (New York, 1941)

SHCBP   *The Complete Poems of Charlotte Brontë and Patrick Branwell Brontë*, edited by T. J. Wise and J. A. Symington (Oxford, 1934)

SHCBM   *The Miscellaneous and Unpublished Writings of Charlotte Brontë and Patrick Branwell Brontë*, edited by T. J. Wise and J. A. Symington, 2 vols. (Oxford, 1938)

†   indicates a reading that has been crossed out

*   indicates a reading that has been corrected without crossing out

**   indicates the correct or upper reading where there is more than one version

( )   titles in round brackets are those given by the Shakespeare Head editors for which there is no manuscript authority

[　]   in the notes indicates an incorrect reading in the original Shakespeare Head text

[?]   following a word indicates a doubtful reading

Where there is only one manuscript this has been assumed, except on rare occasions, to have the correct reading. Where there is more than one manuscript variant readings are recorded, but the latest version has been assumed to be the correct one. The Shakespeare Head text has been used as a base from which the correct reading may be established; there are occasions when it provides the correct reading, agreeing with the latest manuscript, but earlier manuscript variants are recorded.

BRANWELL BRONTË'S POEMS
IN APPROXIMATE
CHRONOLOGICAL ORDER

Dates given are dates of composition except in a few cases where a manuscript is untraceable, but we do have the date of publication.

I

POEMS OF BRANWELL BRONTË
PREVIOUSLY PUBLISHED IN
THE SHAKESPEARE HEAD EDITION

ODE TO THE POLAR STAR

LORD of the Northern fields of heaven,
   May light like thine to me be given
    While I thy praises sing.
Let sordid flatterers cringe and wait
5 Before the rich man's open gate,
   And bow beneath the glare of state,
    And there their offerings bring.

But on some rock's tremendous steep,
High hanging o'er the hoary deep,
10   Let me be seated lone,
And while the tempests round me fly,
Howling across a midnight sky,
Behold thee shining bright and high,
    And silent and alone.

15 Star of the Pole, amid the sea
How many now may look on thee,
    And bless thy light divine;
How often doth the sailor pray,
When tossed by tempests far astray,
20 That thou wouldst guide his wandering way,
    And on his vessel shine?

How often from the abyss of air
Hast thou heard the sailor's prayer?
Lo! yon tall vessel lab'ring amid the storm,
25 But vainly struggling 'gainst his giant arm,
With shattered masts, with sails all rent and riven,
Tossed from the gulphs beneath the black clouds of
    heaven.
Lo! the night increasing shrouds the sky,
While upward burst the waves on high;
30 O'er unseen rocks they rage and roar,
Whit'ning with surf the shaken shore,

High o'er the ship's tall bows they break away,
And fill the air with showers of spray:
Black clouds vast billows drive along,
35 And as they drive she hurries on.
Now on the secret quicksands dashed
And girdled round with foam;
Then from her rocky harbour washed,
And hurled upon the main, 'mid its huge waves to
    roam;
40 Then, then how droops the sailor's soul,
Hopeless he gazes toward the pole,
For tossing on an unknown sea
How may he hope to look on thee?
But lo! the clouds all rent and riven
45 Have to the winds a passage given.
Forth breaks upon his upward sight
The dark blue concave of the night,
Its thousand stars all fixed on high,
And twinkling in the silent sky,
50 High throned in heaven he sees thee shine;
Well known to him thy light divine,
    He sees thee and adores.
Unheeded now may rage the sea,
Secure in thy directing ray
55 He learns to avoid the rocky way,
    And sees his native shores.

    But not alone to him,
Who doth a wanderer o'er the ocean roam,
    Wilt thou bestow thy beam,
60 And guide him toward his home.
The traveller o'er the desert drear
Gazes on thee his heart to cheer;
Though waste on waste expand before,
Nor can his eye a bound explore,
65 Though far behind his native valley lies,
Though unknown scenes his 'wildered sight surprise,

Yet, as he folds his mantle fast
To guard him from the bitter blast
 Swept from the inclement sky,
Unmindful of the gathering night,
70 Upward to thee he strains his sight
Where he beholds thee shining bright—
 His Guardian in the sky.

Blesser of Mortals! Glorious Guide!
Nor turning ever from thy course aside,
75 Eternal pilot, while Time passes by,
While earthly guides decay and die,
 Thou hold'st thy throne,
 Fixed and alone,
In the vast concave of the nightly sky.
80 Kingdoms and states may droop and fail,
 Nor ever still abide;
The mighty moon may wax and wane,
But thou dost silent there remain,—
 An everlasting guide!

       June 26, 1832.

THERMOPYLAE

Book 1st.

I

NOW morning rises broad and bright
 Above the Egean sea,
And gives to heaven returning light,
While hill and valley, plain and height
5 Roll off the iron shroud of night,
 And welcome in the day.
Awake Egean, wake from sleep!
 Behold the sunlight dawn!
Come, join thy waves in glittering light
10 To hail the rising morn!

All Grecia's shores beneath the sun
   With golden lustre glow,
And heaven reflects a dazzling light
   From thy wild waves below.
15 High o'er, the vapours curling off
   The Argolic Mountains rise,
And Attica her arid ridge
   Rears far amid the skies.

II

Now all around this smiling sea
20 One swelling champaign sweeps away,
Shewn in this early morning light
With streams and trees and temples bright.
   Beyond its eastern bound
   Rise the dark hills of Thessaly,
25 Above it beetling awfully,
As proud its guardian walls to be
   They gird the champaign round.
Rise up, Oh hills, still sterner rise!
Still blacker frown against the skies.
30 This morning dawns how fair and gay!
How shore and ocean seem in play
   To hail returning life!
But has not oft an outside fair,
A forehead seeming smoothed from care,
35 Striven to conceal a heart's despair,
   And inward burning strife?

III

A gnawing worm hath Grecia now,
   Though summer-like all round her lie,
Beneath Thessalia's frowning brow,
40   The soft vales smiling on the sky.

Behold! far outward round the plain
Yon mighty host of moving men;
Slow as they wheel in line on line
Their helms and arms and armour shine,
45 Still pressing on each trodden place,
Still closing round each vacant space,
And still, as farther on the sight
Forth flashes up this newborn light,
For mile on mile across the plain
50 Moves on this mighty warrior train.
Behold them joined, one glittering mass,
Thermopylae's tremendous pass
     Above them beetling lone,
While neath it, village, field or tree
55 The eyesight strives in vain to see,
All calmer scenes of nature flee
     As that huge host rolls on.
The sudden shout, the long-drawn hum,
The Trumpet's blast, the thundering drum,
60 Like smoke o'er mountains rolling come
     With mixed and murmuring tone.

IV

Now far and wide the Ensigns fly
Like thousand flashes mid the sky,
Their silken folds all fluttering bright
65 Make wide heaven quiver with varying light.
Behold yon broad, bright crimson shown,
In gold emblazed its gilded sun.
Great Mithras[1] with a borrowed glow
Blazes along the closing row.
70 A thousand suns this fated day
In Ocean's breezes glance and play,
And snowy helm and sun-tipped spear
Above each mountain gorge appear.

[1] The God of the sun among the Persians.

Greece! let me drop one tear for thee,
75　　　Where hath thy light of freedom gone?
I know thy sons will perish free,
Yet what avails a glory flown!
And when thy children all are gone
　　　Where will that light of Freedom be?
80　Where! Thou struck, blasted, lying alone,
Must feel this huge host's tread, and wither 'neath
　　　its throne.

V

I said a mountain's stormy height
Hung beetling o'er that Army bright.
Yes! there thou frown'st, Thermopylae,
85　Stern standard of the brave and free—
High o'er rough Peneus'[2] roaring flood,
O'er swelling hill and shadowed wood,
Thy huge rocks, starting to the sky,
Swell forth a barrier broad and high,
90　And seems as rent by thunder's stroke
Between the ribbed and frowning rock
That path which upward from the shore
Winds high above the torrent's roar.

VI

Now all beneath that bulwark high
95　The whole wide champaign sound with joy.
And Oh! in what unnumbered lines
Yon mighty army shades and shines!
First breaks the spearlight o'er the hill,
Then seems its flash the vale to fill,
100　And still o'er all that wide expanse
One broad, bright sunbeam seems to glance.
Hark to the roar of revelry!

[2] The chief river of Thessaly.

Hark to the ceaseless shouts of joy!
See! how the rising morning wind
105   Swells up each banner's glorious fold.
See! how, before, around, behind,
  Flames forth in crimson and in gold!
  Yon long, long ranks of war unfold;
So now they crowd in burnished ring
110 Around the standard of their king!

VII

That King upon his golden throne
High o'er the tumult shines alone;
Their Xerxes, with insatiate eye,
Roams o'er the hosts which round him lie—
115 Parthians and Medians beneath him stand
Glittering in purple and kinglike band;
Aye many a monarch is in yon train,
Doomed to the sun his beams to wane.
Where far mid the desert the Nile flows on
120 Egypt hath given her shaven son;
The sunscorched Arabian stands haughtily there,
The Parthian lifts his wandering spear,
And glorious India's climes unknown
Sends her dark hostage round that throne.
125 Aye there they crowd, a jewelled throng,
Loud notes of triumph on each tongue;
Yet all in thrice redoubled ring
Prone kneeling 'neath their lord, the King!
He, rising, lord of glory stands,
130 And spreads toward heaven his sceptred hands.

VIII

Ha! Mithras thou in glory now
May'st shed thy halo round my brow.
To thee I vow a sacrifice
Such as hath never to the skies

135   Blazed in accepting flame.
To thee yon Grecian army dies,
To thee I vow its obsequies,—
A Hecatomb, ye favouring skies!
Accept the whole Grecian name!
140   Gods, have a band of traitorous men
Thus braved the lion in his den?
Do twice ten thousand Persians lie
To stiffen 'neath a Grecian sky?
And yet, Achaia's evil star
145   Can shine ascendant through the air.
Well, twice I have seen my warriors fall
Beneath yon heaven-erected wall.
Twice have my troops in vain assayed
To force yon rock's tremendous shade.
150   But not a third time, never more
Shall we roll backward on the shore!
Thou said'st a Goatherd's step might find
A path which up yon dark hill's brow
High toward Thermopylae may wind,
155   To o'erlook the traitor host below.
'Tis well, now Persian strike your blow!
Mardonius,[1] seize thy trustiest brand!
Thou boastest oft, head thou the band
To storm yon heaven-built wall.
160   Let all our choicest troops advance,
Take Parthian javelin, Persian lance,
And heaven for Xerxes call
Vengeance on Greece! aye, let them know
That what hath stayed the coming blow
165   Shall only force it on our foe
With heavier dint to fall.
The meanest cloud which spots the sky
May hide even Mithras' light on high,

[1] A famous Persian, and one of the chief instigators of the expedition against Greece.

Yet, when again breaks out the day,
170   How those vain vapours fade away.
      Now thou who hast betrayed to me
          Thy country and Thy home,
      'Tis meet that I should show to thee
          Thy own reward to come.
175   Ha! base Trachinian[1] deem'st thou, then,
          Because I seize thy way,
      That I will weigh three hundred men
          Against thy craven clay?
      Go, slave, and know a Persian eye,
180   Though it accept the treachery,
          The traitor casts away.
      Thou hast shown my way to victory
      O'er the dead corses of the free,
      And death, base slave, I shew to thee.

                    IX

185   The traitor wretch is born away—
      He casts a wild glance round the sea,
      But dares not face Thermopylae;
          On thy betrayed brow,
      He, who, to the proud spoiler's hand,
190   Hath given the bravest of his land,
      Beneath the glad receiver's hand
          Rolls headless, breathless now.

                    X

      Just then, the sun with sudden light
      Burst full on yon far fronting height,
195   And flashing back in golden lines
      Clear o'er the champaign streams and shines.

---

[1] Tráchis or Tráchin, a town of Thessaly in the district of Malis. It was a Malian named Ephialtes who showed the Persians the mountain path, thus enabling them to fall on the rear of the Greeks who were defending the Pass of Thermopylae.

So all along yon brazen sea
How flame the bright arms gallantly!
See how they spread from side to side,
200 Forth streaming o'er the champaign wide!
And what a cloud of standards stare,
Lighten and darken through the air.
'For Victory, for victory!'
Roars high above the living sea.
205 Aye, ye may shout proud Persians now,
For all hope's garlands bind your brow.
Aye, ye shall gain yon mighty height,
And fight and conquer in that fight.
Oh Greece! in this dark hour of gloom,
210 When round thee yawns yon bloody tomb,
Think, through destruction's dreariest day
Freedom can shine with brightest ray,—
That in the Tyrant's mightiest hour
One God-given sword may shake his power.
215 Now bid thy armèd children see
On thy huge heights, Thermopylae,[1]
Three hundred fight 'gainst millions three.

August 9, 1834.

MISERY

PART I

HOW fast that courser fleeted by,
His archèd neck backward tossed on high,
His snorting nostrils opened wide,
His foam-flecked chest and gory side.

[1] Thermopylae was the only pass by which an enemy could penetrate from Northern into Southern Greece, hence its great importance in Greek history. It is especially celebrated on account of the heroic defence of Leonidas and the 300 Spartans against the mighty host of Xerxes, in 480 B.C.; they only fell because the Persians were shown the path over the mountain, thus enabling them to attack the Greeks in the rear.

Branwell Brontë wrote an earlier poem relating to this subject, entitled 'The Pass of Thermopylae,' dated March 3, 1834.

5   I saw his Rider's darkened form
As on they hurried through the storm.
Forward he pressed, his plume behind
Flew whistling in the wintry wind,
But his clenched teeth and angry eye
10   Seemed wind and tempest to defy,
And eagerly he bent his sight
To pierce the darkness of the night,
And oft he gazed and gazed again
Through the rough blast and driving rain.
15   Look up and see the midnight heaven
Where mass o'er mass continual driven
The wild black storm clouds fleet and change;
Like formless phantoms vast and strange
They bend their gloomy brows from high
20   To pass in midnight darkness by;
And still they pass and still they come
Without a flash to break the gloom.
     I cannot see the foam and spray
That mark that raging torrent's way,
25   But well I hear the ceaseless roar
Where swollen and chafed its waters pour.
There, where yon blackened oaks on high
Blend wildly with the midnight sky,
Tossing their bare and groaning boughs
30   Like some dread fight of Giant foes;—
There, where that glimpse of Moonlight shines,
     From the wild wrack of heaven sent down,
And spreads its silver trembling lines
     Amid the darkness, then is gone;—
35   There stays the Horseman—wide before,
Deep and dark the waters roar,
But down the lone vale far away
Glances one solitary ray.
The sound of winds and waters rise,
40   And sweeps the sleet-shower o'er the skies,
While dreariest darkness all around

Makes still more drear each sight or sound.
But heeds not such that Cavalier:
Reining his trembling Charger there,
45 He halts upon the river's brink,
Where all its wild waves surge and sink,
Shades with his hand his anxious eye
And through the night looks eagerly.
   Why smiled he when that far off light
50 Again broke twinkling on his sight?
Why frowned he when it sunk again
'Mid the rough wrack of stormy rain?
Till brightly flashing forth once more,
It streams and twinkles far before.

55 'Oh through the tempests of this life
       However loud they sound,
   However wild their storms and strife
       May burst and thunder round,
   Though reft and riven each aid or prop,
60 There must be Heaven!—There must be Hope!
   I thought just now that Life or Death
       Could never trouble me,
   That I should draw my future breath
       In silent apathy,
65 That o'er the pathway of my fate
       Though steady beat the storm,
   As I walked alone and desolate
       I'd to that path conform.
   Affection should not cherish me,
70   Or Sorrow hold me down,
   But Despair itself sustain me,
       Whom itself had overthrown.
   I knew that fame and glory
       Were names for shame and woe,
75 That Life's deceitful story
       I had finished long ago,
   That all its novelty was gone,
       And that thus to read again

The same dull page in the same sad tone
80   Was not even change to pain.
Defeat had crushed me into dust,
    But only laid my head
Where head and heart and spirit must
    Be soon for ever laid.
85 My fearless followers all were slain,
    My power and glory gone,
My followers met that fate of man
    And Power—! I am NOW alone!
Not so!—I thought it—till that light
90   Glanced glittering down the glen,
And on my spirit's dreary night
    Flashed brighter back again.
Yes! I had thought I had stood alone,
That I need sigh or weep for none,
95 Had quenched my love in apathy,
Since none could sigh or weep for me.
Yes! But that single silver beam
    Which flashes in my eye
Hath waked me from my dreary dream
100   And bade my darkness fly;
But pardon that the storms of woe
    Have whelmed me in a drifting sea,
With death and dangers struggling so
    That I—a while—forgot even THEE.
105 The moment that I gained the shore,
    And clouds began to disappear,
Even steadier, brighter than before
    THOU shinest, my own—my Guardian Star!'

    'Oh could I speak the long lost feeling,
110 The inward joy its Power revealing,
The glimpse of something yet to come
Which yet shall give a happy Home.
Oh should I speak my thoughts of thee
Whom soon again my eyes shall see.
115 The dove that bore the Olive leaf

Could never bring such glad relief
To wanderers o'er the shoreless main
As in my weariness and pain
That single light hath given to me.
120 My gallant horse, speed swiftly thou,
Soon shall a hand caress thee now,
Grateful that thou hast borne me on
Through deadliest deeds and dangers gone,
A touch thou mayest be proud to own
125 Though thou so oft hast felt my own!
Oh that fair hand and faithful heart
From mine what power can ever part?
What Power?—Ha! well indeed I know
The very fire that burns me now,
130 The very energy of soul
    That to thine arms impels me on,
When once I have gained that heavenly goal
    Will—like a comet from the sun,
Hurl me with power that scorns control
135   Far from thy beams of Happiness,
    Into the expanse of mad distress
Where passion's lightnings burst and battles'
        thunders roll!'

Impetuous then that Horseman sprung
Down the deep bank—His armour rung
140   'Mid the wild water's roar,
And dashing through the old oak trees,
His Courser's hoofs upon the breeze
Their reckless rattle swiftly cease
    In that dark night before!

145 Who that hath felt the feeling wild
    Which struck upon the excited mind
When, perhaps, long since—while yet a child,
    In awful mystery undefined,
Old tales and legends darkly told,
150   While winter nights fell long and drear,

Have made his heart's blood curdle cold
  Their dreary tales to hear,
Of Ancient Halls where Destiny
  Had brooded with its raven wing;
155 Of castles stern whose riotry
  Hid not the gloomy crimes within;
Of Death beds, where the sick man lying
  'Mid anxious list'ners standing by,
Ere he had told the secret, dying,
160   And left a sealèd mystery;
Of Heirs who to some fearful doom
  Succeeded with their ancient Hall;
Of Marriage Feasts where ghosts would come
  The new-made Bride to call;—
He that hath still in memory
165   Kept fast those dreams of childhood's hours,
Who these far visions yet may see
  Of Castle halls and feudal Towers,—
To him I show this stormy Night
  That seems to darken on my sight!

170 Far above their forest trees
  These dreary turrets rise,
And round their walls the midnight breeze
  Comes shrieking from the skies.
Scarce can I note the central tower
175   Amid the impetuous storm,
Till shimmering through the pelting shower
  The moonbeams mark its form.
Far downward to the raving stream
  The woody banks decline,
180 Where waters flashing in the gleam
  Through densest darkness shine.
Those giant oaks their boughs are tossing
  As wild winds wilder moan,
Trunks and leaves confusedly crossing
185   With a ceaseless groan.
And over all the castle walls

Rise blacker than the night,
No sign of man around their Halls
Save that lone turret light.
190 The upward path is wild and steep,
Yet hear that horseman come,
Not toiling up, with cautious creep,
But hotly hasting home.
The steed is to his stables led,
195 But where's the Rider gone?
Up the high turret staircase sped
With gladdened haste alone.
The Ante Room looks hushed and still
With lattice curtained close,
200 The tempests sweeping round the hill
Disturb not its repose.
All's soft and calm, a holy balm
Seems sleeping in the air,
But what on earth has power to charm
205 A spirit chafed by care?
The warrior hastes to seek that power,
He knows the only one
Whose love can soothe his lonely hour
Or hush his rising groan;
210 And where that soft and solemn light
Shines chequering o'er the floor,
He hastens in with armèd tread
Towards the opened door;
And entering—Though a sacred stream
215 Of radiance round him fell,
It could not with its silent beam
His eager spirit quell.

'Maria!'—But the silence round
Would give him no reply,
220 And straightway did that single sound
Without an echo die.

'Where hath my Gentle Lady gone?
I do not find her here.'

Lo, on that stately couch alone
225   Reclines thy Lady fair.
But—cold and pale is her marble brow,
   Dishevelled her sunny hair.
Oh! is it in peaceful slumber now
   That she lieth so silent there?
230 'Heaven bless thy dreams!' Lord Albert cried,
   But his heart beat impetuously,
And as he hasted to her side
   He scarce had power to see.
All wildly the scenes of his former life
235   Flashed back upon his eyes,
And at once a cloud of despair and strife
   Before him seems to arise!
But as the sailor to his ship
   Clings with more frenzied power
240 As louder thundering o'er the deep
   Fresh billows whelm it o'er,
So madly on his only prop
   This war-worn man reclined,
He could not, would not deem his hope
245   Delivered to the wind!

Yet then why is this start of bewildered fright?
   And whence can arise this fear?
Is it not now the depth of night?
   And sleeps not thy Lady there?
250 And art not thou on the Castle height
   From war's alarms afar?
See—is that sleep?—
           —With open eyes
Chilly white and cold she lies!
255 Sunk her cheeks and blanched her lip
   That trembles as with suffering—
She sleeps not till the eternal sleep
   Its dreamless rest shall bring!
Heaven had occupied her mind
260 To onward hasting Death resigned,

But 'mid those strange uncertainties
   That crowd their ghastly phantoms round,
When all our Reason's guiding ties
   Are from the parting soul unbound,
265 She thought when first she heard that tread
   That Death himself was hasting near,
The conjured vision of his form
   Obeyed her ready fancies' fear,
And to her dim eyes seemed to appear,
270   Till—that one word—and all was clear!
Then—sinking Reason rose again,
Then—joined the links of memory's chain,
Then—spite of all her dying pain,
   She felt—she knew her Lord was there!
275 Oh! when across that dreary sea
The light broke forth so suddenly,
What soul can feel, what tongue express
The burst of raptured happiness
   That from her spirit chased its care,
280   For—She was dying! But—He was near!

Ah! surely, swiftly art thou gliding
   Over Death's unfathomed sea,
Dark and dread the waves dividing
   Thee from earth and earth from thee!
285 Life, thy own, thy native land
Parting far on either hand,
   As the mighty waters widen
   Onward to Eternity!
Shores of life, farewell for ever,
290   Where thy happiness has lain,
Lost for ever! Death must sever
   All thy hopes and joys and pain!
Yet, how blest that sound must be
   Which strikes upon thy dying ear
295 From off the dim departing shore,
   Although its landmarks disappear,
Still sounding o'er the eternal roar

The voice of HIM thou hold'st so dear!
'Tis as when the Mariner,
300   Just parted from his native home,
     After a night of dread and fear
Whose storms have riven the waves to foam,
When night's dark hours have wrapt away
All save the sounding of the sea,
305   Morn breaks where all looks new and strange,—
But Hark!—a sweet and sudden change,
For on his ear strikes soft from far
     In Sabbath chime his native bells;
He starts, and bursts the joyful tear
310   For things unutterably dear
     That farewell music tells!

Yet stay—why do I wander so
To wile me from that scene of woe?
     There stood the armèd man,
315   The very madness of Despair
In his red eyeballs' stricken glare,
     His cheek so ghostly wan!
And on her couch his Lady lying
Still and slow and surely dying,
320   Yet, with an enraptured smile
     And glittering in her glassy eye,
And her weak arms she would the while
     Have stretched to clasp him standing by;
But they would not her will obey,
325   And motionless beside her lay.
Then her white lips moved to speak,
     But nothing could she say!
This was Death's triumphant hour,
Grasped by his tremendous power
330   She must pass away!

'Speak Maria!—speak, my love!
     Let me hear thy voice.
Nought on earth or Heaven above
     Could make me so rejoice!

335 Speak, O speak, and say to me
I am not come too late to thee!
Oh tell me that my arm can save
Thy spirit from the hideous grave!
Maria! O my only love
340 Tell me thou wilt not die,
And nought below me or above
Shall feel so blest as I!
O would that I were far away
Alone upon the stormy sea!
345 Might I awake on yonder plain
Where I have left my soldiers slain,
So I could wake and rise and know
That this was but a frightful dream,
That thou at least wert living now
350 In love and life and beauty's beam!
But here's the truth which now I know!
My God, My God, I cannot bear Thy blow!'

All was vain! she moved not, spoke not,
Speech or sound the silence broke not,
355 But he flung him o'er her lying
As he would catch her spirit, dying.
All was vain!—That spirit flies
To God, Who gave it, in the skies!
That within his arms which lay
360 Was but a lifeless form of clay,
No return to his embrace,
Nought of feeling in that face,
Not a wish or power to save
Its own cold members from the grave.
365 Go, Lord Albert, go again,
Drown thought amid a world of storms.
Go—For thy Despair is vain
And thy Hope lies food for worms!

December 18, 1835.

MISERY

Part II

WIDE I hear the wild winds sighing
O'er the hills and far away,
Heaven in clouds before them flying
Through the drear December day,
5 Dull and dark its evening ray,
As o'er the waste the ceaseless rain,
Drives past, is gone, and then again
Sweeps cold and drenching by, in showers of sleety
spray.

And now the watery mountains rise
10 All dimly mingling with the skies,
At times some black brow darkening forth
Cleaved by the tempest from the North,
And then, as fast the clouds sail on,
All its crags and heath knolls gone;
15 The changing veil of sleet drives o'er the waste alone.

Alone I list to hear the sigh
Of the wild blast passing by;
Far away with mournful moan
It bends the heath on the old gray stone,
20 Then rising in the ashgrove's bough
Scatters the withered leaves below;
Blackens the wall with pelting spray
And wails and wanders far away.
Oh when I hear that wintery sound,
25 The very vales of a mountain land,
A thousand feelings crowding round
Start up and rise on every hand,
And wake to life as the wild winds wake,
And pass with them away,

30   Sunbeams that o'er the spirit break
        Amid the dreariest day;
      But hush!—And hark, that solemn wail,
        'Tis past—and yet—'tis on my ear,
      Shrill, piercing through the misty veil
35   Like rain of the departing year!
      Oh hush!—Again and yet again
      Bursts forth that loud and longdrawn strain,
      Soldiers! attend! it calls you back
      From the pursuers' bloody track,
40   And wildly o'er your foeman's fall
      Resounds your evening bugle call!

      The battle is done with the setting sun,
      The struggle is lost and the victory won,
      'Tis over, no sighs, no anguished cries,
45   From the wild wreck of conflict rise.
      The senseless corse on earth reclining
      Nor feels defeat nor knows repining,
      And they who survive in their agony
      Now stiff and spent and speechless lie,
50   With dim eyes wandering toward the sky,
        Yet look and seek no comfort there,
      For here upon this storm-tost heath
      The laboured faintness of the breath,
      The chill approach of Iron Death,
55   Demands a sterner care;
      And well I know that life's last light
      Just bordering on Eternal night,
      When all these souls shall take their flight,
        Must crush these souls with fear.

60   There they lie and wildly o'er them
        Howls the wind with hollow tone,
      While between its banks before them
        Hear the torrent chafe and groan
        Heavily with sullen tone,

65   Yet still advancing swiftly on;
And torn with shot, a shattered tree
    Shakes its bare arms in the bitter gale,
O'er the blood-red eddies that rapidly
    Down the swollen streamlet curling sail;
70 And the blackened stones of a fallen wall
    Dashed down by the iron-hail of war
With their earthy bank above them thrown
    Obstructs the torrent's passage there,
Till angrily its waters roar
75 All white with froth and red with gore;
And—There!—a shattered carcase lies
Without the power to look or rise.
'Tis He!—the Conquered Chieftain—he
Whose look could once give victory,
80 But sightless now—
The shot has torn his eyes away,
And his slashed face is dashed with clay
Cast backward in the eddying Flood
That washes off his bursting blood,
85 The stones across his body thrown
Which as he fell drove following down.
Oh scarce we know the human form
In this chief victim of the storm.
Yet—though thus crushed and torn he be,
90   Though hence he never more shall rise,
Though just as now still streams shall wash
From the crushed bones the wasting flesh,
    There shall he lie, as now he lies.
Yet still! oh still! look down and see
95 How vast may mortal misery be,
For in that bloody battered cell
Still Life and Soul and Memory dwell.
Never when he was fair and young
Did feeling thrill more stern and strong,
100 Never the Hell-hounds of despair
Had wilder power to worry there.

'O could I untormented lie
Without this gnawing agony
That wrings my heart so——!
105   Heavily and slow
The blood ebbs forth, but parts not so the soul:
Hither I came with pain, hence must I go
Still, still in pain!—Is such my changeless doom?
God! shall such destiny unroll,—
110 Its agonies beyond the tomb?
All Dark without, All Fire within,
Can Hell have mightier hold on sin?
But yet, through all, my dying mind
From such a present turns behind
115 To—what has been—and then looks o'er
The dark, dark void of things before,
The land of souls beyond the sable shore!
Oh how my eyes have stretched to see that land!
How even when sunk in life's bewildering roar
120   All my strained thoughts have striven to reach its
            strand,
            Have striven its mysteries to understand,
Though dark indeed the unreturning sea
That separates what lies beyond from me;
Though those vast waves which bear such thou-
            sands thither
125 Have never brought again one spirit hither,
            If spirits those who pass may truly be,
Those fearful passengers, whose sightless eyes
            And blanched lips and tongues which cannot
            move,
May either see the expanse which round them lies,
130   Or tell the scenes which open where they rove.
            Oh might I send across yon sea that Dove
Which bore the Olive branch! Oh might it bear
From hence some token, reward my hovering here,
Even though it were the fruit of bitterness,
135 So I might cease this doubt and fearfulness
While I embark to sail—I know not where,

I scarce know whence—or how—but such distress,
Vain is the hope that it will end!—and then
How vain the wish to know where lies my pain!
140 Oh, it lies here—and if my mind
Survives, it will not lag behind,
And if indeed—I really die,
Lost—in the abyss of vacancy,
Why *then* the sum of all will be
145 That I on earth have lived to see
Twice twenty winters beat on me,
Not one whole day of happiness
And year on year of mad distress!

'They say when on the bed of death
150 The wasted sick man lingering lies,
His breast scarce heaving with his breath,
And cold his hand and quenched his eyes,
See! how resignedly he dies.
Aye! what a look of peace and love
155 That glazed eye casts to heaven above:
Even those white lips will scarcely quiver
Though he must leave this world for ever,
And though his children around him stand
'Tis not for them that outstretched hand.
160 Angels shall press those clay cold fingers
In the unknown void round which he lingers.

'Ha! does the *victim* reason so
When bound beneath that fatal blow?
No! There indeed he lies inert,
165 For death's cold frost congeals his heart,
Yet while that dim and dazing eye
Can wander o'er one stander by,
While those mute lips, that silent tongue
Can one short broken gasp prolong,
170 While in that whirled and burning brain
Reason's last spark can wax and wane,
So long across that parting soul

Unmixed—unmingled—torments roll;
Ha—look on death with smiling eye,
175 Ha—content and peaceful die,
Ha—no, like fire one burning strife
Convulses each riven string of life,
And could those lips be moved to say,
Could those stiff hands be clasped to pray,
180 That only voice and prayer would be,
"Oh save me from that fatal sea
Where Hell and Death join agony!"

'I am dying, and what a rayless gloom
Seemed dark'ning round my dreary tomb.
185 I know no hope—I see no ray
To light me on my heavenly way.
There was a light—but it is gone.
There was a Hope—but all is o'er,
And friendless, sightless, left alone,
190 I go where thou hast gone before,
And yet I shall not see thee more.
Ha! say not that the dying man
Can only think of present pain,
Oh no! Oh no! it is not so,
195 For where, Maria, where art THOU!
O do I seem to see thee now?
Thy smiling eyes and shining brow,
Thy sunny cheek and golden hair,
In all thy beauty beaming there?
200 All through the noontide of my years
How thou didst enter all my fears
And hopes of joy, and smiles and tears!
How often have thy bright blue eyes
Driven sorrow shrinking from its shrine,
205 And banished all my misery
Before one heavenly look of thine!
How often has that look divine
Roused up this heart from bitterness,
Or bowed it in its worst distress

210 To kneel before thy shrine!
Oh, once we thought to pass together
Through stormiest change of wind and weather,
And thou wouldst never shrink from me,
And I could never part with thee
215 I clasped within my arms, and thou,
Lying on my breast thine ivory brow,
Unthought, uncared for storm or shine
While I was thine and thou wert mine.
When troubles hastened thickening on,
220 When every hope of rest seemed gone,
When 'mid the blight of hating eyes
I stood bewildered, sick with woe,
What was the star which seemed to rise
To light me on and guide me through?
225 What was that form so heavenly fair,
Untouched by time, unmarked with care,
To whose fond heart I clung to save
My sinking spirit from its grave?
Maria! hadst thou never been,
230 This hour I should not living be,
But while I strove with fate, between
The strife thou camest to set me free,
And wildly did I cling to thee.
I could not, would not, dared not part,
235 Lest hell again should seize my heart.

'Can I forget how toward my eye
Still ever gazed, for guidance, thine,
As if I were thy star on high,
Though well I knew 'twas thou wert mine.
240 That azure eye, that softened smile,
That heavenly voice whose tones to me
The weariest wintriest hours could wile,
And make me think that still might be
Some years of happiness with thee;
245 That thou, amid my life to come,
Shouldst be my hope, my heaven, my home,

But—we are sundered—thee, thy grave,
And me, this dreary wild will have.
Whate'er the world to come may be
250   I must never look on thee.
If there's no God, no Heaven, no Hell,
Thou within thy grave must dwell—
I, left black'ning in the storm—
Both a banquet for the worm.
255   If there *is* a heaven above,
        Thou in bliss art shining there
At the wondrous throne of love,
        Angel bright and angel fair:
From Heaven thou wanderest like the Dove
260   To the wild world of waters here,
But nevermore o'er it to rove,
        Thou hast left this site of sin and care,
        Back to thine Ark, while I staid where
The vilest mass of carnage lay,
265   A Raven rushing on the prey
And Hell's dread night must close my day!
        *   *   *   *   *
          *   *   *   *   *

'Why, why will the parted return to our heart
        When the sods have grown green on their tomb?
Oh, why will the twilight be first to depart
270   When it only gives depth to the gloom?
Oh why, in the snow and storms of December,
        When the branches lie scattered and strewn,
Do we oftest and clearest and brightest remember
        The sunshine and summer of June?
275   Oh why, mid the hungry and cottageless waste
        Do we dream of the goblet filled high?
Why will our spirits when famishing taste
        Such visionlike revelry?
Moralist, speak!—is't in life's deepest sorrow
280   That these gleams of the past which hath vanished
        away,

Though misery and mourning await on the morrow,
    May strengthen to bear through the shades of to-day?
Since we have had our sunshine, we must have our
    storm
First with the angel, and last with the worm.
285 Christian, speak—dost thou point to the sea
And show me the mariner drifting away,
Behind him the shores of his desolate home,
Around him the billows all crested with foam.
Yet he casts not a look upon ocean or shore,
290 But fixes his eyes on his haven before.
Sayest then, thou should now smile on his joy and his
    sorrow,
And press toward Heaven, his Haven of to-morrow?
Aye Man! on let him press till that heaven shall break
    In lightnings and thunders and tempest and gloom.
295 Then let the Spirit in safety speak!
    Where is the rest beyond the tomb?
    Where are the joys of his heavenly home?
Then let the moralist seek for his strength
    And smile on the past in its visionlike form.
300 Then let the Christian, anchored at length,
    See light in the darkness and sun through the storm.
Away with all this false disguise,
View midnight truth with noonday eyes,
The past has had a single joy,
305 But when the past is long gone by,
When cares have driven cares away,
When general darkness clouds the day,
That single star amid the sky
Will shed a brighter light on high,
310 And in the horizon only one
Is yet the ALL that can be shewn.
Well o'er me shining let it be
That thus one glimmering I may see
Fixed far above to show my gloom,
315 And light my spirit to its Tomb!

'Yet how I wander! grasping now
At the glorious dream of a world to come,
Then recalling back, I scarce know how
Upon that hideous, hopeless gloom,
320   THE NOTHINGNESS within the tomb.
Thinking of THEE, and then again
Shrinking within my present pain.
All wide, all wandering—This is death,
And I would calmly meet him now,
325   As then I'd feel my shivering breath
As I have felt my life blood flow,
But for the thought—
              Oh, what's to come!
God, if there be a God, look down,
330   Compassionate my call!
Oh, clear away thine awful frown,
        Oh, hearken to my call!
Nay—all is lost—I cannot bear
In mouldering dust to disappear,
335   And Heaven will not the gloom dispel,
Since were there one, my home were Hell—
No Hope, no Hope, and Oh, farewell.
The form so long kept treasured here
Must thou then ever disappear?
340   Gone, nay but kept in memory's shrine,
Now dying again as memory dies.
First passes from earth my star divine,
And now 'tis passing from the skies.
Thou art alone and Heaven is gone,
345   And sights and sounds and all are gone.

'Oh, what a state is life—I am dying,
And how like A DREAM is EXISTENCE FLYING.'

See through the shadows of the night,
        Burst hotly, hasting onward there,
350   A wounded charger vast and white
        All wild with pain and mad with fear.

With hoofs of thunder on he flies
Shaking his white mane to the skies,
Till on his huge knees tumbling down,
355   Across the fallen chieftain thrown,
With a single plunge of dying force
His vast limbs cover Albert's corse.

March 2, 1836.

This long poem was written by Branwell Brontë at the age of 18
years. On April 8, 1836, he submitted it for publication to the Editor
of *Blackwood's Magazine*. (See *The Brontës: Their Lives, Friendships and
Correspondence*. Shakespeare Head Edition, Vol. I, p. 135.) Portions of
it are quoted by Mrs Oliphant in *Annals of a Publishing House: William
Blackwood and His Sons*, Vol. II, p. 183.

ELRINGTON

THE sunshine of a summer sun
On the proud domes of Elrington
Glows with a beam divinely bright
In one unquenched, unvaried light,
5   And high its archèd windows rise,
As if to invite the smiling skies;
And proud its mighty columns show
Between them ranked in haughty row;
And sweet and soft the solemn shade
10   By the o'erarching portals made.

The stately halls of Elrington
May fitly meet that glorious sun,
For fêtes and feasts are given to-day
To noble Lords and Ladies gay;
15   And that vast city of the sea
Which round us lies so endlessly
Has hither poured its proudest train
To worship mirth and fly from pain.

34

The sunshine of a summer's sun
20 Glows o'er the graves of Elrington,
Where, city-girt spreads wide around
The flower and foliage-laden ground.
All round the hot and glaring sky
Bespeaks a mighty city nigh;
25 And through each opening in the shade
Palace and temple crown the glade.
So here, as an oasis stands
'Mid the wide waste of Egypt's sands,
This glorious vision of a grove,
30 With flowers beneath and fruits above,
Lies in that city's human sea
Whose streets stretch round so ceaselessly.

Oh! who could pass unnoticed by
This scene of nature's royalty?
35 Instead of birds to warble there,
Ethereal music fills the air,
Breathed from these halls thrown open wide
To admit the ever-changing tide
Of Earth and Afric's hope and pride.

May 17, 1836.

These lines were printed as Emily's in *The Complete Poems of Emily Brontë*, edited by Clement K. Shorter, 1910.

MY Ancient ship upon my Ancient sea
Begins another voyage—Nay thou'rt gone,
But whither pending? who is gone with thee?
Since parted from thee I am left alone,
5 Unknowing what my Rover's fate may be,
Into its native world of tempests thrown,
Lost like a speck from my diverted eye
Which wilder, mightier visions must survey;

Lost, and unnoticed—far away the roar
10 Of southern waters breaking to the wind,
With restless thunder rolling still before
As the wild gale sweeps wilder on behind,
And every vision of old Afric's shore
As much forgot and vanished out of mind
15 As the wild track thou markedst so long ago
From those eternal waves which surge below.

Gone—'tis a word which through life's troubled
        waste
Seems always coming, and the only one
Which can be called the *present*. Hope is past
20 But hate and strife and love and peace are gone
Before we think them, for their rapid haste
Scarce gives us time for one short smile or groan
Ere that thought dies, and new ones come between
It and our heart with some as fleeting scene.

25 And yet there is, or seems at least to be,
A general base of thought that colours all,
So though each one be different, all agree
In the same melancholy shade-like pall,
Even as the shadows look the same to me
30 Though cast I know, from many a varying wall
In this vast city—Hut and Temple sharing
In the same light, and the same darkness wearing.

Not that I deem all life a course of shade,
Nor all the world a waste of streets like these:
35 From youth to age a mighty change is made,
As from this city to the Southern seas:
For years through youthful hope our course is laid,
For years in sloth, a sea without a breeze,
For years amid the stir of civil jar,
40 For years within some silent sleepless care:

Changing, and still the same, yet swiftly passing,
'Tis here, 'tis there, 'tis nowhere, oh! my soul,
Is there no rest from such a fruitless chasing
Of the wild dreams that ever round thee roll!
45 Each as it comes the parting thought defacing,
Yet all still hurrying to the self-same goal—
Gone ere I catch them, but their path alone
Stretching afar toward *one* for ever gone!

What have I written—nothing, for 'tis over,
50 And seems as nothing in the single cloud
That shadows it, and long has seemed to hover
O'er all the crossing thoughts that overflowed
In this wrecked spirit. Oh, my ocean Rover!
Well may'st thou plough the deep so free and proud.
55 Thou bear'st the uniting tie of ceaseless dreams,
The fount, the confluence of a thousand streams.

I do not see myself again
A wanderer o'er the Atlantic main.
I do not backward turn my eye
60   Toward sleepless sea and stormy sky.
Oh, no! these banished visions rest
In far woodlands of the west,
And there let Hesperus arise
To watch my treasure where it lies.
65   The present scenes, the present clime
Forbid the Dreams of olden time.
The present thoughts, the present hour
Are rife with deeds of sterner power,
And who shall be my leading star
70   Amid the howling storm of war?

Hark! Listen to the distant gun
From the battlefield of Edwardston.
It breaks upon the awful roar
    Which stuns my ears around,

75   And on their shout of Victory
            Strikes with a hollow sound.
        My struggles all are crowned with power
        And fortune gives a glorious hour.
        Men who hate me kneel before me;
80   Men who kneel are forced to adore me;
        My name is on a million tongues,
        The million babbles of my wrongs,
        And twenty years of tyrant pride
        Which strove this modern God to hide
85   At last have vanished in the rays
        Of his unquenched, unclouded blaze.
        Oh! Is not Jesus come again
        Over his thousand saints to reign!
        To free the world from error's chain,
90   While sin and Satan vainly spit
        Their venomed fury from the pit
        Where they may lie...[1]
        Till Heaven descends...
        Their reign is past, their power is gone,
95   For fallen is Mighty Babylon.
                                    [*July*, 1836.]

In a prose manuscript dated July 22, 1836, belonging to the An-
grian cycle of stories, Branwell Brontë relates how Zamorna, King of
Angria, after his defeat at the Battle of Edwardston by Alexander
Percy, Earl of Northangerland, was 'placed in the ROVER, under
S'death, who directly set sail to banish him two thousand miles off on
the rocks of Ascension Isle.'
    In the autumn of 1834, Northangerland himself had been driven
out of Angria by Zamorna, and become 'a wanderer o'er the Atlantic
main.' In the above lines he muses on the fate of his ship, and his own
altered circumstances, and exults in his victory at the Battle of
Edwardston.
    These lines were printed as Emily's in *The Complete Poems of Emily
Brontë*, edited by Clement K. Shorter, 1910.

[1] Here there is an ink-stain on the manuscript obliterating a few words.

MEMORY

MEMORY! how thy magic fingers,
With a wild and passing thrill,
Wake the chord whose spirit lingers,
Sleeping silently and still,

5   Fast asleep and almost dying,
Through my days of changeless pain,
Till I deem those strings are lying,
Never to be waked again.

Winds have blown, but all unknown;
10   Nothing could arouse a tone
In that heart which like a stone
Senselessly has lain.

All seemed over—friend and lover
Strove to waken music there;
15   Flow the strings their fingers over,
Still in silence slept the air.

Memory! Memory comes at last,
Memory of feelings past,
And with an Æolian blast
20   Strikes the strings resistlessly.

[*July*, 1836.]

There is an earlier draft of this poem, besides which Branwell has written the following note:

'I am more terrifically and infernally and idiotically and brutally STUPID than ever I was in the whole course of my incarnate existence.

'The above precious lines are the fruits of one hour's most agonizing labour between ½ past 6 and ½ past 7 in the evening of Wednesday, July 1836.'

The lines were printed as Emily's in *The Complete Poems of Emily Brontë*, edited by Clement K. Shorter, 1910.

STILL and bright, in twilight shining,
Glitters forth the evening star;
Closing rosebuds, round me twining,
    Shed their fragrance through the air;
5 Slow the river pales its glancing,
Soft its waters cease their dancing,
Calm and cool the shades advancing
    Speak the hours of slumber near!
Why this solemn silence given
10   To the close of fading day?
Feels the earth the hush of heaven?
    Can the expanse of nature pray?
And when daylight's toil is done,
Grateful for summer sunshine gone,
15 Can it before the Almighty's throne
    Its glad obeisance pay?
Such a hush of sacred sadness
    Wide around the weary wild,
O'er the whirl of human madness
20   Spreads the slumbers of a child.
These surrounding sweeps of trees
Swaying to the evening breeze
With a voice like distant seas
    ·Making music mild.
25 Percy Hall above them lowering,
    Darker than the dark'ning sky,
With its halls and turrets towering
    Wakes the wind in passing by.
Round that scene of wondrous story
30 In their old ancestral glory
All its oaks so huge and hoary
    Wave their boughs on high.

Among these Turrets there is one
The soonest dark when day is done,
35 And when Autumn's winds are strongest
Moans the most and echoes longest.

So—on the steps that lie before
A solitary archèd door,
In that lone gable far away
40   From sights and sounds of social joy,
Fronting the expanse so dim and grey
   There sits a lonely boy.
One hand is in his curling hair
   To part it from his brow,
45 And that young face so soft and fair
   Is lifted heavenward now.
On the cold stone he has laid him down
   To watch that silver line
Beneath the power of twilight's frown
50   In the wide west decline.
For heaven still guides his azure eyes
   Toward its expanse so wild,
As veiled in darkness there he lies,
   A little Angel Child!

55 Oh who has known, or who can tell
   The Fountain of those feelings high
Which, while in this wild world we dwell,
   At times will lift us up on high,
   In a celestial sympathy
60 With yon lone vault, yon starry dome,
   As if the spirit deemed the sky
Was even on earth its only home,
   And while the eye is dim with tears,
   The feelings wrapt in dreams sublime,
65 How dead seem earthly hopes and fears,
   How all forgot the soul to time!
And yet the soul can never say
   What are the thoughts which make it glow.
We feel they *are*, but *what are* they?
70   'Tis this which we must never know
While lingering in this world of woe.

Yet did man's soul descend from heaven
With feelings by its Maker given
All high, all glorious, all divine,
75   And from his hand perfected gone
With such a bright reflected shine
    As the full moon bears from the sun.
But then—the soul was clothed in clay,
So straight its beauty passed away,
80 And through a whirl of misery driven
Earth's shadow came 'tween it and heaven.
A darkened orb the moon became,
Lost all its lustre, quenched its flame!
Or entering on this morbid life,
85 The clouds of war, the storms of strife,
Continual passing, veil it round
With gloomy wreaths of shade profound.
So, only shining fitfully,
A single gleam of light we see,
90 As pass the clouds on either hand
To show the clear calm heaven beyond.
Yet at one moment soars our soul
    Into those wayward dreams divine,
Till back again the darkness roll
95   And hide the uncertain shine.
Yet shall a time come rapid on
When all these clouds that round us frown,
From Heaven's vast vault all past and gone,
Leave the full moon in glory there,
100 To shine for ever bright and fair.
When this dull clay is cast away
These THOUGHTS shall shine with cloudless ray
And we shall understand what now
    .   .   .   .   .[1]

In yon lone child's uplifted eyes
105   Such dreams can scarce be dim,

[1] Line undecipherable.

So late upon those morbid skies
   The moon has risen to him;
So late his soul has passed from heaven
   That it can scarce forget
110 The visions bright whose hallowed light
   Is round its musings yet.
Silent he sits on the darkened stone,
   With night around him rolling,
As if to him that hollow moan
115   From the old tree tops were calling.
He listens to the eerie wind
   Around his Father's dwelling,
Till later following on his mind
   More glorious thoughts seem swelling.
120 For both his little hands were stretched
   In rapture to the sky,
When wilder from the wilderness
   Each blast came howling by
Toward clouds all southward resting wide
125   Above the Atlantic sea,
While o'er them far the darksome air
   Is haloed lustrously.
He fears some wondrous sight
   To him were opening soon,
130 Till, lo!—that sudden shining light,
   'The Moon, the glorious Moon!'

Oh, soft and sweet is the silver beam
   That floods the turret high,
While fairy woodlands round it seem
135   All shining gloriously.
Each window glitters cold and clear
   Upon the southern tower,
And—though the shade is darker made
   Around his lonely bower—
140 Yet o'er his face a solemn light
   Comes smiling from the sky,

And shows to light the lustre bright
  Of his uplifted eye.
The dimless, heedless carelessness
145   Of happy Infancy,
Yet such a solemn tearfulness
  Commingling with his glee,
The parted lips, the shining hair
  Cast backward from his brow,
150 Without a single shade of care,
But bathed amid that moonlight air,
  Oh, who so blest as thou!
The moon in glory o'er the grove
  Majestic marches on,
155 With all the vault of heaven above
    To canopy her throne;
And from her own celestial rest,
Upon the dark wood's waving crest
  Serenely she looks down,
160 Yet beaming still, as if she smiled,
Most brightly on that beauteous child.
But what thought he as there he lay
  Beneath the archèd door,
Amid the ever trembling play
165   Of moonshine through the bower,
Gazing with blue eyes dimmed with tears
To that vast vault of shining spheres,
  Till its mysterious power
Makes the bright drops unnoticed break
170 In dewy lustre o'er his cheek?

'Oh, how I could wish to fly
Far away through yonder sky,
O'er those trees upon the breeze
  To a paradise on high!
175 Why am I so bound below
That I must not, cannot go,

Lingering here for year on year
  So long before I die?
Now how glorious seems to be
180 Heaven's huge concave stretched o'er me.
But—Every star is hung so far
  Away from where I lie.
I love to see that Moon arise—
It suits so well the silent skies.
185 I love it well, but cannot tell
  Why it should make me cry.
Is't that it brings before me now
Those wondrous times gone long ago,
When Angels used from Heaven to come
190 And make this earth their happy home?
When Moses brought from Egypt's strand
God's favoured tribes through seas and sand
Victorious to the promised land!
When Salem rose, her Judah's pride,
195 Where David lived and Jesus died!
Is't that I know this very moon
Those vanished wonders gazed upon,
'When Shepherds watched their flocks by night,
  All seated on the ground,
200 And angels of the Lord came down,
  And glory shone around?'
Is't that I think upon the sea,
Just now lit beaming beauteously,
Where I so oft have longed to be,
205 But never yet have been?
Is't that it shines so far away
On Lands beyond that Ocean's spray,
Mong lonely Scotland's hills of grey
And ENGLAND's groves of green!
210 Or is't that through yon deep blue dome
It seems so solemnly to roam,
As if upon some unknown Sea,
  A vessel's stately form,

It o'er the waves was wandering free
215   Through calm and cloud and storm!
I cannot tell but it's in heaven,
    And though I view it here
Till I am mouldering dust to dust,
My parted spirit never must
220   Behold its brightness near.
I am crying to think that mighty throng
Of Glorious Stars to heaven belong,
That they can never, never see
A little earthly child like me;
225   Still rolling on, still beaming down,
And I unnoticed and unknown,
Though Jesus once in ages gone
    Called children to his knee.
So, where He reigns in glory bright
230   Above these starry skies of night,
Amid his paradise of light,
    Oh, why might I not be!
Oft, when awake on Christmas morn,
In sleepless twilight laid forlorn,
235   Strange thoughts have o'er my mind been borne
    How he has died for me;
And oft, within my chamber lying,
Have I awaked myself with crying
From dreams where I beheld him dying
240   Upon the accursed tree;
And often has my mother said,
While on her lap I laid my head,
She feared for time I was not made,
    But for Eternity!
245   So I can read my title clear
    To mansions in the skies,
And let me bid farewell to fear
    And wipe my weeping eyes.
I'll lay me down on this marble stone
250   And set the world aside,

To see upon its ebon throne
　　Yon moon in glory ride.
I'll strive to pierce that midnight vault
　　Beyond its farthest star,
255　Nor let my spirit's wanderings halt
　　'Neath Eden's crystal bar;
For sure that wind is calling me
　　To a land beyond the grave,
And I must not shrink upon the brink
260　　Of Jordan's heavenly wave;
But I'll fall asleep in its waters deep,
　　And wake on that blest shore
Where I shall neither want or weep
　　Or sigh or sorrow more.
265　Oh, Angels come! Oh, Angels come!
And guide me to my Heavenly Home!'

Guide thee to heaven!—Oh, lovely child,
Little knowest thou the tempests wild
Now gathering for thy future years
270　Their blighting floods of bitter tears.
Little thou knowest how long and dread
Must be thy path ere thou art laid
Within thy dark and narrow bed,
Or how, then, thou wilt shrink to be
275　Launched out upon Eternity,
All those celestial visions flown,
All Hope of Heaven for ever gone!
　　This passionate desire for Heaven
Is but the beam of brightness given
280　Around thy spirit at its birth,
And not yet quenched in clouds of earth,—
The inward yearnings of the soul
Toward its original sad goal,
Before that goal is hid from sight
285　Amid the gloom of mortal night.
To that just entering into Time
This world is like a stranger clime,

Where—nothing kindred—nothing known—
Leaves thy young spirit all alone
290 To spend its hours in thinking on
The native home whence it has gone.
    But—Oh! at last a time will come
When Heaven is lost, and earth is home;
Where pleasures glimmering on thy sight
295 As soon as seen shall sink in night,
Whilst thou pursuest them through the gloom,
Sinking like willows to the tomb.
This light shall change to lightning then,
This love of Heaven to Hell of men.
300 So if thou seekest a glorious name
Thy path shall lead through blood and flame,
From crime to crime, imparting healing,
Blessed thyself and others blessing;
For that which from on high is thrown
305 Will always fall most rapid down,
And sink the deepest—So with thee,
Thy quick and passionate heart shall be
But farther plunged in misery.
Then those around thee oft may find
310 Earth and its joys to suit their mind,—
For dust to dust, the sons of earth
Will love the land that gave them birth,
Yet never thou, or if thou dost
Full quickly thou shalt find it Dust!

315 He sleeps!—in slumber calm and deep,
An infant's blest and balmy sleep,
Dreaming of heaven those closèd eyes,
And glorious visions of the skies,
And tremblingly their fringes lie
320 On the young cheek of infancy;
The softened curls of golden hair
Just moving in the moonlight air;
But his white brow so sweetly still,
So free from every shade of ill,

325   Shall it be so for ever?—No!
Who in this world would wish it so.
Yon is the image of a man
Destined to lead the foremost van
Of coming time, and in his hand
330   The future chooses to command.
'Tis he whose never dying name
Shall see a future world of flame.
PERCY! awake thee from thy sleep.
Awake! to bid thy country weep.

August 13, 1836.

This is the poem which Branwell Brontë sent to William Words-
worth. In his letter to Wordsworth of January 19, 1837 (see *The
Brontës: Their Lives, Friendships and Correspondence*, Shakespeare Head
Edition, Vol. I, pp. 151–152), he writes:

'What I send you is the Prefatory Scene of a much longer sub-
ject, in which I have striven to develop strong passions and weak
principles struggling with a high imagination and acute feelings,
till, as youth hardens towards age, evil deeds and short enjoyments
end in mental misery and bodily ruin. Now, to send you the whole
of this would be a mock upon your patience; what you see does not
even pretend to be more than the description of an imaginative
child.'

Twenty lines, beginning 'So where he reigns in glory bright,' were
quoted by Mrs Gaskell in *The Life of Charlotte Brontë*, Chapter VIII.

SLEEP, mourner, sleep!—I cannot sleep,
My weary mind still wanders on;
Then silent weep—I cannot weep,
   For eyes and tears seem turned to stone.

5   O might my footsteps find a rest!
O might my eyes with tears run o'er!
O could the world but leave my breast
   To lapse in days that are no more!

And if I *could* in silence mourn
10   Apart from lying sympathy,
And man's remarks or sighs or scorn,
   I should be where I wish to be.

For nothing nearer Paradise
   Ought for a moment to be mine:
15 I've far outlived such real joys—
   I could not bear so bright a shine;

For I've been consecrate to grief—
   I should not be if that were gone—
And all my prospect of relief
20   On earth would be to grieve alone!

To live in sunshine would be now
   To live in Lethe every thought;
What I have seen and been below
   Must first be utterly forgot:

25 And I can not forget the years
   Gone by as if they'd never been;
Yet if I will remember—tears
   Must always dim the dreary scene.

So there's no choice—However bright
30   May beam the blaze of July's sun,
'Twill only yield another sight
   Of scenes and times forever gone.

However young and lovely round
   Fair forms may meet my cheerless eye,
35 They'll only hover o'er the ground
   Where fairer forms in darkness lie;

And voices tuned to Music's thrill,
   And laughter light as marriage strain,
Will only wake a ghostly chill,
40   As if the buried spoke again.

All—all is over, friend or lover
    Cannot awaken gladness here;
Though sweep the strings their music over,
    No sound will rouse the stirless air.[1]

45   I am dying away in dull decay,
    I feel and know the sands are down,
And Evening's latest, lingering ray
    At last from my wild heaven is flown.

Not now I speak of things whose forms
50   Are hid by intervening years,
Not now I pierce departed storms
    For bygone griefs and dried-up tears.

I cannot weep as once I wept
    Over my Western Beauty's grave,
55   Nor wake the woes that long have slept
    By Gambia's towers and trees and wave.

I am speaking of a later block,
    A death—the doom of yesterday;
I am thinking of my latest shock,
60   A noble friendship torn away.

I feel and say that I am cast
    From hope, and peace, and power, and pride—
A withered leaf on Autumn's blast;
    A shattered wreck on ocean's tide,

65   Without a voice to speak to me
    Save that deep tone which told my doom
And made my dread futurity
    Look darker than my vanished gloom;

Compare this stanza with stanza 4 of 'Memory,' p. 290.

Without companion save the sight,
70   For ever present to my eye,
Of that tempestuous winter night
That saw my angel Mary die.

January 13, 1837.

A later and unfinished version of this poem, written *c.* 1845–1847, is
contained in a manuscript in the Brontë Parsonage Museum, Haworth.
The poem was printed as Emily's in *The Complete Poems of Emily
Brontë*, edited by Clement K. Shorter, 1910.

'WELL! I will lift my eyes once more
       The Western heaven to wonder o'er,
Though I had thought them closed for ever—
Had thought that last, long look should sever
5   My thoughts from all this upper air!
But—Who can still the Spirit's care
Or hush the Griefs contending there?

'What! shining still? Oh thou canst shine
       With light and heat unchangeably,
10   Even though descends Thine orb divine
       On this wild world of misery!
Bright journeyer on a path like mine,
Companion of my dark decline,
       Thus let me welcome Thee!
15   And Oh! behind my native West
While thou descendest to thy rest,
To that far land I love the best,
       Might I but, following, flee!—

'My noble West! My Native Home!
20   How all my feelings round thee roam
       Since not even death can kill
The thoughts which from my Infancy
Have twined thee round my memory!
But I can feel thy Majesty
25   And, dying, I'll love thee still!

'Glorious in Heaven that sun goes down
  Lost in his own unclouded blaze,
And glorious is the splendour thrown
  Round his declining rays!
30 Glorious where chief, his central light
  Crowns those dim hills so far away,
Till all their summits float from sight
  Amid a sunbright sea!

'Though Life with me is waning low,
35 I feel my Heart expanding now
And tears are trembling in my eyes
While gazing on those glorious skies,
This dreadful Death forgot awhile,
These lips can frame one farewell smile;
40 And all is mingling now
Into a strange, celestial glow;
The Summer clouds, the sunlit trees,
The Blackbird's song, the Evening breeze,
The raptured thoughts that fill my brain,
45 Even this, my Bed of fevered pain,
All float in wildered maze around me;
All confounded, all confound me!

'Nature, I know, smiles fresh and fair,
And bright the Heavens and still the air,
50 But basking in those dreamlike skies,
Afar, a sea of glory lies
With all its Isles of Paradise
  Revealed before my sight;
And kissed by Evening's Westering blaze
55 And melting in its golden haze
They wander weakening in my gaze
  In strange unsteady light!

'Oh why is such a dreamy feeling
Over my dying spirit stealing?
60 Is this the dizzying whirl of death?

Does Memory with my parting breath
　　Yield up her trust to him?
Oh God! Oh God! and must I go?
Is this the voice that warns me to
65　　Awaken from my dream?

'I know not the reality
Which when awake these eyes must see
　　To look upon for ever,
But I *do* know the thrilling ties
70　Which bind my spirit to those skies,
And which my dying agonies
　　In vain may strive to sever.

'I cannot wake! My spirit seems
As if, amid unearthly dreams,
75　　Its course were borne away
From out this Ark of Wretchedness,
O'er blighting waves of bitterness,
For some green olive branch of peace
　　A weary flight to stray.

80　'Lost Bird! upon yon stormy sea
　　I seem to see thee hovering,
Where buried Nature's sepulchre
　　The waste of waves is covering,
And thy white wings are glistening there
85　　As thou for rest wert yearning;
But there's no hope in that dark air
　　To soothe thee, back returning;
Submerged thy native forests lie
　　With leafless branches torn;
90　So homeward through that wintry sky
　　Return, Lost Bird, Return!'

So that sweet sufferer spoke—Her mind
　　Seemed passing fast from earth
In forms and fancies undefined,
95　　To give its feelings birth
In glimpses of a spirit shore,

The strength of eyesight to restore,
  Which coming death denied,
That while the world was lost to her
100 Her soul might rove a wanderer
  Through visional wonders wide.

And strange it is how oft in death,
  When reason leaves the brain,
What sudden power the fancy hath
105   To seize the falling rein.
It cannot hold a firm control,
But it can guide the parting soul,
  Half leading and half led,
Through dreams whose startling imagery
110 Hide with their feigned reality
  The tossed and fevered bed.

It seems as to the bleeding heart
  With dying torments riven
A quickened life in every part
115   By fancy's force was given;
And all those dim disjointed dreams
Wherewith the failing memory teems
  Are but the bright reflection
Flashed upward from the scattered glass
120 Of mirror broken on the grass,
  Which shapeless figures in each piece
  Reveals without connection.

And is her mirror broke at last
  Who motionless is laid
125 To await her hour approaching fast
  Upon her dying bed?
Are her wild dreams of western skies
The shattered wrecks of memories
  That glitter through the gloom
130 Cast o'er them in the cold decay
Which signs the sickening soul away
  To meet its early tomb?

What pleasant Airs upon her face
    With freshening coolness play,
135 As they would kiss each transient grace
        Before it fades away;
    And backward rolled each deep red fold
    Begirt with tasselled cords of gold
        The Open Arch displays
140 O'er towers and trees that Orb divine
    His own unclouded light decline
        Before her glist'ning gaze.

    On pillows raised, her drooping head
        Confronts his glorious beam,
145 And all her tresses backward strayed
        Look golden in the gleam,
    But her wan lips and sunken cheek
    And full eyes eloquently speak
        Of sorrows gathering near,
150 Till those dark orbs o'erflowing fast
    Are shadowed by her hand at last
        To hide the streaming tear.

    Oh, say not that her vivid dreams
        Are but the shattered glass
155 Which but because more broken gleams
        More brightly on the grass.
    Her spirit is the unfathomed lake
    Whose face the sudden tempests break
        To one tormented roar,
160 But as the wild winds sink in peace
    All those disturbèd waves decrease
    Till each far down reflection is
        As lifelike as before.

    She thought when that confusion crossed
165   Upon her dying mind,
    'Twas sense and soul and memory lost
        Though feeling burned behind;

But that bright heaven has touched a chord
And that wide west has waked a word
170   Can still the spirit's storm,
Till all the griefs that brought her here,
Each gushing with a bitterer tear,
Round her returning sight appear
In more tremendous form.

175   'Land of the West! Thy glorious skies,
Their dreamy depths of azure blue,
Their sunset Isles of Paradise
That float in golden glory through
Those depths of azure o'er my sight
180   This musing moment seem to expand,
Revealing all their radiance bright
In Cloud Land, gorgeous Land!

'Land of the West—Thine Evening Sun
Brings thousand voiceless thoughts to mind
185   Of what I've said and seen and done
In years by time long left behind.
And forms and faces lost for ever
Seem arising round me now,
As if to bid farewell for ever
190   Before my spirit go.

'Oh! how they gush upon my heart
And over flow my eyes;
I must not keep, I cannot part
With such wild sympathies,
195   I know it's called a sin and shame
To mourn o'er what I mourn,
I know 'twill blacken o'er my name
And desecrate my urn;

'I know that I must soon decay
200   Without a single tear;
My friendships buried with my clay
And love forgotten there.

I know that I must meet my God
    Before an hour has flown,
205 To seek my sentence from His word
    For all the deeds I've done.

'I know!—But Oh! Thou Western Sky
    Take all my thoughts with thee!
And fly, my spirit, fleetly fly
210   Across that Western sea!
And raise my head that, when the shade
    Of Death comes darkning o'er me,
The mighty king may find me laid
    With my Sweet West before me.

215 'Yet still my Heart, how wild thou art
    That throbb'st so anxiously,
Where with the whole world though I part,
    I cannot part with thee.
And though the thoughts which ought to stay
220   Will fastest, farthest flee,
The thoughts I ought to keep away
    The closest cling to me!

'And comes the vision back again
    Which I should strive to quell
225 With all its wildly welcome pain
    In might Invincible;
And I must wake these tears for Him
    Whose heart is parted far,
The worship of my fevered dream,
230   My life's bright Western Star!

'And must the dart that shed thy blood
    Be consecrate by thee?
Say—shall all Lethe's dreary flood
    Wash out His memory?

235   My God has left me—But my Heart
        Through life to death is THINE,
        Nor can Eternal Torments part
        Thy Memory from Mine!'

                            February 9, 1837.

Stanzas 14, 15, 19, 20, 21, were printed as the work of Emily Brontë
in *The Complete Poems of Emily Brontë*, edited by Clement K. Shorter,
1910.

ALONE she paced her ancient Hall,
        While Night around hung dark and drear
And silent,—even her footsteps' fall
        Mocked echoless the aching ear
5   That ever watched but nought could hear,
And through the windows arched on high
        Alone looked forth the opening where
        Their mullions mingled with the sky
In midnight's cheerless vacancy,
10   Each lingering moment winged with fear
And filling her with dread unknown,
        Till scarce she dared to stop alone
        Although she felt she could not go,
That aimless dread had chilled her so!
15   And motionless with clasped hands there
        Against a Grecian pillar leaning
        She gave her spirit to the hour,
Gazing the unfathomed darkness o'er
        As if for signs of ghostly meaning;
20   And oh!—one wild wish seized(?) her brain—
        Might she but look on future years
        She felt she'd courage to sustain
All their array of phantom pain
        So it should end her doubts and tears,
25   For fast despair and hope combined
        Were bringing all the past to mind:

And—whispered Hope—the sun before
Might show more bright than sorrows o'er;
And nought *can come*—chimed in Despair—
30 More darksome than those sorrows were.
And then at every sound her soul
    Woke in those eyes that gazed to see
Phantoms amid the gloom unroll
    Her future History.

35 There is a time—when earthly aid
    Glides from the sinking soul away,
Wherein 'twill desperate call . . .[1]
    On Earth-born gods of empty sway;
And then, unmoored, with anchor lost,
40 O'er years of life's wide ocean tost,
Twill make a land of clouds and find
All . . .[1] in phantoms of the mind;
And so it was with her who there
Waited for help from forms of air.
45 She would have smiled in happier years
    To think of such a vain relief,
    But little knew she then how grief
Can move the soul to hopes and fears,
Far, far away from Reason's road
50 Wide wandering from the Throne of God!

Against the pillar leaned her cheek
    Even colder than that marble stone,
And fast she felt the tear drops break
From her strained eyes that wandered wide,
55 Reft like her heart of aim or guide,
    For something they might rest upon.
They wandered till they ached and then
Closed heavily with wearied pain,
And pressed one hand her burning brow
60   And one dropped coldly by her side,

[1] Word undecipherable.

And gathering fast, her voiceless woe
  Began to dim all thought beside,
Till faded in her deep distress
Even the eerie consciousness
65 Of where she stood—that lonely room
And midnight hour and phantom gloom
All mingling in a strange decay
All subsiding far away!
It was as if the world to her
70   Was sinking in a vast profound
  With clouds and darkness whirling round,
And thunders bursting on her ear.
But if her sudden start brought back
Her senses to that former track,
75 'Twas lost as soon and wrapt again.
She seemed above a dreary main
With tired wing wandering, and beneath,
The deep unfathomed waves of death,
Herself the only living thing
80 O'er that wide water hovering;
And seemed as though she lighted on
A floating form to her unknown,
Some wretched relic of the sea
Unnoticed, festering to decay,
85 Its uncurled hair with seaweed tangled,
Its bleaching cheek by seabirds mangled,
And grave worms nestling in the eyes
Turned sightless to the unpitying skies;
From whence upon the dreary dream
90 Came sudden down a single beam—
Enough for her—that beam revealed
All that the kinder clouds concealed—
The face, the form—one moment shewn,
All death despoiled—but ALL HIS OWN!
95 Her Hope, her Heaven lay there!—'Tis gone,
All gone that lonely lingering light,
Gone—drowned in one unchanging night

Whose deep dead clouds of darkness lie
Around their grim and lowering sky
100 With bitter blasts, whose moaning scream
Aroused her from the dreary dream;
And hardly roused her, for 'twas vain
To wake the wearied sense again,
And though she knew 'twas Phantasy
105 Whose fancied visions mock the eye,
She could not combat with it—still
That dreary dream seemed visible,
And even her struggles to get free
From such unreal imagery,
110 Her painful chasing from the soul
Thoughts far beyond its lost control,
Her frightful doubts, lost reason's reign
Was passing from her wildered brain,
All but increased the weight of care
115 And fixed the visions firmer there.
'Twas dead of night, and yet the sun
    Seemed strongly struggling through the gloom,
'Twas that old Hall, and yet he shone
On some far mansion not her own,
120   And in an unremembered room,
    The antechamber to her tomb:
For life around her seemed to swim
Like phantoms in a fever dream,
Mingled with wild realities
125 That struck upon her dizzied eyes
As sudden strikes the racking pain
That wakes the sleeping wretch again;
Till half she saw each curtained fold
    Gathered above the bed of death,
130 And half the being might behold
    That came to stop her fleeting breath.
He stood between her and the sun,
    All things in dizzy whirl save him—
A shadowy something, dark and dun,

135 Who back to the declining beam
Pointed with warning hand, to show
That as it sunk, so she must go,
Nor hope of respite there—subsided
Evening's beam to night—and glided
140 Her soul into forgetfulness
Of every pleasure or distress,
Till each cold member turned to clay,
And each faint feeling passed away,
Till fluttered forth her latest breath
145 And all seemed everlasting death.
She slept, and not even death could bring
A more unbroken slumbering.
No! not even now—Within that grave
Whose marble floors yon Minster aisle,
150 Can she a rest more peaceful have
From worldly wrongs and tears and toil!

O'er these cold bones so lowly laid
In that far tomb forgotten now,
Be slow thy step and soft thy tread
155 And long thy lingering look below!
There sleeps the soul that knew no sleep,
There throbs no more the burning brow,
There eyes of grief have ceased to weep,
There passion's storms are silent now!
160 These walls have heard the guns whose roar
Broke the Enchanter's mightiest spell,
These Towers have seen the strife which bore
Down from his throne the Invincible.

That roof had echoed back the knell
165 Of buried Hopes and pride and power,
When burst the storm on Parthas shore
That quenched Rebellion's torch in gore.
But THEE—not even that thundrous swell
Aroused from darkness!—though, afar,
170 Fell stricken Afric's Morning Star.

No—not though thine own PERCY fell!
Could that dread voice awake thee—Thou
  Slept mouldering on amid the yell
Of thousands trampled neath the foe,
175 Whose sudden shouts of victory won
Left thee alone to slumber on!

But—whence this dreamy wandering?—Back
Through vanished years retrace our track
From darkness into such a gloom
180 As might befit the darkest tomb!
No—Hours have passed, and as they fly
Time brings his changes ceaselessly.
'Tis the first dawn of summer morn,
  And looms the light o'er Alnwick's hill
185 In one long gleam that seems to stream
  Through darkness visible!
And hover round this lordly room
Realities half hid in gloom
That makes them visions—But the eye
190 Seeks for one fair reality,
Now long a vision!—there she lies!
In silence closed her weary eyes;
But nought can hide the loveliness
Of her fair form of youthful grace,
195 Whose soft curls shade the marble cheek
  Yet dewy with the undried tear,
Whose one fair hand her eyelids hide,
And one drops moveless by her side,
All still as she no more might wake
200   To morning's trembling air!

Brightened at last that summer morn,
And sudden on its breezes born
Out rushes o'er the rustling grove
The skylark's happy song of love,
205 Like Hopes that soaring up on high
Look brighter near their kindred sky,

And next about its fragrant bough,
Even close that window's arch below,
All round the echoing walls prolong
210 An answer to the Blackbird's song.
Who—when the earliest sounds they hear
Are tones so soft and sweet and clear—
Oh, who would think this world a den
Of warring, weeping, wretched men!-
215 But soft!—Her ears have caught the strain
That calls her back to life again.

Oh! that it called to hope—her eyes,
Like sunshine smiling out through rain,
Gaze strangely on that daylight air,
220 Unrecognizing aught around,
For something in that thrilling sound
Awoke her—not pertaining there,
    Something that spoke of far off skies
And vanished years—a passing glance
225   Towards a long lost paradise
Cast back across this world's expanse,
Soon hid by clouds and only leaving
For what is past a fruitless grieving!
So her that Blackbird's happy voice
230 Recalled to thoughts of perished joys
That lightning-like before her flow
And lost as soon in darkness too!
She rises—proudly calm and cold,
    Nay, even the shadow of a smile
235 Bespeaks her outward looks controuled
    All prying gazers to beguile;
Scarce marked her buoyant footsteps fall
While passing through that Lordly Hall;
Scarce seen the tear drop in her eye
240 That greets the morn so carelessly.

                                    March 1, 1837.

ON CAROLINE

T H E light of thy ancestral hall,
  Thy Caroline, no longer smiles:
She has changed her palace for a pall,
  Her garden walks for minster aisles:
5 Eternal sleep has stilled her breast
  Where peace and pleasure made their shrine;
Her golden head has sunk to rest—
  Oh, would that rest made calmer mine!

To thee, while watching o'er the bed
10 Where, mute and motionless, she lay,
How slow the midnight moments sped!
  How void of sunlight woke the day!
Nor ope'd her eyes to morning's beam,
  Though all around thee woke to her;
15 Nor broke thy raven-pinioned dream
  Of coffin, shroud, and sepulchre.

Why beats thy breast when hers is still?
  Why linger'st thou when she is gone?
Hop'st thou to light on good or ill?
20 To find companionship alone?
Perhaps thou think'st the churchyard stone
  Can hide past smiles and bury sighs:
That Memory, with her soul, has flown;
  That thou can'st leave her where she lies.

25 No! joy *itself* is but a shade,
  So well may its remembrance die;
But cares, life's conquerors, never fade,
  So strong is their reality!
Thou may'st forget the day which gave
30 That child of beauty to thy side,
But not the moment when the grave
  Took back again thy borrowed bride.

[1837.]

CAROLINE

CALM and clear the day declining,
　　Lends its brightness to the air,
With a slanted-sunlight shining,
　　Mixed with shadows stretching far:
5　Slow the river pales its glancing,
Soft its waters cease their dancing,
As the hush of eve advancing
　　Tells our toils that rest is near.

Why is such a silence given
10　　To this summer day's decay?
Does our earth feel aught of Heaven?
　　Can the voice of Nature pray?
And when daylight's toils are done,
Beneath its mighty Maker's throne,
15　Can it, for noontide sunshine gone,
　　Its debt with smiles repay?

Quiet airs of sacred gladness
　　Breathing through these woodlands wild,
O'er the whirl of mortal madness
20　　Spread the slumbers of a child:
These surrounding sweeps of trees
Swaying to the evening breeze,
With a voice like distant seas,
　　Making music mild.

25　Woodchurch Hall above them lowering
　　Dark against the pearly sky,
With its clustered chimneys towering,
　　Wakes the wind while passing by:
And in old ancestral glory,
30　Round that scene of ancient story,
All its oak-trees, huge and hoary,
　　Wave their boughs on high.

'Mid those gables there is one—
The soonest dark when day is gone—
35 Which, when autumn winds are strongest,
Moans the most and echoes longest:
There—with her curls like sunset air,
Like it all balmy, bright, and fair—
Sits Harriet, with her cheek reclined
40 On arm as white as mountain snow;
While, with a bursting swell, her mind
Fills with thoughts of 'Long Ago,'[1]
As from yon spire a funeral bell,
Wafting through heaven its mourning knell,
45 Warns man that life's uncertain day
Like lifeless Nature's must decay;
And tells her that the warning deep
Speaks where her own forefathers sleep,
And where destruction makes a prey
50 Of what was once this world to her,
But which—like other gods of clay—
Has cheated its blind worshipper:
With swelling breast and shining eyes
That seem to chide the thoughtless skies,
55 She strives in words to find relief
For long-pent thoughts of mellowed grief.

'Time's clouds roll back, and memory's light
Bursts suddenly upon my sight;
For thoughts, which words could never tell,
60 Find utterance in that funeral bell.
My heart, this eve, seemed full of feeling,
Yet nothing clear to me revealing;
Sounding in breathings undefined
Æolian music to my mind:
65 Then strikes that bell, and all subsides
Into a harmony, which glides
As sweet and solemn as the dream

---

[1] Compare these first five stanzas with the first 36 lines of 'Still and bright, in twilight shining,' p. 291.

Of a remembered funeral hymn.
This scene seemed like the magic glass,
70 Which bore upon its clouded face
Strange shadows that deceived the eye
With forms defined uncertainly;
That Bell is old Agrippa's wand,
Which parts the clouds on either hand,
75 And shows the pictured forms of doom
Momently brightening through the gloom:
Yes—shows a scene of bygone years—
Opens a fount of sealed-up tears—
And wakens memory's pensive thought
80 To visions sleeping—not forgot.
It brings me back a summer's day,
Shedding like this its parting ray,
With skies as shining and serene,
And hills as blue, and groves as green.

85 'Ah, well I recollect that hour,
When I sat, gazing, just as now,
Toward that ivy-mantled tower
Among these flowers which wave below!
No—not these flowers—they're long since dead,
90 And flowers have budded, bloomed, and gone,
Since those were plucked which gird the head
Laid underneath yon churchyard stone!
I stooped to pluck a rose that grew
Beside this window, waving then;
95 But back my little hand withdrew,
From some reproof of inward pain;
For *she who loved it* was not there
To check me with her dove-like eye,
And something bid my heart forbear
100 *Her* favourite rosebud to destroy.
Was it that bell—that funeral bell,
Sullenly sounding on the wind?

Was it that melancholy knell
  Which first to sorrow woke my mind?
105 I looked upon my mourning dress
  Till my heart beat with childish fear,
And—frightened at my loneliness—
  I watched, some well-known sound to hear.
But all without lay silent in
110 The sunny hush of afternoon,
And only muffled steps within
  Passed slowly and sedately on.
I well can recollect the awe
  With which I hastened to depart;
115 And, as I ran, the instinctive start
With which my mother's form I saw,
  Arrayed in black, with pallid face,
  And cheeks and 'kerchief wet with tears,
As down she stooped to kiss my face
120 And quiet my uncertain fears.

'She led me, in her mourning hood,
  Through voiceless galleries, to a room,
'Neath whose black hangings crowded stood,
  With downcast eyes and brows of gloom,
125 My known relations; while—with head
Declining o'er my sister's bed—
My father's stern eye dropt a tear
Upon the coffin resting there.
My mother lifted me to see
130 What might within that coffin be;
And, to this moment, I can feel
The voiceless gasp—the sickening chill—
With which I hid my whitened face
In the dear folds of her embrace;
135 For hardly dared I turn my head
Lest its wet eyes should view that bed.
"But, Harriet," said my mother mild,
"Look at *your* sister and my child

One moment, ere her form be hid
140 For ever 'neath its coffin lid!"
I heard the appeal, and answered too;
For down I bent to bid adieu.
But, as I looked, forgot affright
In mild and magical delight.

145 'There lay she then, as now she lies—
    For not a limb has moved since then—
In dreamless slumber closed, those eyes
    That never more might wake again.
She lay, as I had seen her lie
150   On many a happy night before,
When I was humbly kneeling by—
    Whom she was teaching to adore:
Oh, just as when by her I prayed,
    And she to heaven sent up my prayer,
155 She lay with flowers about her head—
    Though formal grave-clothes hid her hair!
Still did her lips the smile retain
    Which parted them when hope was high,
Still seemed her brow as smoothed from pain
160   As when all thought she could not die.
And, though her bed looked cramped and strange,
    Her *too* bright cheek all faded now,
My young eyes scarcely saw a change
    From hours when moonlight paled her brow.
165 And yet I felt—and scarce could speak—
    A chilly face, a faltering breath,
When my hand touched the marble cheek
    Which lay so passively beneath.
In fright I gasped, "Speak, Caroline!"
170   And bade my sister to arise;
But answered not her voice to mine,
    Nor ope'd her sleeping eyes.
I turned toward my mother then
    And prayed on her to call;

175 But, though she strove to hide her pain,
  It forced her tears to fall.
  She pressed me to her aching breast
  As if her heart would break,
  And bent in silence o'er the rest
180 Of one she could not wake:
  The rest of one, whose vanished years
  Her soul had watched in vain;
  The end of mother's hopes and fears,
  And happiness and pain.

185 'They came—they pressed the coffin lid
  Above my Caroline,
  And then, I felt, for ever hid
  My sister's face from mine!
  There was one moment's wildered start—
190 One pang remembered well—
  When first from my unhardened heart
  The tears of anguish fell:
  That swell of thought which seemed to fill
  The bursting heart, the gushing eye,
195 While fades all *present* good or ill
  Before the shades of things gone by.
  All else seems blank—the mourning march,
  The proud parade of woe,
  The passage 'neath the churchyard arch,
200 The crowd that met the show.
  My place or thoughts amid the train
  I strive to recollect, in vain—
  I could not think or see:
  I cared not whither I was borne:
205 And only felt that death had torn
  My Caroline from me.

  'Slowly and sadly, o'er her grave,
  The organ peals its passing stave,
  And, to its last dark dwelling-place,
210 The corpse attending mourners bear,

While o'er it bending, many a face
'Mongst young companions shows a tear.
I think I glanced toward the crowd
That stood in musing silence by,
215   And even now I hear the sound
Of some one's voice amongst them cry—
"I am the Resurrection and the Life—
He who believes in me shall never die!"

'Long years have never worn away
220 The unnatural strangeness of that day,
When I beheld—upon the plate
Of grim death's mockery of state—
That well-known word, that long-loved name,
Now but remembered like the dream
225 Of half-forgotten hymns divine,
My sister's name—my Caroline!
Down, down, they lowered her, sad and slow,
Into her narrow house below:
And deep, indeed, appeared to be
230 That one glimpse of eternity,
Where, cut from life, corruption lay,
Where beauty soon should turn to clay!
Though scarcely conscious, hotly fell
The drops that spoke my last farewell;
235 And wild my sob, when hollow rung
The first cold clod above her flung,
When glitter was to turn to rust,
"Ashes to ashes, dust to dust!"

'How bitter seemed that moment when,
240   Earth's ceremonies o'er,
We from the filled grave turned again
    To leave her evermore;
And, when emerging from the cold
    Of damp, sepulchral air,

245 As I turned, listless to behold
    The evening fresh and fair,
How sadly seemed to smile the face
    Of the descending sun!
How seemed as if his latest race
250   Were with that evening run!
There sank his orb behind the grove
    Of my ancestral home,
With heaven's unbounded vault above
    To canopy his tomb.
255 Yet lingering sadly and serene,
    As for his last farewell,
To shine upon those wild woods green
    O'er which he'd loved to dwell.

'I lost him, and the silent room,
260   Where soon at rest I lay,
Began to darken, 'neath the gloom
    Of twilight's dull decay;
So, sobbing as my heart would break,
    And blind with gushing eyes,
265 Hours seemed whole nights to me awake,
    And day as 'twould not rise.
I almost prayed that I might die—
    But then the thought would come
That, if I did, my corpse must lie
270   In yonder dismal tomb;
Until, methought, I saw its stone,
    By moonshine glistening clear,
While Caroline's bright form alone
    Kept silent watching there:
275 All white with angel's wings she seemed,
    And indistinct to see;
But when the unclouded moonlight beamed
    I saw her beckon me,

And fade, thus beckoning, while the wind
280 Around that midnight wall,
To me—now lingering years behind—
Seemed then my sister's call!

'And thus it brought me back the hours
When we, at rest together,
285 Used to lie listening to the showers
Of wild December weather;
Which, when, as oft, they woke in her
The chords of inward thought,
Would fill with pictures that wild air,
290 From far-off memories brought;
So, while I lay, I heard again
Her silver-sounding tongue,
Rehearsing some remembered strain
Of old times long agone!
295 And, flashed across my spirit's sight,
What she had often told me—
When, laid awake on Christmas night,
Her sheltering arms would fold me—
About that midnight-seeming day,
300 Whose gloom o'er Calvary thrown,
Showed trembling Nature's deep dismay
At what her sons had done:
When sacred Salem's murky air
Was riven with the cry,
305 Which told the world how mortals dare
The Immortal crucify;
When those who, sorrowing, sat afar,
With aching heart and eye,
Beheld their great Redeemer there,
310 'Mid sneers and scoffings die;
When all His earthly vigour fled,
When thirsty faintness bowed His head,
When His pale limbs were moistened o'er

With deathly dews and dripping gore,
315 When quivered all His worn-out frame,
As Death, triumphant, quenched life's flame,
When upward gazed His glazing eyes
To those tremendous-seeming skies,
When burst His cry of agony—
320 "My God!—my God!—hast Thou forsaken me!"

'My youthful feelings startled then,
As if the temple, rent in twain,
Horribly pealing on my ear
With its deep thunder note of fear,
325 Wrapping the world in general gloom,
As if her God's were Nature's tomb;
While sheeted ghosts before my gaze
Passed, flitting 'mid the dreary maze,
As if rejoicing at the day
330 When death—their king—o'er Heaven had sway.
In glistening charnel damps arrayed,
They seemed to gibber round my head,
Through night's drear void directing me
Toward still and solemn Calvary,
335 Where gleamed that cross with steady shine
Around the thorn-crowned head divine—
A flaming cross—a beacon light
To this world's universal night!
It seemed to shine with such a glow,
340 And through my spirit piercing so,
That, pantingly, I strove to cry
For her, whom I thought slumbered by,
And hide me from that awful shine
In the embrace of Caroline!
345 I wakened in the attempt—'twas day;
The troubled dream had fled away;
'Twas day—and I, alone, was laid
In that great room and stately bed;

No Caroline beside me! Wide
350 And unrelenting swept the tide
Of death 'twixt her and me!'
.   There paused
Sweet Harriet's voice, for such thoughts caused—

.   .   .   .   .

[1837.]

In a letter to J. B. Leyland, written in January, 1848, Branwell
Brontë writes:
    'When you return me the manuscript volume which I placed in
your hands will you (if you can easily lay your hands on it) enclose
that MS. called "Caroline"—left with you many months since—
and which I should not care about any more than about the volume,
only I have no copies of either.'
    It seems that Leyland did not return the MS. as the poem is printed
by F. A. Leyland in *The Brontë Family*, Vol. I, pp. 214–226.

HARRIET I

HOW Edenlike seem Palace Halls
    Where Youth and Beauty join,
To waken up their lighted walls
    With looks and smiles divine.
5 How free from care the perfumed air
    About them seems to play,
How glad and bright appears each sight,
    Each sound how soft and gay!

'Tis like the Heaven which parting days
10   In summer's pride imbue
With beams of such imperial blaze,
    And yet so tender too.
But, Parting day, however bright
    It still is—Parting day!
15 The Herald of descending night,
    The Beacon of decay!

So when my mind recalls to me
The Hour in years gone by,
When such a scene of Majesty
20   First met my wondering eye,
I think—within that Lordly Dome
How soon its glory fell,
And Woe and darkness made their home
Where joy was wont to dwell.

25 I think—till o'er the unknown main
Departed spirits glide,
And bring before my eyes again
That warning night of pride.
So turn from yon bright clouds that spread
30   Those sunset skies behind,
And look with me and thou shalt see
The sunset of the mind!

A hundred lustres light the Hall
Where power and pleasure reign,
35 And gilded roof and mirrored wall
Reflect their rays again;
And, entering from the starless night,
So dazzling seems this blaze of light,
That scarce the eye may know
40 Who form the proud patrician throng
Whose glittering mazes pour along
With such imperial show:
Till, slowly on the senses stealing,
Saloons and galleries seem revealing
45 Columns clad in many a fold
Of costly crimson ribbed with gold,
Ancient arches ranked between,
And long drawn lighted halls within,
Where mid the ever varying dance
50 Visions of loveliness advance,
Beheld one moment, but an age
Wipes not such sights away, and when

Long years of Life's corroding pain
Has hardened every feeling, still
55   The vision shall have power to assuage
The troubled heart, and warm the chill
   Of sad and stoic Age![1]

There is in such a magic hour
Something of so divine a power
60 That the full heart and thrilling eye
O'erflow with sudden tears of joy,
For we feel at once there lingers still,
Like evening sunshine o'er a hill,
A glory round Life's pinnacle,
65 And, though our fortunes lie below
The splendour of that sunny brow,
Still will Ambition beckon on
To It, a Height which may be won,
And Hope still whispers in the ear,
70 'Others have been, thou mayst be there,
But 'scape the shade of humble birth
And something of Heaven is thine on Earth!'

Amid this Royal Bower of Love
   One Vision seems to glow
75 Of a resounding Dome above
   And a gathered crowd below,
Whose glancing plumes and curling hair
   Beneath the lights on high
Wave gladly to each perfumed air
80   That sighs so sweetly by;
But all assembled in a ring,
As still as they were worshipping
Beneath the eye of Heaven divine
At some blest Martyr's Holy shrine;
85 And whither wafts the sacred sound
Which makes this trancèd quiet round,

---

[1] 'Of Life's most Northern stage' (alternate line in MS.)

And lures these stealing footsteps on
    Before its Heaven-born breathings die,
Till peals from its ascending tone
90   Tumultuous Melody!—
    Whose is the Minstrelsy?
Sounding in chords abrupt and loud,
Or in the Bosom of the crowd
    Subsiding Mournfully?

95   The Minstrel sits begirt by eyes
That gaze on him with mute surprise,
But away with that last quivering note
His own wrapt spirit seems to float;
For silent droops his curling head
100   O'er which the lights a halo shed,
And on the keys that 'neath them lie
His eyes are fixing vacantly;
Unheard by him the sounds that come
Resounding from the lighted Dome
105   Of distant dance and laughter gay,
For his bent brow and looks of gloom
    Show feelings wandering far away;
But there is something in his face
Beyond its outward form of grace—
110   A forehead dark with frowns of ire,
An eye of fierce, unholy fire,
A lip of scorn—but all o'erspread
With the chill whiteness of the dead,
And noble though the features be
115   They are marked with hidden treachery,
And sickness left from hours gone by
Of riot and debauchery.

A sudden welcome wakes his ear
In tones that sound familiar,
120   So from his dreams he starts to know
The faces of the princely row,
Forgotten—though they round him stand,

And though so bright the beauteous band
Whose soft approving glances swim
125   With tears of rapture, roused by him,
And whose red lips so softly parting
Smile upon his sudden starting.—
Then, He knows his power revealed
In Them, though from themselves concealed;
130   His power upon each Beauty's soul
That bows to feeling's soft controul,
Unconscious that her real shrine
Is that high front and face divine!

Tall and erect the Minstrel rises
135   With placid calmness, that disguises
Each treacherous hope within his breast,
For there, to greet their Noble Guest,
The Lord and Lady of the Hall
Are both arrived at Music's call.
140   He—a man severe to sight
Of mighty bone and manly height,
With restless eyes and raven hair
Dashed from his forehead broad and bare.
She, oh! could I paint her form—
145   A sunbeam wedded to the storm!
With such a look of friendship shining
    Through her bright and dewy eye,
That not the silken lock declining
Could o'ershade its brilliancy,
150   No, not even the shadows passing
    Through her heart and o'er her brow
Could avail in wholly chasing
    Thence, its soft and sunny glow.
Strange that she, thus formed to be
155   The banisher of misery,
Should have one cloud of care or sadness
To overcast her smiles of gladness;
But—where feeling most appears,

There springs the fullest fount of tears,
160 Since on this earth the seeking eye
Meets more of sorrow than of joy;
And Lady! thus the youthful bloom
    From thy soft cheek so soon declined,
    And thus so oft thy inward mind
165 Seemed looking forward to the tomb!
For early hopes, in thee so strong,
With early scenes and times were gone,
And—wedded to an Iron Breast
    Whose feelings ne'er replied to thine,
170 For thy far forests of the west
    Long days of summer saw thee pine;
And Halls in stateliest grandeur drest
    Could ne'er thy sorrowing soul resign
    To cold content, when those far skies
175 Hold all thy Spirit's sympathies!

But let us to that night return—
    And, mid that noble company,
    Beside the minstrel standing—why
Did her fair cheek with blushes burn?
180 Oh what awoke the sudden red
That o'er its sorrowing paleness spread?
And when her lips a greeting tried,
    What broke their quick and trembling tone?
And, oh! when his to her replied,
185   Why—through their tears—her dark eyes shone?
    He said—'I thought you'd scarce have known
A face and form so changed as mine,
    But, through the shade that years have thrown,
It seems that still the past can shine!
190 Yet time has marked us both with care,
And are our friendships what they were?
My old regards accept from me
As wrecks of many a stormy sea,
And I'll forgive if you've forgot—

195 For ships in harboured rest will rot
Sooner than those whose tattered sails
Have braved wild waves and wrecking gales——
With wandering look the lady stood,
    As if his voice she hardly heard—
200 As if her inmost thoughts would brood
    On thought more deep than spoken word,
And then she said—still tremblingly,
    'Percy!—We heard that you were far
Across the stormy northern sea
205   Still sailing, but we knew not where,
Though every wind that swept the sky
Recalled you to my memory,
    And every hour reminded me
Of happier skies and brighter weather
210 When we used to walk together—
I—unconscious as a child
How years of winds and waters wild
Should separate—
             Oh, Sir, forgive
The weakness of this woman's tear,
215 For—as we stand together here,
    Old Times and Memories will revive!'
So Harriet with her heart alive
To other hours of vanished bliss,
But dead to all the pomp of this,
220   Stood by her Noble friend whose eye
Lit with a look of double meaning,
As if some thought of darkness screening
    With a strange smile of treachery—
And yet—to hers replying, for his
225 Was not the heart which could, unmoved,
Behold the mind of one he loved
So changed—So saddened—
                  There she stood,
Leaning against his instrument,
230   And the unbidden flush of blood

Dying from off her cheek that bent
  To hide, in vain, the sudden flood
Of sorrows long suppressed till now!—
But what a shadow crossed his brow,
235 Whose eyes upon her beauty fell
With a reflected light of Hell,
That woke in every gazer's mind
A fear of something undefined;
And Percy knew it, so, to chase
240   The dampness o'er that circle lying,
He called the demon from his face,
And, with an air of winning grace
  Over the keys his fingers trying,
He struck a chord of sudden sound
245 That gathered quick his listeners round.

'Harriet' he said, 'Shall hear a song—
  O'er many a wave has swelled its strain!—
  And often it has brought again
The hours when she and I were young!'
250   He smiled, and straight his fingers woke
A solemn change of swelling tone
  That with an aimless seeming broke,
As if at random round him thrown—
Such music as the Atlantic gale
255 Had often sounded in his sail,
Till all its chords began to join
With his deep voice in melody divine.

SONG[1]
Air: 'Auld Lang Syne.'

SONG BY PERCY

SHOULD Old Acquaintance be forgot
As Time leaves years behind?
260 Should Life's for ever changing lot
Work stronger on the mind?

Should Space that severs Heart from Heart
The Heart's first love destroy?
Should Time that bids the youth depart
265 Bid youthful Memories die?

Oh! say not that these coming years
Can fresh Affections bring,
For friendship's Hopes and friendship's fears
From deeper fountains spring.

270 Their feelings to the Heart belong,
Their token—glistening eyes,
While later friendship on the tongue
Arises, lives and dies!

And passing crowds may smiles awake
275 The passing hour to cheer,
But—only *old Acquaintance' sake*
Can ever wake a Tear!

So the stately Minstrel sung,
Turning as that last note rung
280 To mark the impression of his song
Upon the mute surrounding throng,
And, when he turned, his eyes were brightning
With a fervour so divine

[1] A slightly different version of this song was sent by Branwell to J. B. Leyland in the year 1842. See *The Brontë Family*, by F. A. Leyland, Vol. II, p. 24.

That many a soft heart felt like lightning
285   The thrill of their poetic shine,
While thrilled indeed that Lady's hand
By his a single moment pressed,
As softly smiling he addressed
His *old Acquaintance* and his best
290   And last and *only* friend!

Oh how that voice seemed music's own,
As yet again with winning tone
He said—'Our spirits vainly strive
To keep old friendships still alive,
295 If happy hearts and pleasant hours
Our pathway strew with countless flowers,
For such a constant joy destroys
The memory of former joys.—
'Tis care and sorrow round us strewn
300 That give us back the pleasures gone,
As darksome nights, not sunny days,
Awake the far-off Beacon's blaze,
And minds content, from happy home
May never find a cause to roam,
305 While hearts, fair Lady, such as mine,
   Continual tossed from storm to storm,
   The vanished Hopes, the parted form
Will still remember—still repine!
And these thoughts—deeming you were true,
310 Have lit the fire which warmed me through
Many a dark day of maddened slaughter,
And many a night of stormy water;
So, though declares my altered brow
That as I was, I am not now,
315 If your fair eyes my heart could see,
That is as it was wont to be!'—

So burst in such impassioned tide
   Those words, breathed from a burning mind
   That little cared for ill designed

320 If but the hour was gratified
With conquering passion, hate or pride;
And Harriet dared not—could not think
Her yielding heart on ruin's brink,
When every look and word from him
325 Awoke some sweet remembered dream
Of Auld Lang Syne—of happy youth,
Of summer skies and sunny smiles,
When after treacheries and wiles
Stained not the Soul's unsullied truth.
330 'Tis true she saw the shade severe
Impressed by many a stormy year
Collected on his forehead high,
And o'er his deep unquiet eye,
But in its glance of dissolute joy
335 That truly sparkled to destroy,
Her fond heart traced with answering thrill
The old impassioned feeling still.
So she replied with solemn sweetness
Such as thrilled the Listener's ear—
340 Sorrow she was used to witness,
And had shaken hands with care!
But o'er that deluge of Distress
Oh! should she dream that Hope would bear
One welcome olive branch of Peace
345 To save her future from Despair!—
'Twas sweet to join the broken chain
Of old associations gone,
By such a meeting once again,
To the long Future coming on!

350 But—! There she stopped, for trusted not
Her heart to speak of him who stood
Apart, in black and brooding mood,
The gloomy partner of that Lot
Which he embittered with a life
355 Of wild debauchery and strife,

And serpent-like revenge—
                              Oh well
    To Percy's heart was Hector known!
    His comrade dear in riot gone,
360 And now his foe implacable,
    For He—while Percy, far away,
    Was tossing over Norway's sea,
    For his broad Lands found ample grace
    Before Her friends and father's face,
365 So she was sacrificed to be
    The Bride of wrath and treachery,
    However much her sunny soul
    Might shrink beneath his harsh controul;
    However hate, neglect or pride
370 Should cast her dreams of comfort wide!
    'And now' thought Percy, home returned—
        With Spirit practised to destroy—
    While every nerve for vengeance burned,
        'If I my thoughts on ought employ
375 Save how to wake the ancient flame,
    Till headlong Passion end in shame
    To him who dared my prize to take—
    May I no more have power to wake
        A look of love from Woman's eye!———'
380 Yes—Percy saw, and Percy's soul
        Felt all the flame he wished to inspire,
    Till doubly spurning all controul
        He plunged in that destroying fire
    And gave his fiery heart the rein,
385 Heedless of punishment or pain!

    But—turn we to that magic sound
    Where whirled the dance on music round,
        Mid merry laughter through the room
        While echoed back the regal Dome
390 That busy hum of social sound,
    And mirrors gave in mimic nature

Many a fairy form and feature
And lustres gloriously supplied
The light by midnight hours denied.
395 While—there they two together stood,
No one near them—all alone
In a bright world of their own,
Whose sunny light no cloud subdued
With worldlike shadow—Heard by them,
400 The whirl of pleasure round them flying
On their enraptured ear fell dying
Like an incoherent Dream!
But Recollections crowding came
To re-awake the smouldering flame,
405 And, as on each refulgent head
A glorious glow those lustres shed,
How glanced in Harriet's eyes a shine
That made their tearful looks divine
Beneath those golden locks, that shaded
410 The Angel brow their curls invaded,
While mutely mild her soft lips smiled
To note the change on Percy made
By long, long years of waters wild
Whose storms she thought had given that shade
415 Of passing sternness o'er his face,
Though never yet in woman's eye
Did marks of ills and wars gone by
A Noble Countenance deface.
His voice too had a deeper tone
420 Than that her earlier years had known,
While her blue eyes more sadly shone
Than in departed days,
But both indeed seemed passing fair,
In rapt communion standing there,
425 And o'er them lingered many a gaze
From forth the giddy, passing maze,
And many a heart of rank and power
Did homage to that lovely flower,

Whose very whiteness far outshone
430 The redder roses round her strewn.

But—wherefore will Time's warning finger
    Sign these happy hours away?
Cares and sorrows always linger—
    Cannot these a moment stay?
435 Yet, Great Destroyer, whose will is dooming
    All the world to be Thy prey,
Know thine own last hour is coming
    Faster still with our decay!
For since that fateful night had birth
440 A score of years have past from earth,
And thou, whose Avarice nought will leave,
Art so much nearer to thy grave!

Now slowly through that mighty Hall
    The sound of mirth and music dies,
445 And softly signs of parting fall
    From lips and hands and eyes.
Corridors receive the tide
Underneath their Arches wide,
And many a chariot's wheels are heard
450   Departing through the starless night,
And many a whispered farewell word
    Shall long through memory glisten bright.
And many, oh many a heart sinks down
    From forced smiles, vainly kept so long
455   Amid the mazes of the throng,
To gnawing care or sullen frown.
Till now, at last, the lustres bright
Gleam on a floor of lonely light!
And all alone fair Harriet stands
460   Beneath their beams all dimly waning,
    Of that proud crowd the last remaining,
With wandering eyes and clasping hands,
Entranced—as if all living things
    Were but the shadows of a dream,

465   Till o'er her blue eyes humid gleam
The o'erwrought gush of feeling springs,
An outburst of the soul's surprise
When buried Hopes so sudden rise,
And then so soon depart.—He is gone!
470   That glorious face, that noble form,
Returning from so many a storm
To bring her back a lifetime flown,
And then to leave her thus alone!—
She had not spoken the farewell word,
475   She scarce his own farewell had heard,
But in her hearing something rung
As if he had said—'Oh wait not long,
For spite of Fate—if I am thine,
Thou art, thou wilt—thou shalt be mine!'

August 27–November 9, 1837.

A variant version of the first three stanzas of this poem, and the
thirteen lines beginning 'There is something in this glorious hour'
were printed as Emily's in *The Complete Poems of Emily Brontë*, edited
by Clement K. Shorter, 1910. The first four stanzas were printed as
the work of Branwell Brontë in *The Orphans and Other Poems*, privately
printed for Mr. T. J. Wise in 1917.

HARRIET II

AT dead of Midnight, drearily
  I heard a voice of horror say
'O God, I am lost for ever!'—
And then the bed of slumber shook
5   As if its troubled sleeper woke
  With an affrighted shiver;
While in her waking burst a sigh
  Repressed with sudden fear,
As she gasped faintly—'Where am I?—
10   Oh help!—Is no one here?'

No one was there—And, through the dark,
Only a last and trembling spark,
Left from the dying taper's light,
With red gloom specked the void of night,
15 Which, scarcely wakened from her dreaming,
　　She gazed at as this far off world,
　　From whence her spirit's flight seemed hurled,
Through Heaven's vast void so feebly gleaming!
Quick came that thought, and, quickly gone—
20 She found herself laid there alone,
While heard my ear the choking sob
As that dread truth, with 'wildering throb,
Seemed as its force would stop the breath
Of her who woke to wait for death!
25 There, both her hands as cold as clay
Pressed her damp forehead, while she lay
All motionless, beneath the power
Which weighs upon life's latest hour.
Short, short had been her fevered slumber,
30 　And filled with dreams of that dread shore
　　Where she must wait her Judge, before
Another hour that night might number!
And fails my pen to paint the room
So deeply veiled in utter gloom
35 Where she unseen, unwatched, unknown,
And thought and feeling almost gone,
Gasped breathless, 'neath The Mighty Foe,
And watched each moment for the blow!

'O God!'—she murmured forth again,
40 　While scarce her shattered senses knew
　　What darkness shrouded from her view—
'Oh, take from me this sick'ning pain!—
That frightful dream, if 'twas a dream,
　　Has only wakened me to die;
45 Yet death and life confounded seem
　　To inward thought and outward eye!

'Tis not the Agony of death
That chills my breast and chokes my breath;
'Tis not the flush of fevered pain
50 That dizzies so my burning brain—
Which makes me shudder to implore Thee
When my soul should bow before Thee;
I shrink not from the eternal gloom
That waits my *body* in the tomb—
55 Oh no!—'Tis something far more dread
Which haunts me on my dying bed!—
I have lost—long lost—my trust in Thee!
   I cannot hope that Thou wilt hear
   The unrepentant sinner's prayer!
60 So, whither must my spirit flee
For succour through Eternity?
Beside me yawns that awful void,
And, of the joys I once enjoyed,
Not one remains, my soul to cheer,
65 When I am launched all aidless there!

'Eternity!—oh, were there none!—
   Could I believe what some believe,
   Soon might my spirit cease to grieve
At the cold grave and churchyard stone!
70 But—God!—To appear before Thy face
In all a sinner's nakedness,
Without one little hour to spare
To make that sinner's sins more fair,
   Without the slightest power to shun
75   Thine Eye whose lightning looks upon
   All things I've thought and deeds I've done.
Repentance past, and useless prayer—
How can my *spirit* live to stand
That look, and hear that Dread Command
80   Which even Archangels shrink to hear?
That voice whose Terrors none can tell
"Depart, Lost Spirit, into HELL!"

Great God! To-*night*, shall fires infernal
  Hold me down in hideous pains
85   With devils bound in burning chains,
And fires and pains and chains ETERNAL?
O Christ! When Thou wert crucified
Thou heardst the felon at Thy side,
And in his bitterest agony
90 Thou promisedst him a Heaven with Thee!
But, he repented and confessed
Ere Thou wouldst give his anguish rest;
And, oh!—In my last hour, do *I*—
Thus wretchedly afraid to die—
95 *Dare I* repent?—*Can I* repent?—
When with my very life are blent
  The feelings that have made me sin,
Who have scorned Thy name to atone my crime?—
Repent!—Ah, no! My Sands of Time
100   Sink far too swiftly to begin!—
Can I repent?—*Can* I forget
The face, the form, scarce vanished yet?—
The only vision which has proved
There's aught in this world worth being loved!
105 Can I forget the Noble Name
For which I lost my earthly fame?—
Can I forget—when harshly round
Parents and friends and kindred frowned;
When Home was made a Hell of strife
110 By those who gave and shared my life?
When far had fled the inward peace
Which gives the troubled spirit ease?
When—Heaven's and Earth's affections reft
Nor present Hopes, nor future, left?
115 Can I forget the Glorious Star
That cheered me through the weary war?—
Those long long hours of rapt communion,
  'Mid the quiet Moonlight grove,
Those wild hopes of future union

120 Gilding o'er my guilty love!—
Even the bursts of maddened mourning
If I was his Happy Bride
Lost amid the joys returning
When once more he sought my side!—

125 'Oh, I led a life of sinning
At her beck, whose soul was sin;
Yet my spirit ceased repining
If a look from him 'twould win!—
Bright that band with hellish glory
130 Circling round *Augusta's Throne,*
Dark those hearts whose influence o'er me
Led me in and lured me on!—
All their Mirth I knew was hollow,
Gain and guilt their path and aim,
135 Yet I cared not what might follow—
Deaf to warning, dead to shame.
What to me if Jordan Hall
Held all Hell within its wall,
So I might in his embrace
140 Drown the misery of disgrace!

'God! *Thou* knowest my inward thought
Through many a dreary after-day
When, to another sold away,
Could never with my Hand be bought!
145 Or, if a moment's madness gave
My heart to throb—a Tyrant's slave,
Still—still how often true to one
Whom still I thought for ever gone
I'd sadly sit and silent weep
150 While all the wide world seemed asleep—
Thinking upon that surging sea
That tossed his vessel far away!

'Oh, wast thy curse—when sneers and scorn,
From a stern jesting fiend, had worn

155 My soul, so long dispirited
    And chafed between disgust and dread—
    Oh, wast thy curse, that fatal night,
    Which once more brought him to my sight,
    When all the room went whirling round
160 As first I heard his music sound,
    When all my veins ran living flame
    As first—for years—he named my name,
    As first I pledged my broken faith
    To fly with him to—friendless death!
165 I'd spent my life in search for pleasure,
    I thought that hour I'd found the treasure;
    All else I lost to gain that one
    And—when I gained it—It was gone!—
    Then Honour left me!—peace of mind
170   Fled with it, and conscience came
        To gnaw my heart with ceaseless flame
    And wither all it left behind.
    Oh, for a while—a little while,
    While I could gain a single smile
175 From him—my Star of Happiness,
    I knew not how to feel distress,
    'Twas then the dreadful death-blow came,
    'Twas when he left me to my shame,
    When sudden ceased my Star to shine,
180 That happy hopes—that joys divine,
    As they were centred, passed with him,
    And—I awakened from my dream!—
    Sure, never bore a human frame,
        Unmaddened, agonies like me,
185 Who have lain as if Hell's hottest flame
        Was kindled by that agony,
    Till day and night has o'er me flown
    Alike unnumbered and unknown;
    Tossing on my tearless pillow
190 As if it were Hell's burning billow;
    Straining eyes that wept no longer

Weak'ning down while woe waxed stronger!

'Where—in such an hour of pain—
Where were friends and flatterers then?
195   Where were hearts that would have died,
So they perished by my side?
Where were knees that joyed to kneel
Waiting on my slightest will?
Tongues and thoughts that seemed to be
200   Only framed to speak of me!
Ah!—The wide world holds them still;
   All is whirling round the same;
     The same feigned words and fancies flame,
But waiting on another's will!
205   Then and now as once they shone
Thousand lights are beaming down,
And dizzy dance and thrilling song
Still gather many a noble throng!—
   There was but a single change;
210   One was lost—and no one heeded,
For along the glittering range
   No one felt that ONE was needed.
Faces blushed to name her name,
Silence hushed the Adulterer's shame,
215   Little cared they how she grieved
   O'er her monstrous wickedness.
Hardly knew they if she lived
   Through her desolate distress!
Three short words might speak her lot—
220   *Fallen, Forsaken,* and *Forgot!'*

There she stopped, for, spent and broken,
The last deep accents she had spoken
Fell as if no more could come
From lips with utter anguish dumb!
225   There she stopped, but even the bed
Trembled with her dying dread,

And for a while she moaning lay
As if she'd weep her heart away.
Now and then a broken word
230 Amid her sobbing might be heard—
Some name perhaps that childhood knew
And yet to fleeting memory true;
Some thought perhaps of far off time
Before these hours of grief and crime
235 Had changed that voice of music mild
Into a key so sadly wild!

Could HE have bent above her head,
    Even he whose guilt had laid her there,
One burning drop he must have shed
240   Those old yet altered tones to hear,
    Like west winds breathing on his ear
    The Memory of climes afar!
She thought herself old scenes among,
Where Recollection lingering hung
245 In life's last hour to bid farewell
To what her heart had loved so well.
Methought she called on 'Caroline!'
    As long ago she used to cry
When laid at rest in eve's decline—
250   Till Caroline all smilingly
Would bend above her golden head
    And sing to sleep the guileless child.—
Oh! had she known this change so dread,
    Fair Caroline had never smiled
255 To see her sister's blue eyes close
And kiss her lips to sweet repose!
But let us haste to present woe
From pleasures perished long ago.—
As Harriet lay, the spark of red
260 In her spent taper vanishèd;
So turning toward the wall her head
She murmured—

'Ah! So all depart
From blasted hopes and broken heart!
265 I thought IT might have been my end,
But nought a sinner will attend
To the dark flood!—They're gone—all gone!—
Where's PERCY?'—
                        With that word again
270 Like bowstring loosened from its strain
Her wandering spirit sprung!—That tone
Called voice and vigour back—
                        'Who's gone?—
O Percy! Percy! *where* art thou?—
275   I've sacrificed my God for thee,
And yet thou wilt not come to me!—
How thy strong arm might save me now!
My heart would chase away despair;
I'd hope, I'd live, if thou wert there!
280 Percy, *where* art thou—tell me where?—
He's far away—and minds no more
Than the spent surge of Norway's shore
His 'Own loved Harriet'—Halls of light,
And beauteous forms and beaming eyes
285   Echo and look this very night
To his rich floods of harmonies!
He smiles and laughs!—Amid the throng
None smile so much or laugh so long.
Ah! Lady, fly that witchery,
290 Or thou wilt soon be fallen as I!
Ah, fair and frail, the tender tale
Must then again o'er thee prevail?—
And wilt thou kneel to such a god?
And darest thou bear his chast'ning rod?
295 What though this mighty dome contain
So bright a scene, so fair a train—
But my own head whirls dizzily
For these are visions that I see!
Save me! I'm falling!—Was *that* him?

300 Methought I saw a sudden beam
Of passing brightness through the room
Like lightning vanish—Percy, come!
Leave me not in the dark; 'tis cold,
    And something stands beside my bed—
305 Oh, loose me from its icy hold
    That presses on me! Raise my head—
    I cannot breathe!'—
                She'd scarcely said
That word, when sudden o'er her frame
310 Again the chilly trembling came,
And died upon her palsying tongue
The charmèd words adored so long;
And, all relaxed, her hands unclasped,
And faint and fainter still she gasped—
315 Why fell that silence?—Hush! I hear
    A wing-like winnowing—'tis the wind
In the Cathedral Towers afar—
    But it came strangely on my mind
Like one departing. . . .
                .   .   .   .
                        [*eleven asterisks in author's MS.*]
320 I waited through the waning night
Until the first pale hue of light
    Won wanly o'er the gloom;
I watched the forms of things arise
Like midnight spectres to my eyes,
325 While all things showed like mysteries
    About the silent room.
I looked intently on the bed
Where that unhappy Lady laid,
    But naught distinct could see;
330 I felt a sense of awful fear
Thus to be left so lonely there,
I hardly dared to gaze on her
    When seen more plain by me.
Oh, did she sleep or was she dying? —

335 The curtain drawn obscured her lying,
But all distinct each window pane
Was starting into form again;
And longer here I must not stay,
For daylight makes me speed away,
340 And yet the task was given to me
To watch her through her agony.
So back I drew the curtain shade,
And started at the noise I made.
There, then, her gentle cheek declined;
345 All white her neck and shoulders gleamed,
White as the bed where they reclined.
As peaceful slumbering she seemed,
As if in Heaven her spirit dreamed,
Till lo! a stronger morning glowed,
350 And all the solemn vision showed
Hands clasped—cheeks sunk—
—But Oh that brow,
I saw it and I knew it now!
I knew it in . . .

[Here the text abruptly ends.]

May 14, 1838.

Branwell Brontë sent a transcript of the second part of 'Harriet' to
Hartley Coleridge on April 29, 1840, but in that transcript he made
many variations in the text, and omitted the concluding portion from
'I waited through the waning night.' In his letter to Coleridge, Bran-
well states that the piece 'is only the sequel of one striving to depict
the fall from unguided passion into neglect, despair and death. It
ought to shew an hour too near those of pleasure for repentance, and
too near death for hope.'
    The poem is here printed from the manuscript in the Brontë Par-
sonage Museum, Haworth.

NOW—but one moment, let me stay:
   One moment, ere I go
To join the ranks whose Bugles play
   On Evesham's woody brow.

5   One calm hour on the brink of life
   Before I dash amid the strife
      That sounds upon my ear;
   That sullen sound whose sullen roll
   Bursts over many a parting soul—
10   That deep-mouthed voice of war!

Here am I standing lonely 'neath
   The shade of quiet trees,
That scarce can catch a single breath
   Of this sweet evening breeze.

15   And nothing in the twilight sky
   Except its veil of clouds on high,
      All sleeping calm and grey;
   And nothing on the summer gale
   But the sweet trumpet's solemn wail
20   Slow sounding far away.

That and the strange, uncertain sound
   Scarce heard, yet heard by all;
A trembling through the summer ground,
   A murmuring round the wall.

These lines were printed as Emily's in *The Complete Poems of Emily Brontë*, edited by Clement K. Shorter, 1910.

OH, all our cares these noontide airs
   Might seem to drive away,
So glad and bright each sight appears,
   Each sound so soft and gay;
5   And through the shade of yonder glade,
   Where thick the leaves are dancing,

While jewels rare and flow'rets fair
   A hundred plumes are glancing.
For there the palace portals rise
10   Beyond the myrtle grove,
Catching the whitest, brightest dyes
   From the deep blue dome above.
But here this little lonely spot,
   Retires among its trees,
15 By all unknown and noticed not,
   Save sunshine and the breeze.

These lines were printed as Emily's in *The Complete Poems of Emily Brontë*, edited by Clement K. Shorter, 1910.

FRAGMENT

AS if heartsick at scenes of death, the day
   From Albuera's hills has passed away,
Not with its customed gift of farewell light
To feed our hopes through the dark paths of night,
5   But mingling battle smoke with driving rain,
And howling blasts with shrieks of mortal pain.

Was that the Moon?—Methought I saw her shine
As hurrying clouds disclosed one beam divine,
But her mild face befits not such an hour,
10   So intervened the increasing sleet and shower,
And heaven above again looked charged with woe
And darkness veiled the scenes on earth below.

THERE'S many a grief to shade the scene,
   And hide the starry skies;
But all such clouds that intervene
   From mortal life arise.

5 And—may I smile—O God! to see
Their storms of sorrow beat on me,
    When I so surely know
That Thou, the while, art shining on;
That I, at last, when they are gone,
10 Shall see the glories of Thy throne,
    So far more bright than now.

January 23, 1838.

DEATH TRIUMPHANT

OH! on this first bright Mayday morn,
    That seems to change our earth to Heaven,
May my own bitter thoughts be borne,
    With the wild winter it has driven!
5 Like this earth, may my mind be made
    To feel the freshness round me spreading,
    No other aid to rouse it needing
Than thy glad light, so long delayed.
    Sweet woodland sunshine!—none but thee
10   Can wake the joys of memory,
Which seemed decaying, as all decayed.

O! may they bud, as thou dost now,
    With promise of a summer near!
Nay—let me feel my weary brow—
15   Where are the ringlets wreathing there?
Why does the hand that shades it tremble?
    Why do these limbs, so languid, shun
    Their walk beneath the morning sun?
Ah, mortal Self! couldst thou dissemble
20   Like Sister-Soul! But forms refuse
    The real and unreal to confuse.
But, with caprice of fancy, She
Joins things long past with things to be,

Till even I doubt if I have told
25   My tale of woes and wonders o'er,
Or think Her magic can unfold
A phantom path of joys before—
Or, laid beneath this Mayday blaze—
Ask, 'Live I o'er departed days?'
30   Am I the child by Gambia's side,
Beneath its woodlands waving wide?
Have I the footsteps bounding free,
The happy laugh of infancy?

May, 1838.

SIR HENRY TUNSTALL

(THE WANDERER)

BIBLIOGRAPHICAL NOTE

In the Ashley Library of Mr T. J. Wise is a manuscript which is described in 'A Brontë Library' as:

'*The Wanderer*. A Tale in Verse. By Emily Jane Brontë. Bradford, 1838.

'The original Holograph Manuscript, extending to twelve closely written large octavo pages of white paper, measuring $7\frac{7}{8}$ by 5 inches. The poem, which is unpublished, comprises 509 lines, mostly in rhymed couplets, but with a lyric of five four-line stanzas introduced. The whole is written in the usual minute script affected by the Brontë children, and is dated "Bradford, July 31st, 1838."...

'*The Wanderer* is an early draft of *Sir Henry Tunstall*, printed as by Branwell in the *De Quincey Memorials*, 1891. Apparently either Branwell adopted his sister's work when composing the latter poem, or Emily for some unknown reason transcribed her brother's verses in their original form.'

In the note-book used by Branwell Brontë during the time he was employed on the railway at Luddendenfoot, and which he took home with him to Haworth in 1842, is his first draft of part of a letter which he wrote to the editor of *Blackwood's Magazine* on September 6, 1842. The letter accompanied a long poem which he had written when he was living in Bradford in the summer of 1838, and to which he gave the title of *Sir Henry Tunstall*. The entry in the note-book reads as follows:

'The piece endeavours, I fear feebly enough, to describe the harsh contrast between the mind changed by long absence from home, and the feelings kept flourishing in the hearts of those who have never wandered, and who vainly expect to find the heart returning as fresh as when they had bidden it farewell.'

Part of the poem was printed in *Annals of a Publishing House: William Blackwood and His Sons*, 1897, by Mrs Oliphant, and in *De Quincey Memorials*, 1891, by Alexander Japp, more than five hundred lines of the poem are printed, the text being derived from a copy of the poem which Branwell sent to De Quincey on April 15, 1840.

'TIS only afternoon—but midnight's gloom
    Could scarce seem stiller, in the darkest room,
Than does this ancient mansion's strange repose,
So long ere common cares of daylight close.
5 I hear the clock slow ticking in the Hall;
And—far away—the woodland waterfall
Sounds, lost, like stars from out the noonday skies—
And seldom heard until those stars arise.
    The parlour group are seated all together,
10 With long looks turned toward the threat'ning weather,
Whose grey clouds, gathering o'er the moveless trees,
Nor break nor brighten with the passing breeze.
    Why seems that group attired with such a care?
And who's the visitor they watch for there?
15 The aged Father, on his customed seat,
With cushioned stool to prop his crippled feet,
Averting from the rest his forehead high
To hide the drop that quivers in his eye;
And strange the pang which bids that drop to start;
20 For hope and sadness mingle in his heart;
A trembling hope for what may come to-day—
A sadness sent from what has passed away!
Fast by the window sits his daughter fair;
Who, gazing earnest on the clouded air,
25 Clasps close her mother's hand, and paler grows
With every leaf that falls, or breeze that blows:

Sickened with long hope bursting into morn
Too long for her, with longer pining worn!
Even those young children o'er the table bent;
30   And on that map with childish eyes intent,
Are guiding fancied ships through ocean's foam,
And wondering—'what he's like'—and 'when he'll
    come.'
Ah! many an hour has seen yon circle pore
O'er that great map of India's far-off shore,
35   And sigh at every name the paper gave
Lest it might mark their well-beloved warrior's grave
Oft have their eyes a burning tear let fall
O'er Ganges' mimic tide or Delhi's wall;
Oft have their hearts left England far away
40   To wander o'er the wastes of red Assaye!

.   .   .   .   .

But long that house has lost all trace of him,
Whose very form in memory waxes dim.
Long since his childhood's chosen friends have died;
The shaggy pony he was wont to ride—
45   The dog so faithful to its Master's side—
The rooks and doves that hover round the door
Are not the same his young hand fed of yore;
The flowers he planted many seasons past
Have drooped and died and disappeared at last;
50   For him afar, tempestuous seas had torn,
Before the children round that map were born:
And, since, so many years have passed between
The voiceless farewells of that parting scene,
That scarce they saw it then through gathering tears
55   So dim as now through intervening years.
'But still'—said Mary—'still I think I see
The Soldier's plumed helmet bent o'er me,
The arm that raised me to a last embrace,
The calmness settled o'er his youthful face,
60   Save when I asked 'how soon he'd come again'—
And all that calm was lost a moment then!—

Our Father shook his hand, but could not speak,
Our weeping Mother kissed his sunny cheek,
Our Sisters spoke not—'twas a mute farewell,
65 And yet no voice could speak it half so well.
We saw our *Henry* on his charger spring,
We heard his swift hoofs o'er the pavement ring,
There—long we stopped—as if he still was there—
Hand clasped in hand, and full eyes fixed on air:
70 He scarce seemed gone so long as we beheld
The chequered sunshine and the open field,
But—when we turned within—when closed the door
On that bright Heaven—we felt that *all* was o'er;
That never more those rooms should hear his call,
75 That never more his step should cross that Hall.
We sat together till the twilight dim,
But all the world to us seemed gone with him.
We gathered close, but could not drive away
The dreary solitude that o'er us lay.
80 We felt when *one* has left the home fireside
It matters not though all be there beside,
For still all hearts will wander with that one,
And gladness stays not when the heart is gone,
And—where no gladness is a crowd may feel alone.

    .   .   .   .   .

85 'Since then how oft we've sat together here
With windows opening on the twilight air,
Silently thinking of the climes afar
Beneath the shining of that evening star,
Dear as a friend unto our loneliness
90 Because it seemed to link those lands with us.
He saw it, perhaps, when time's and ocean's tide
So many years had sundered from our side,
And 'twas the same he used to look upon
While all beside so different had grown.
95 Our wood, our house, ourselves, were not the same
As those that floated through his boyhood's dream.
Is he too changed?—Alas, the cannons' roar,

The storms and summers of that burning shore,
May have made the last great change!—Too well I
  know!
100 Even *our* calm woods cannot escape *that* blow!
We cannot greet him if again he come
With the same group that made his ancient home—
The Heart that he loved best is clad in clay—
She is laid in lasting rest—she is far away!'

105   So Mary spoke—but she said nothing now,
Turning so earnestly her pallid brow
On the dull Heavens to which they all were turning
With looks that could not clear the shade of mourning
Worn far too constantly upon each face
110 For that one day of feverish hope to chase;
That day, determined from Madeira's shore,
When they their wanderer might behold once more;
Not now the boyish ensign he had gone,
But full of honours from his foes o'erthrown.
115 Time after time fresh tidings of his fame
Had roused to life his aged Father's frame,
When the old Man would raise his gushing eye,
And lose his sighs of grief in smiles of joy.
  At last, that letter with *Sir Henry's* crest
120 The tidings of his swift approach expressed,
A Victor General to his England's shore—
At last—that sixteen years' suspense seemed o'er.
At last—the fresh-rolled walks, the shaven lawn
That long a look of such neglect had worn,
125 The rooms so fairly decked—the expectant calm
O'er all things brooding like a magic charm,
At last, proclaimed the mighty moment come
When hope and doubt should both give place to doom.
  Stay—what was that which broke the hush pro-
    found?—
130 Like rapid wheels I heard its murmur sound.
Why are the servants' footsteps heard within

So sudden intermixed with hasty din?
What pales each cheek—what lights each swimming
    eye
Through the close circle of that company?

   ·   ·   ·   ·   ·

135   I cannot paint the start of mute surprise,
The tears that flashed in scarce-believing eyes,
The long embrace—the silence eloquent
Of more than language ever could give vent;
The Father's face that said, 'Thy will be done—
140 Take me if fit since Thou hast given my son;'
The Mother's look, too fond to turn above
Her Son beholding with a mother's love;
The Sister's eyes that shone in youth's o'erflow
Of feelings such as age could never know,
145 With whom this world was not the earth it seems,
But all surrounded by the light of dreams,
With whom even Sorrow took a heavenly die,
Since where it darkened Hope seemed shining by;
So thus, while, speechless, held in *His* embrace,
150 She saw, she knew, her long-lost Henry's face,
She let past times part—hurrying down the wind,
And years of vain repinings leave her mind.
    Not so Old Age—for Sorrow breaks it in,
And—used to harness—it can ill begin
155 Existence o'er again. Dissolved in tears
Of heartfelt gratitude, the head of years
Was bowed before that Soldier—but in vain
Each parent strove to shake off Sorrow's chain;
Their eyes were dim to present joys—yet still
160 Past joys to them were far more visible.
They saw their first-born's golden locks appear
Shining behind the cloud of memories dear;
They looked—and was this war-worn warrior Him?
Ah! how the golden locks waned dark and dim!
165 Their innocence destroyed—for India's clime
Had touched him with the iron hoar of time;

Wast him?—they gazed again—a look, a tone
Can sometimes bring the past—'twas Henry—'twas
   their own!

They did not mark his restless glances roam
170 As if he sought but could not find his home;
They did not mark the sternness of his cheek
Even if to smiles its muscles chose to break;
They only saw the stately Soldier's form
Confirmed, not altered by the battle's storm;
175 They only saw the long-lost face again,
Darkened by climate, not by crime or pain.
    But what *He* thought it would be hard to tell,
Since worldly life can mask the heart so well,
Can hide with smiles a sorrow-eaten cheek,
180 Can bitter thoughts in cheerful accents speak,
Can give to icy minds heart-eloquence,
And 'clothe no meaning in the words of sense'—
Words he poured forth of warm and welcome greet-
    ing,
For—'Heaven,' he said, 'smiled in this happy meet-
    ing.'—
185 By turns he wandered o'er each long-lost face—
By turns he held them in a fast embrace—
Then Mary saw—though nought her parents knew—
For youthful love has eyes of eagle view—
She saw his features in a moment alter,
190 Their rapture vanish and their fondness falter;
And—in that moment—Oh, how cold seemed all
The mind that lurked beneath that passion's pall!
A corse beneath a gilded shroud—the corse
Of him who left them on his battle-horse
195 Sixteen long years ago!—
                —Sir Henry broke
A sudden pause where only glances spoke,
With a request for one half-hour alone
To call his spirits to a steadier tone,

200 And moderate their swell. He left them then
　　To spend that time in calling back again
　　The ancient image to their wildered view,
　　To mark the difference 'twixt the old and new:
　　But—strange—whene'er they strove to realize
205 The form erewhile enshrined in their eyes,
　　The visioned Idol of each vanished year—
　　How *like* a vision did it now appear!
　　They could not bear to see it shrink from view,
　　Like a vain dream—but never came the new
210 Before the old—thus on a sudden faded
　　When by life's stern realities invaded.
　　Changed—like life's dreary path from youth to
　　　　years,
　　And dull as age. The twilight hour appears,
　　The hour ordained by God for man's repose,
215 Yet often made by man an hour of woes,
　　A summing-up of daylight's toils and grief,
　　Of moody musing, not of mild relief.

　　　·　　　·　　　·　　　·　　　·

　　That dull hour darkened in the boding sky,
　　And bore the breeze in mournful murmurs by,
220 With promise of a storm. Within the room
　　No cheerful candle shone to cheat its gloom,
　　Nor cheerful countenance smiled—for only one
　　Lone tenant held it, seated still as stone—
　　Sir Henry Tunstall—with a vacant gaze,
225 As if his mind were wandering through a maze
　　Of alien thoughts, though on that very bed
　　Long years ago had lain his infant head
　　In sleep unstained by sorrow. Still there hung—
　　Wrecks of a time when all the world looked young—
230 His guns—his rods—wherewith he'd often trod
　　The breezy hills or wandered by the flood,
　　And breasted mountain winds, and felt within
　　The first bold stirrings of the Man begin.
　　There, pictured as of yore, the self-same wall

235   Showed England's victory, and her Hero's fall
        On cold Canadian hills. With strange delight,
        In other days the child would fix his sight,
        Whene'er he wakened, on that time-dimmed view,
        And inly burn to be a hero too;
240   Would fill his spirit with the thoughts divine
        Of the loud cannon, and the charging line,
        And Wolfe, departing 'mid commingling cries
        To join immortal spirits in the skies!
        'Twas that dim print that over Indian seas
245   First led his feet and fixed his destinies.
        So why on what was childhood's chief delight
        Will manhood hardly deign to bend his sight?
        The old print remains—but does the *old mind* remain?
        Ah World!—why wilt thou break enchantment's
              chain!—

250   Bending his brows, at last Sir Henry said—
        'Well, *now* I know that Time has really sped
        Since last my head has in that chamber lain—
        That nothing has my *Now* to do with *Then!*
        Yes—now at last I've reached my native home,
255   And all who loved me joy to see me come,
        And memory of departed love is nigh
        To cast a holier halo round their joy.
        I have seen my Father full of honoured days,
        Whom last I saw adorned with manhood's grace,
260   Who has lived since then long winters but to see
        Once more—his first-born—world-divided me.
        I have seen those re-kindle, that have mourned
        For me. I have seen those grey locks that have turned
        From raven black for me. I have seen Her too—
265   The first I loved on earth—the first I knew—
        She who was wont above that very bed
        To bend with blessings o'er my helpless head;
        I have seen my Sister—I have seen them all—
        All but myself. They have lost *me* past recall,

270 As I have them. And vainly have I come
These thousand leagues—my Home is not my Home.
'Yet—let me recollect myself—for strange
And vision-like appears this sudden change;
In what consists it? I am still the same
275 In flesh and blood, and lineaments and name.
Still wave the boughs of my ancestral trees,
Still these old gables front the western breeze,
Still hang these relics round this chamber lone,
I still can see—can call them still my own.

    .   .   .   .   .

280 'They fancied, when they saw me home returning,
That all my soul to meet with them was yearning,
That every wave I'd bless which bore me hither;
They thought my spring of life could never wither,
That in the dry the green leaf I could keep,
285 As pliable as youth to laugh or weep;
They did not think how oft my eyesight turned
Toward the skies where Indian sunshine burned,
That I had perhaps left an associate band,
That I had farewells even for that wild Land;
290 They did not think my head and heart were older,
My strength more broken, and my feelings colder,
That spring was hastening into autumn sere—
And leafless trees make loveliest prospects drear—
That sixteen years the same ground travel o'er
295 Till each wears out the mark which each has left before.

'So—old affection is an empty name
When nothing that we loved remains the same,
But while we gaze upon the vapour gay,
The light that gave it glory fades away.
300 And—Home Affection—where have we a home?
For ever doomed in thought or deed to roam,
To lay our parents in their narrow rest
Or leave their hearthstones when we love them best;
Nay, sometimes scarce to know we love at all,

305 Till o'er love's object Death has spread its pall!—
     I feel 'tis sad to live without a Heart,
     But sadder still to feel dart after dart
     Rankling within it—sad to see the dead,
     But worse to see the sick man's tortured bed.
310   'Well I have talked of change—but oh, how changed
     Am I from him who o'er those dim hills ranged
     With trusty dog—poor Rover!—where art thou?
     I seem to see thee looking upward now
     To thy young Master's face, with honest eye
315 Shining all over with no selfish joy.'

                .   .   .   .   .

         He paused with heavy eye, and round the room
     Looked, through the shadows of descending gloom,
     Like one heart-sick, for 'twas a bitter task
     The hollowness of spirit to unmask
320 And show the wreck of years. To change his mind
     He took a book lying by, in which to find
     Some other course for thought—and, turning o'er
     Its leaves, he thought he'd known that book before;
     And on one page some hand had lightly traced
325 These lines, by Time's dim finger half-effaced:—

         'My Father and my childhood's guide,
            If oft I've wandered far from Thee,
         Even though Thine only Son has died
            To save from death a child like me,

330   Oh! still, to Thee when turns my heart
            In hours of sadness—*frequent now!*
         Be still the God that once Thou wert,
            And calm my breast and clear my brow.

         I am now no more a guileless child
335   O'ershadowed by Thine angel wing,
         For even my dreams are far more wild
            Than those my slumbers used to bring;

I farther see, I deeper feel,
 With hopes more warm, but heart less mild,
340 And ancient things new forms reveal,
 All strangely brightened or despoiled;

 I am entering on life's open tide,
 So fare ye well lost shores divine!
 And, O my Father!—deign to guide
345 Through its wild waters—CAROLINE!'[1]

.   .   .   .   .

Long o'er that dark'ning page Sir Henry pondered,
Nor from its time-worn words his eyesight wandered;
Yet scarce he comprehended what they were,
For other words were sounding in his ear—
350 Sent to him from the grave far-off and dim,
As if from Heaven a spirit spoke to him,
That bade the shadows of past time glide by
Till present times were hidden from his eye
By their strange pictured veil—scene after scene
355 Sailing around him of what once had been.—
He saw a Drawing-room revealed in light
From the red fireside of a winter night,
With two fair beings seated side by side,
The one arrayed in all a soldier's pride,
360 The other sadly pale, with angel eyes,
O'er whose fair orbs a gushing gleam would rise
Whenever, tremblingly, she strove to speak,
Though scarce a sound the voiceless calm would break,
So silent seemed despair.—He took her hand
365 And told her something of a distant land
Soon to be won with fame, and soon again
Of his return victorious o'er the main,
 'Oh no!'—at last she said—'I feel too well
The hollow vanity of all you tell.
370 You'll go, you'll join the ranks by Ganges' flood,

[1] These verses are printed in The Brontë Family, by F. A. Leyland, Vol. I, pp. 211–212, with the title: 'Caroline's Prayer, or the Change from Childhood to Womanhood.'

You'll perhaps survive through many a field of blood,
You'll perhaps gain fame's rewards—but nevermore
Those far-off climes *my* Henry shall restore
To England's hills again. Another mind—
375   Another heart than that he left behind—
And other hopes he'll bring—if hope at all
Can outlive fancy's flight and feeling's fall
To flourish on an iron-hardened brow.—
The Soldier may return—but *never Thou!*
380   And, further, know, our meeting must not be,
For even thyself wilt not be changed like me.
I shall be changed, my Love, to change no more;
I shall be landed on a farther shore
Than Indian Isles—a wider sea shall sever
385   My form from thine—a longer time—*For ever!*
Oh! when I am dead and mouldering in my grave,
Of me at least some dim remembrance have,—
Saved from the sunken wrecks of ancient time,
Even if to float o'er thoughts of strife and crime:
390   Then on the grave of Her who died for thee
Cast one short look—and, oh! Remember Me!'

'Alas, Lost Shade! why should I look upon
The mouldering letters of thy burial-stone!
Why should I strive thine image to recall,
395   And love thy beauty's flower and weep its fall?
It cannot be—for far too well I know
The narrow house where thou art laid below.
I know its lifeless chill, its rayless gloom,
Its voiceless silence, and its changeless doom.
400   I know that if from weeds I cleared thy name
And gazed till memories crowding round me came
Of all that made the sunshine of my home,
'Twould be of no avail—*Thou* couldst not come
That I might almost think I saw thee stand
405   Beside me—almost feel thy fairy hand.
Still would that form be pressed 'neath earth and stones

And still that hand would rest in dust and bones.
No, Caroline—the hours are long gone by
When I could call a shade reality,
410 Or make a world of dreams, or think that one
Was present with me who, I knew, was gone.
No—if the sapling *bends* to every breeze,
Their force shall rather *break* the full-grown trees.
If Infancy will catch at every toy,
415 Pursuits more solid must the Man employ.
He feels what *is*, and nought can charm away
The rough realities of present day.
    Thou art dead—I am living—my word is not thine,
So keep thy sleep—and, Farewell, Caroline!

     .   .   .   .   .

420   'Yet—while I think so, while I speak farewell,
'Tis not in words the dreariness to tell
Which sweeps across my spirit—for my soul
Feels such a midnight o'er its musings roll
At losing—though it be a vapour vain—
425 What *once* was rest to toil and ease and pain.
I knew not, while afar, how utterly
These memories of youth were past from me.
It seemed as if, though business warped my mind,
I could assume them when I felt inclined;
430 That though like dreams they fled my wakened brain,
I, if I liked, could dream them o'er again.
I did not think I *could* be seated here,
After the lapse of many a toilsome year
Once more returning to accustomed places
435 Amid the smiles of "old familiar faces;"
Yet shrinking from them—hiding in the gloom
Of this dull evening and secluded room,
Not to recall the spirit of the boy,
But all my world-worn energies to employ
440 In pondering o'er some artifice to gain
A seat in council or command in Spain.

'Well—world, oh world!—as I have bowed to thee
I must consent to suffer thy decree;
I asked—Thou'st given me my destiny;
445   I asked—when gazing on that pictured wall,
Like England's Hero to command or fall;
I asked when wandering over mountains lone,
Some day to wander over lands unknown;
I asked for gain and glory—place and power;
450   Thou gavest them all—I have them all this hour;
But I forgot to ask for youthful blood,
The thrill divine of feelings unsubdued,
The nerves that quivered to the sound of fame,
The tongue that trembled o'er a lover's name,
455   The eye that glistened with delightful tears,
The Hope that gladdened past and gilded future years;
So—I have rigid nerves and ready tongue,
Fit to subdue the weak and serve the strong;
And eyes that look on all things as the same,
460   And Hope—no, callousness, that thinks all things *a
name!*
So, Caroline—I'll bid farewell once more,
Nor mourn, lost shade; for though thou'rt gone be-
fore,
Gone is *thy* Henry too—and didst not thou,
While just departing from this world below,
465   Say thou no longer wert a guileless child,
That all old things were altered or despoiled?—
And—hadst thou lived—thine angel heart, like mine,
Would soon have hardened with thy youth's decline—
Cold, perhaps, to me, if beating, as when laid
470   Beneath its grave-stone 'neath the churchyard shade.
.   .   .   .   .

'I home returned for rest—but feel to-day
Home is no rest—and long to be away,
To play life's game out where my soldiers are,
Returned from India to a wilder war
475   Upon the hills of Spain—again to ride
Before their bayonets at Wellesley's side,

Again to sleep with horses trampling round,
In watch-cloak wrapped, and on a battle-ground;
To waken with the loud commencing gun,
480 And feed life's failing flame and drive the moments on—
There is our aim—to *that* our labours tend—
Strange we should love to hurry on our end!
But so it is, and nowhere can I speed
So swift through life as on my battle-steed!'

485 He ceased—unconsciously declined his head,
And stealingly the sense of waking fled,
Wafting his spirit into weeping Spain:
Till—starting momently—he gazed again,
But all looked strange to his beclouded brain:
490 And all was strange—for, though the scenes were known,
The thoughts that should have cherished them were gone,
Gone like the sunshine—and none others came
To shake the encroaching slumbers from his frame,
So, while he lay there, twilight deepened fast,
495 And silent, but resistless, hours swept past,
Till chairs and pictures lost themselves in gloom,
And but a window glimmered through the room,
With one pale star above the sombre trees,
Listening from Heaven to earth's repining breeze.
500 That Star looked down with cold and quiet eye,
While all else darkened, brightening up the sky,
And though his eye scarce saw it, yet his mind,
As, half awake and half to dreams resigned,
Could scarce help feeling in its holy shine
505 The solemn look of sainted Caroline,
With mute reproachfulness reminding him
That faith and fondness were not all a dream;
That form, not feeling, should be changed by clime;
That looks, not love, should suffer hurt by time;
510 That o'er life's waters, guiding us from far,
And brightening with life's night, should glisten
    Memory's Star.

April 15, 1840.

BLACK COMB

FAR off, and half revealed, 'mid shade and light,
Black Comb half smiles, half frowns; his mighty
   form
Scarce bending into peace, more formed to fight
A thousand years of struggles with a storm
5 Than bask one hour subdued by sunshine warm
To bright and breezeless rest; yet even his height
Towers not o'er this world's sympathies; he smiles—
While many a human heart to pleasure's wiles
Can bear to bend, and still forget to rise—
10 As though he, huge and heath-clad on our sight,
Again rejoices in his stormy skies.
Man loses vigour in unstable joys.
Thus tempests find Black Comb invincible,
While we are lost, who should know life so well!

(*circa* 1840.)

OH Thou, whose beams were most withdrawn
When should have risen my morning sun,
Who, frowning most at earliest dawn,
   Foretold the storms through which 'twould run;

5 Great God! when hour on hour has passed
   In an unsmiling storm away,
No sound but bleak December's blast,
   No sights but tempests, through my day,

At length, in twilight's dark decline,
10   Roll back the clouds that mark Thy frown,
Give but a single silver line—
   One sunblink, as that day goes down.

My prayer is earnest, for my breast
   No more can buffet with these storms;
15 I must have one short space of rest
   Ere I go home to dust and worms;

I must a single gleam of light
   Amid increasing darkness see,
Ere I, resigned to churchyard night,
20   Bid day farewell eternally!

My body is oppressed with pain,
   My mind is prostrate 'neath despair—
Nor mind nor body may again
   Do more than call Thy wrath to spare,

25 Both void of power to fight or flee,
   To bear or to avert Thy eye,
With sunken heart, with suppliant knee,
   Implore a peaceful hour to die.

When I look back on former life,
30   I scarcely know what I have been,
So swift the change from strife to strife
   That passes o'er the 'wildering scene.

I only feel that every power—
   And Thou hadst given much to me—
35 Was spent upon the present hour,
   Was never turned, my God, to Thee;

That what I did to make me blest
   Sooner or later changed to pain;
That still I laughed at peace and rest,
40   So neither must behold again.

August 8, 1841.

✓THE TRIUMPH OF MIND OVER BODY

MAN thinks too often that the ills of life,
Its ceaseless labour, and its causeless strife,
With all its train of want, disease, and care,
Must wage 'gainst spirit a successful war;
5   That when such dark waves round the body roll,
Feeble and faint will prove the struggling soul;
That it can never triumph or feel free,
While pain that body binds, or poverty.

No words of mine have power to rouse the brain
10   Oppress'd with grief—the forehead bowed with pain;
For none will hear me if I tell how high
Man's soul can soar o'er body's misery:
But, where Orations, eloquent and loud,
Prove weak as air to move the listening crowd,
15   A single syllable—if timely spoken—
That mass inert has roused—its silence broken,
And driven it, shouting for revenge or fame,
Trampling on fear or death—led by a *single name!*

So now, to him whose worn-out soul decays
20   Neath nights of sleepless pain or toilsome days,
Who thinks his feeble frame must vainly long
To tread the footsteps of the bold and strong;
Who thinks that—born beneath a lowly star—
He cannot climb those heights he sees from far;
25   To him I name one name—it needs but one—
NELSON—a world's defence—a Kingdom's noblest son!

Ah! little child, torn early from thy home
Over a weary waste of waves to roam;
I see thy fair hair streaming in the wind
30   Wafted from green hills left so far behind;
Like one lamb lost upon a gloomy moor,
Like one flower tossed a hundred leagues from shore.

Thou hast given thy farewell to thine English home,
And tears of parting dim thy views of fame to come.

35   I seem to see thee, clinging to the mast,
     Rocked roughly o'er the northern ocean's waste;
     Stern accents only shouted from beneath,
     Above, the keen winds bitter biting breath,
     While thy young eyes are straining to descry
40   The Ice blink gleaming in a Greenland sky,
     All round the presages of strife and storm
     Engirdling thy young heart and feeble form.

     Each change thy frame endured seemed fit to be
     The total round of common destiny;
45   For next—upon the Wild Mosquito shore
     San Juan's guns their deadly thunders pour,
     Though, deadlier far, that pestilential sky
     Whose hot winds only whisper who shall die.
     Yet, while—forgotten all their honours won—
50   Strong frames lay rotting neath a tropic sun,
     And mighty breasts heaved in deaths agony,
     Death only left the storm-worn *Nelson* free.

     Death saw him laid on rocky Teneriffe,
     Where stern eyes sorrowed on their bleeding chief
55   Borne down by shot and beaten back by fate,
     Yet keeping front unblenched and soul elate.

     Death saw him, calm, off Copenhagen's shore,
     Amid a thousand guns' heaven-shaking roar,
     Triumphant riding o'er a fallen foe
60   With hand prepared to strike, but heart to spare the blow.

     Death touched, but left him, when a tide of blood
     Dyed the dark waves of Egypt's ancient flood,
     As mighty L'Orient fired the midnight sky
     And first bedimmed Napoleon's destiny;
65   When in that blaze flashed redly sea and shore,
     When far Aboukir shook beneath its roar,

When fell on all one mighty pause of dread
As if wide heaven were shattered overhead,
Then—From the pallet where the hero lay—
70 His forehead laced with blood and pale as clay—
He rose—revived by that tremendous call—
Forgot the wound which lately caused his fall,
And bade the affrighted battle hurry on,
Nor thought of pain or rest till victory should be won!

75   I see him sit—his coffin by his chair—
With pain-worn cheek and wind dishevelled hair,
A little, shattered wreck, from many a day
Of cares and storms and battles passed away;
Prepared at any hour God bade, to die,
80 But not to stop or rest or strike or fly;
While—like a burning reed—his spirit's flame
Brightened, as it consumed his mortal frame.
He knew his lightning course must soon be o'er,
That death was tapping at his cabin door,
85 That he should meet the grim yet welcome guest
Not on a palace bed of downy rest,
But where the stormy waters rolled below,
And, pealed above, the thunders of his foe;
That no calm sleep should smooth a slow decay
90 Till scarce the mourners knew life passed away,
But stifling agony and gushing gore
Should fill the moments of his parting hour;
He knew—but smiled—for, as that polar star
A thousand years—as then—had shone from far,
95 While all had changed beneath its changeless sky—
So, what *to* earth belonged *with* earth should die;
While he—all soul—would take a glorious flight,
Like yon—through time—a still and steady light;
Like yon, to England's sailors given to be
100 The guardian of her fleets—the Pole Star of the sea!

    A Vessel lies in England's proudest port
Where venerating thousands oft resort,

And, though ships round her anchor, bold and gay,
They seek her only, in her grim decay;
105   They tread her decks—all tenantless—with eyes
Of awe-struck musing—not of vague surprise;
They enter in a cabin, dark and low,
And o'er its time-stained floor with reverence bow:
Yet nought appears but rafters, worn and old,
110   No mirrored walls—no cornice bright with gold:
Yon packet steaming through its smoky haze
Seems fitter far to suit the wanderer's gaze;
But—'tis not present time they look at now,
They look at six and thirty years ago:
115   They see where fell the 'Thunderbolt of war'
On the storm swollen waves of TRAFALGAR;
They read a tale to wake their pain and pride
In that brass plate, engraved—'HERE NELSON DIED!'

As 'wise Cornelius' from his mirror bade
120   A magic veil of formless clouds to fade,
Till gleamed before the awe-struck gazer's eye
Scenes still to come or passed for ever by;
So let me, standing in this darksome room,
Roll back a generation's gathered gloom,
125   To shew the morn and evening of a sun
The memory of whose light still cheers old England on.

Where ceaseless showers obscure the misty vale,
And winter winds through leafless osiers wail,
Beside a stream with swollen waves rushing wild,
130   Sits—calm amid the storm—yon fair haired child.
He *cannot* cross, so full the waters flow—
So bold his little heart, he *will not* go;
Patient of hindrances, but deeming still
Nothing impossible to steadfast will;
135   While from the old Rectory, his distant home,
'All hands' to seek their darling truant roam,
And *one*—his mother—with instinctive love,
Like that which guides aright the timid dove—

Finds her dear child—his cheeks all rain bedewed,
140 The unconscious victim of those tempests rude,
And, panting, asks him why he tarries there?
Does he not dread his fate—-his danger fear?
That child replies—all smiling in the storm—
'Mother—what is this Fear?—I never saw its form!'
145 Ah! oft, since then, he heard the tempests sound,
Oft saw far mightier waters surging round,
Oft stood unshaken—death and danger near,
Yet saw no more than then the phantom Fear!

Now wave the wand again—Be England's shore
150 Sunk far behind the horizon's billowy roar;
And Lo! again this cabin dark and grim,
Beheld through smoke wreaths, indistinct and dim!
'Where is my child' methinks the mother cries:
No! far away that mother's tombstone lies!
155 Where is her child? He is not surely here,
Where reign, undoubted sovereigns, Death and Fear?

A prostrate form lies, neath a double shade
By stifling smoke and blackened timber made,
With head that backward rolls, whene'er it tries
160 From its hard, thunder shaken bed to rise.
Methought I saw a brightness on its breast,
As if in royal orders decked and dressed;
But its wan face, its grey locks crimson died,
Have surely nought to do with power or pride;
165 For death his mandate writes on its white brow—
'Thine earthly course is run—come with me now!'
Stern faces o'er this figure weeping bend
As they had lost a father and a friend,
While, all unanswered, burst yon conquering cheer,
170 Since He—their glorious chief is dying here.
They heed it not—but, with rekindled eye,
As He, even Death would conquer ere he die,
He asks—'What was't?—What deed had England
done?

What ships had struck?—Was victory nobly won?
175   Did Collingwood—did Trowbridge face the foe?
Whose ship was first in fight—who dealt the sternest
    blow?'

I could not hear the answer—lost and drowned
In that tremendous crash of earthquake sound,
But, I could see the dying Hero smile,
180   As pain and sickness vanquished—bowed, awhile,
To *soul*, that soared—prophetic—o'er their sway,
And saw, beyond death's night Fame's glorious day;
That deemed no bed so easy as a tomb
Neath old Westminster's hero sheltering gloom,
185   That knew the laurel round his dying brow
Should bloom for ever as it flourished now,
That felt, this pain once o'er, to him was given
Honour on earth and happiness in heaven:
That was a smile as sweet as ever shone
190   O'er his wan face in childhood's sunshine gone;
A smile which asked as plainly—'What is fear?'
As then unnoticed, though as then, so near.

Now faint and fainter rolled the cannons sound
On his dull ear—each object, wavering round,
195   Mocked his dim eye—nor face, nor form seemed
    known;
He only felt that his great work was done,
That one brave heart was yearning at his side,
So, murmuring 'Kiss me, Hardy'—Nelson smiling died!

Oh! When *I* think upon that awful day
200   When all I know or love must fade away—
When, after weeks or months of agony,
Without one earthly hope to succour me,
I must lie back, and close my eyes upon
The farewell beams of the descending sun;
205   Must feel the warmth I never more may know
Mock my fast freezing frame of pain and woe,

Must feel a light is brightening up the sky
As shining clouds and summer airs pass by;
While I—a shrouded corpse, my bed must leave
210   To lie forgotten in my narrow grave,
The world all smiles above my covering clay;
I silent—senseless—festering fast away:
And, if my children, mid the churchyard stones,
Years hence, shall see a few brown mouldering bones;
215   Perhaps a skull, that seems, with hideous grin,
To mock at all this world takes pleasure in,
They'll only from the unsightly relics turn,
Or into ranker grass the fragments spurn;
Nor know that *these* are the remains of him
220   Whom they'll remember, like a faded dream,
As one who danced them on a father's knee
In long departed hours of happy infancy.

Then—then I ask—with humble—earnest prayer—
O Mighty Being! give me strength to dare
225   The certain fate, the dreadful hour to bear,
As thou didst NELSON! mid the battles roar
Lying, pale with mortal sickness—choked with gore,
Yet, thinking of thine England—saved, that hour,
From her great foeman's empire crushing power;
230   Of thy poor frame so gladly given, to free
Her thousand happy homes from slavery;
Of stainless name for her—of endless fame for thee.

Give me—Great God!—give all who own thy sway
Soul to command, and body to obey:
235   When dangers frown—a heart to beat more high;
When doubts confuse—a more observant eye;
When fortunes change—a power to bear their blight;
When Death arrives—to Life, a calm *'good night.'*
We are Thy likeness—Give us on to go
240   Through Life's long march of restlessness and woe,
Resolved thy Image shall be sanctified
By holy confidence—not human pride.

We have our task set—Let us do it well;
Nor barter ease on earth with pain in Hell.
245 We have our Talents, from thy treasury given—
Let us return thee good account in heaven.

I know this world, this age is marching on;
Each year more wondrous than its parent gone;
And shall *I* lag behind it sad and slow?
250 With wish to rise but void of power to go?
Forbid it God! Who hast made me what I am;
Nor, framed to honour, let me sink in shame;
But, as yon Moon, which *seems* mid clouds to glide,
Whose dark breasts ever strive her beams to hide,
255 Shines, *really*, heedless of their earth-born sway,
In her own heaven of glory, far away;
So may my soul which seems, to eyes below,
Involved in life's thick mists of care and woe,
Far—far remote—from holy calm look down
260 On clouds of fleecy shine or stormy frown;
And while mankind its beams so shaded see,
Gaze steadfast on this life's inconstancy,
And find itself—like her—at home in heaven with THEE.

NORTHANGERLAND.

The first draft of this poem appears in Branwell's manuscript note-book kept at Luddendenfoot (1841-1842), with the title 'Lord Nelson.' It is the poem mentioned in Chapter III of *Pictures of the Past*, by F. H. Grundy, 1879. Referring to the time when he was acquainted with Branwell Brontë, Grundy writes:

'He wrote a poem called "Brontë," illustrative of the life of Nelson, which, at his special request, I submitted for criticism to Leigh Hunt, Miss Martineau and others. All spoke in high terms of it.'

The heading of the poem in Grundy's copy refers to Nelson's Neapolitan title of 'Duke of Brontë,' conferred on him by the King of Naples in August, 1879. In Branwell's final draft of the poem he gave it the title of 'The Triumph of Mind over Body.' The first draft of the poem was printed in the *Brontë Society Transactions*, Vol. VII, Part xxxvii.

SONNET

MAN thinks too often that his earth-born cares
    Bind chains on mind and can overcome its sway,
That faint and feeble proves the soul which wars
    Against its storm struck prison-house of clay;
5   But henceforth know that on its dreary way,
Whate'er of Ills with all its race it shares,
    Though pain and poverty becloud its day,
And want begins and sadness ends its years,
Soul still can brighten through its mortal gloom—
10   As THINE did, JOHNSON, England's trueborn son,
Who in thy garret or a lordling's room
Calmly let hunger creep or pride strut on,
Intent on manly thoughts and honours won,
'Mid hours as darksome as thy dreaded Tomb.

September 3, 1841.

AMID the world's wide din around,
    I hear from far a solemn sound
That says, 'Remember me!
And though thy lot be widely cast
5   From that thou picturedst in the past
Still deem me dear to thee,
Since to thy soul my light was given
To give thy earth some glow of heaven,
And, if my beams from thee be driven,
10   Dark, dark, thy night will be!'
What was that sound? 'Twas not a voice
From Ruby lips and Sapphire eyes,
Nor echoed back from sensual joys,
Nor a forsaken fair one's sighs.
15   I, when I heard it, sat amid
The bustle of a Town-like room

'Neath skies, with smoke-stain'd vapours hid—
　　By windows, made to show their gloom.
　　The desk that held my Ledger book
20　Beneath the thundering rattle shook
　　　Of engines passing by;
　　The bustle of the approaching train
　　Was all I hoped to rouse the brain
　　　Or startle apathy.
25　And yet, as on the billow swell
　　A Highland exile's last farewell
　　　Is borne o'er Scotland's sea,
　　And solemn as a funeral knell,
　　I heard that soft voice, known so well,
30　　Cry—'Oh, remember me!'

　　Why did it bring such scenes to mind
　　As Time has left so long behind?—
　　Those summer afternoons, when I
　　Lay basking 'neath a glorious sky,
35　Some noble page beneath me spread,
　　Some bright cloud floating overhead,
　　And sweet winds whispering in the tree
　　Of wondrous prospects meant for me!
　　Why did it bring, my eyes before,
40　The hours spent wandering on the moor,
　　Beneath a grey and iron sky,
　　　With nothing but the waters still
　　To break the stern monotony
　　　Of withered heath and windless hill?—
45　While fancy, to the heedless child,
　　Revealed a world of wonders wild—
　　Adventures bold and scenes divine
　　Beyond the horizon's gloomy line—
　　Until he thought his footsteps trod
50　The pathless plains round Volga's flood,
　　Or paced the shores of Grecia's sea,
　　Or climbed the steep of Calvary.

Why did I think I stood once more
At night beside my father's door?—
55   And, while far up in heaven the moon
     Through clear and cloud was driving on,
     A moment dark but bursting soon
     Upon the heaven she made her own,
     I often times would think that she
60   Was some bold vessel o'er a sea
     'Mid unknown regions gliding—
     Perhaps with Parry in the north
     On strange discovery venturing forth,
     On stormy waters riding;
65   Perhaps with Sinbad 'mid those Isles
     Where Genii haunt and sunshine smiles;
     Perhaps—and nobler still than these—
     With Vincent guarding England's seas
     From might of foreign war;
70   Or bearing Nelson o'er the wave
     To find a glorious Hero's grave
     On deathless Trafalgar!

September 11, 1841.

ON LANDSEER'S PAINTING

'The Shepherd's chief mourner'—A Dog keeping watch at twilight over its master's grave.

THE beams of Fame dry up Affection's tears,
   And those who rise forget from whom they spring.
   Wealth's golden glories—pleasure's glittering
     wing—
   All that we follow through our chase of years—
5   All that our hope seeks—all our caution fears,
   Dim or destroy those holy thoughts which cling
   Round where the form we loved lies slumbering;
   But not with *Thee*—our slave—whose joys and cares
   We deem so grovelling—power nor pride are thine

10 Nor our pursuits or ties yet, o'er this grave
    Where lately crowds the form of mourning gave,
      I only hear THY low heartbroken whine—
      I only see THEE left, long hours to pine
  For *him* whom thou, if Love had power, wouldst save.

THE man who will not know another,
    Whose heart can never sympathize,
Who loves not comrade, friend, or brother,
    Unhonoured lives—unnoticed dies:
5 His frozen eye, his bloodless heart,
  Nature, repugnant, bids depart.

  O Grundy, born for nobler aim,
  Be thine the task to shun such shame;
  And henceforth never think that he
10 Who gives his hand in courtesy
  To one who kindly feels to him,
  His gentle birth or name can dim.

  However mean a man may be,
  Know man *is* man as well as thee;
15 However high thy gentle line,
  Know he who writes can rank with thine;
  And though his frame be worn and dead,
  Some light still glitters round his head.

  Yes! though his tottering limbs seem old,
20 His heart and blood are not yet cold.
  Ah, Grundy! shun his evil ways,
  His restless nights, his troubled days;

But never slight his mind, which flies,
Instinct with noble sympathies,
25 Afar from spleen and treachery,
To thought, to kindness, and to thee.

In *Pictures of the Past* (pp. 78–79), Francis H. Grundy, referring to the above poem, writes: 'On one occasion he (Branwell) thought that I was disposed to treat him distantly at a party, and he retired in great dudgeon. When I arrived at my lodgings the same evening I found the following, necessarily an impromptu.'

THE desolate earth, the wintry sky,
The ceaseless rain-showers driving by—
The farewell of the year—
Though drear the sight, and sad the sound,
5 While bitter winds are wailing round,
Nor hopes depress, nor thoughts confound,
Nor waken sigh or tear.

For, as it moans, December's wind
Brings many varied thoughts to mind
10 Upon its storm-drenched wing,
Of words, not said 'mid sunshine gay,
Of deeds, not done in summer's day,
Yet which, when joy has passed away,
Will strength to sorrow bring.

15 For, when the leaves are glittering bright,
And green hills lie in noonday night,
The present only lives;
But, when within my chimnies roar
The chidings of the stormy shower,
20 The feeble present loses power,
The mighty past survives.

I cannot think—as roses blow,
And streams sound gently in their flow,
   And clouds shine bright above—
25   Of aught but childhood's happiness,
Of joys unshadowed by distress
Or voices tuned the ear to bless
   Or faces made to love.

But, when these winter evenings fall
30   Like dying nature's funeral pall,
   The Soul gains strength to say
That—not aghast at stormy skies—
That—not bowed down by miseries,—
Its thoughts have will and power to rise
35   Above the present day.

So, winds amid yon leafless ash,
And yon swollen streamlet's angry dash,
   And yon wet howling sky,
Recall the victories of mind
40   O'er bitter heavens and stormy wind
And all the wars of humankind—
   Man's mightiest victory!

The darkness of a dungeon's gloom,
So oft ere death the spirit's tomb,
45   Could not becloud those eyes
Which first revealed to mortal sight
A thousand unknown worlds of light,
And that *one* grave shines best by night
   Where Galileo lies.

50   But—into drearier dungeons thrown,
With bodies bound, whose minds were gone—
   Tasso's immortal strain,
Despite the tyrant's stern decree,
Mezentius-like—rose fresh and free
55   And sang of Salem's liberty
   Forgetful of his chain;

And thou, great rival of his song,
Whose seraph-wings so swift and strong
   Left this world far behind,
60 Though poor, neglected, blind and old,
The clouds round Paradise unrolled
And in immortal accents told
   Misery must bow to mind.

See, in a garret bare and low,
65 While mighty London roars below,
   One poor man seated lone;
No favourite child of fortune he,
But owned as hers by Poverty,
His rugged brow, his stooping knee,
70   Speak woe and want alone.

Now, who would guess that yonder form,
Scarce worth being beaten by life's storm,
   Could e'er be known to fame?
Yet England's love and England's tongue,
75 And England's heart, shall reverence long
The wisdom deep, the courage strong,
   Of English *Johnson's* name.

Like him—foredoomed through life to bear
The anguish of the heart's despair
80   That pierces spirit through—
Sweet Cowper, 'mid his weary years,
Led through a rayless vale of tears,
Poured gentle wisdom on our ears,
   And his was English too.

85 But Scotland's desolate hills can show
How mind may triumph over woe,
   For many a cottage there,

Where ceaseless toil from day to day
Scarce keeps grim want one hour away,
90   Could show if known how great the sway
Of spirit o'er despair.

And he, whose natural music fills
Each wind that sweeps her heathy hills,
Bore up with manliest brow
95   'Gainst griefs that ever filled his breast,
'Gainst toils that never gave him rest,
So, though grim fate Burns' life oppressed,
His soul it could not bow.

December 15, 1841.

O GOD! while I in pleasure's wiles
Count hours and years as one,
And deem that, wrapt in pleasure's smiles,
My joys can ne'er be done,

5   Give me the stern sustaining power
To look into the past,
And see the darkly shadowed hour
Which I must meet at last;

The hour when I must stretch this hand
10   To give a last adieu
To those sad friends that round me stand,
Whom I no more must view.

For false though bright the hours that lead
My present passage on,
15   And when I join the silent dead
Their light will all be gone.

Then I must cease to seek the light
Which fires the evening heaven,
Since to direct through death's dark nigh
20   Some other must be given.

December 19, 1841.

The above is the latest of the dated poems written by Patrick Bran-
well Brontë during the time that he was employed at Luddenden
Foot. The note-book used by him at this time contains several pencil
sketches, some of which are apparently roughly-drawn portraits of
Branwell's acquaintances; and one of them at least is a rough sketch of
his own head. One unfinished drawing, a portrait of a man seated in an
arm-chair, occupies the whole of one page. Two names, written in
Greek letters, appear on this page: 'Johannes Murgatroides' above
the drawing, and 'George Richardson' below it. For a full transcript
of the Luddenden Foot note-book, containing replicas of the draw-
ings, see *The Brontë Society Transactions*, Vol. VII, Part xxxvii.

THE AFGHAN WAR

WINDS within our chimney thunder,
    Rain-showers shake each window-pane,
Still—if nought our household sunder—
    We can smile at wind or rain.
5 Sickness shades a loved one's chamber,
    Steps glide gently to and fro,
Still—'mid woe—our hearts remember
    We are there to soothe that woe.

Comes at last the hour of mourning,
10   Solemn tolls the funeral bell;
And we feel that no returning
    Fate allows to such farewell:
Still a holy hope shines o'er us;
    We wept by the One who died;
15 And 'neath earth shall death restore us;
    As round hearthstones—side by side.

But—when all at eve, together,
   Circle round the flickering light,
While December's howling weather
20   Ushers in a stormy night:
When each ear, scarce conscious, listens
   To the outside Winter's war,
When each trembling eyelash glistens
   As each thinks of *one* afar—

25 Man to chilly silence dying,
   Ceases story, song and smile;
Thought asks—'Is the loved one lying
   Cold upon some storm-beat isle?'
And with death—when doubtings vanish,
30   When despair still hopes and fears—
Though our anguish toil may banish,
   Rest brings unavailing tears.

So, Old England—when the warning
   Of thy funeral bells I hear—
35 Though thy dead a host is mourning,
   Friends and kindred watch each bier.
But alas! Atlantic waters
   Bear another sound from far!
Unknown woes, uncounted slaughters,
40   Cruel deaths, inglorious war!

Breasts and banners, crushed and gory,
   That seemed once invincible;
England's children—England's glory,
   Moslem sabres smite and quell!
45 Far away their bones are wasting,
   But I hear their spirits call—
'Is our Mighty Mother hasting
   To avenge her children's fall?'

England rise! Thine ancient thunder
50   Humbled mightier foes than these;

Broke a whole world's bonds asunder,
Gave thee empire o'er the seas:
And while yet one rose may blossom,
Emblem of thy former bloom,
55   Let not age invade thy bosom—
Brightest shine in darkest gloom!

While one oak thy homes shall shadow,
Stand like it as thou hast stood;
While a Spring greets grove and meadow,
60   Let not Winter freeze thy blood.
Till this hour St George's standard
Led the advancing march of time;
England! keep it streaming vanward,
Conqueror over age and clime!

May, 1842.

This poem was first published in the *Leeds Intelligencer* on May 7,
1842. It is the only composition of Branwell's which is known to have
been printed during his lifetime.

THE EPICUREAN'S SONG

THE visits of Sorrow
  Say, why should we mourn?
Since the sun of to-morrow
  May shine on its urn;
5   And all that we think such pain
Will have departed—then
Bear for a moment what cannot return.

For past time has taken
  Each hour that it gave,
10   And they never awaken
  From yesterday's grave;
So surely we may defy
Shadows, like memory,
Feeble and fleeting as midsummer wave.

15   From the depths where they're falling
     Nor pleasure, nor pain,
     Despite our recalling,
     Can reach us again;
     Though we brood over them,
20   Naught can recover them,
     Where they are laid they must ever remain.

     So seize we the present,
     And gather its flowers,
     For—mournful or pleasant—
25   'Tis all that is ours;
     While daylight we're wasting,
     The evening is hasting,
     And night follows fast on vanishing hours.

     Yes—and we, when night comes,
30   Whatever betide,
     Must die as our fate dooms,
     And sleep by their side;
     For *change* is the only thing
     Always continuing;
35   And it sweeps creation away with its tide.

                                        [1842.]

AZRAEL, OR DESTRUCTION'S EVE

'BROTHERS and men! one moment stay
     Beside your latest patriarch's grave,
While God's just vengeance yet delay,
     While God's blest mercy yet can save.
5   Will you compel my tongue to say,
     That underneath this nameless sod
Your hands, with mine, have laid to-day
     The *last* on earth who walked with God?

'Shall the pale corpse, whose hoary hairs
10   Are just surrendered to decay,
Dissolve the chain which bound our years
To hundred ages passed away?
Shall six-score years of warnings dread
Die like a whisper on the wind?
15   Shall the dark doom above your head,
Its blinded victims darker find?

'Shall storms from heaven *without* the world,
Find wilder storms from hell *within?*
Shall long-stored, late-come wrath be hurled;
20   Or,—will you, can you turn from sin?
Have patience, if too plain I speak,
For time, my sons, is hastening by;
Forgive me if my accents break:
Shall *I* be saved and *Nature* die?

25   'Forgive that pause:—one look to Heaven
Too plainly tells me, he is gone,
Who long with me in vain had striven
For earth and for its peace alone.
He's gone!—my Father—full of days,—
30   From life which left no joy for him;
Born in creation's earliest blaze;
Dying—himself, its latest beam.

'But he is gone! and, oh, behold,
Shown in his death, God's latest sign!
35   Than which more plainly never told
An Angel's presence His design.
By it, the evening beams withdrawn
Before a starless night descend;
By it, the last blest spirit born
40   From this beginning of an end;

'By all the strife of civil war
    That beams within yon fated town;
By all the heart's worst passions there,
    That call so loud for vengeance down;
45 By that vast wall of cloudy gloom,
    Piled boding round the firmament;
By all its presages of doom,
    Children of men—Repent! Repent!'

    The patriarch ceased, and rung his voice
50 Like knell of iron from the skies;
But echo none the earth returned
Whose blinded sons with anger burned,
As silent swayed their mighty tide
Around the grave from side to side.
55 All eyes were bent, with threatening gloom,
On Him who prophesied their doom;
And one arose—upon whose face
Passions and crimes had left their trace,
Contending with a tameless pride
60 That Man and God alike defied.

'Be Thine,' he cried with trumpet voice
    While hoarse applauses rolled—'Be Thine
The task to embitter human joys:
    To raise, to cherish them, be mine!
65 Die with the Head that now has died
    The miseries of a time gone by;
Descend with him; the Tyrant's pride;
    Rise from his ashes, Liberty!
Take him—the type of old things past—
70 His death—our chain, dissolved at last—
I grant it—take that cloudy gloom
For omen of the storm to come—
Take all thy Types—But know thy age
Looks blindly on life's lettered page.

75   Dim eyes see darkness even in day,
       And wrinkled brows scare smiles away.
       Age always thinks the past was bright
       And—like itself—deems present, night.
       Is't fit that he whose memory fails,
80   Save when repeating old world tales—
       That he who scarce the present knows
       Should prophesy of future woes?

       'Oh Human Heart! how waywardly
       From truth to error thou wilt flee![1]
85   We say this world was made by One
       Who's seen or heard or known by none.
       We say that *He*, the Almighty God
       That framed Creation with a nod,
       His wondrous work so well fulfilled
90   That—in an hour—it All rebelled!—
       That though He loves our race so well
       He hurls our spirits into Hell—
       That though He bids us turn from sin
       He hedges us, with tempters, in—
95   That though He says the world shall stand
       Eternal—perfect—from His hand,
       He is just about to whelm it o'er
       With utter ruin—evermore!—
       And all for deeds that we have done,
100   Though He has made us every one—
       Yes, WE—the image of His form!—
       We!—The dust to feed the worm!

       'Away with all such phantasies!—
       Just trust your reason and your eyes!—
105   Believe that God exists when I
       Who, here—this hour—His name deny,
       Shall bear a harder punishment
       Than those whose knees to Him have bent.

       [1] *Alternative reading:* From truth to error still thou'lt flee!

Believe that He can rule above
110 When you shall see Him rule below;
Believe that He's the God of love
When He shall end His children's woe;
Believe that this firm earth we tread,
And that vast canopy overhead—
115 Believe that they have stood for ever,
And that they shall for ever stand—
Till something *really* strive to sever
The earth from Heaven—the sea from land.
Believe that hoar descending hairs
120 Are far more sage than youthful years,
When rotting planks shall prove to be
More fruitful than a forest tree.
Old Man!—a truce to dotard dreams,
And turn from Heaven thy hazy eyes—
125 A Thought for Earth far more beseems
Than childish gazing at the skies.
'Tis Earth—not Heaven—shall shortly rise;
'Tis Man—not God—shall soon avenge;
And if there be a paradise
130 We'll bring it in the coming change!—
To-morrow morn, my country-men,
We meet within that City's wall—
Let us our Liberty regain—
Be that the "Breaking of our chain"—
135 Then if all Heaven its terrors rain
We'll smile upon them all!'

As Azrael ceased, throughout the throng
Uprose a tumult loud and long
That howled about the Man of God
140 And laughed his sorrowing looks to scorn;
Nor could he speak one warning word
Away by surging thousands borne.
One look he cast—one withering look
At Azrael, whose triumphant eye

145 Could scarce withstand its mute rebuke,
      Even in his hour of Victory.
    Then swayed the tide on either side,
    And each apart were sundered wide;
    But o'er the thousands Azrael's form
150 Shone like a Beacon through a storm;
    And o'er the tumult Azrael's voice
    Swelled like a trumpet through the skies.
    On toward the wall he bade them tend,
      And fast the concourse hurried on,
155   Forgot Methuselah's burial stone,
      Where only Noah mourned alone
    Above his father and his friend!

            .   .   .   .   .

    Why walks within his palace hall
      Lord Azrael, silent and alone,
160   While back its roof of marble stone
    Returns his footstep's measured fall?—
    Why gathers in his restless eye
      A shadow of such troubled meaning—
      Why, sometimes at the window leaning
165 So anxious looks he on the sky?—
    Why comes so sad the evening down?—
    Why sleeps so dark the Mighty town?—
    And why *does* every palace dome
    Seem mourning 'mid the misty gloom,
170 While the wind whistles wild and low
    About each pillared portico?—
    'Twas but an hour since thousands roared
      For Azrael o'er Methuselah's grave;
    They why is He, so late adored,
175   Untended by a single Slave?—
    His ears yet ring with uproar loud,
    The Applauses of a maddened crowd;
    He has left the streets choked up with men
    Whose shouts might call him back again.

180 Alone, he has left them, but his eye
Shows that his mind has company;
And, pacing o'er the dark'ning floor,
On mighty thoughts he seems to pour.
At length, the solemn silence breaking,
185 As if a Spirit heard him speaking,
So clenched his hands, so fixed his look,
So earnest every word he spoke.

Azrael (*solus loquitur*):
'There is no God—I know there's none!
190 Neither of spirit nor of stone;
No Holy Hill nor Idol Shrine
Has ever held a Power Divine;
Nor Heaven above *nor hell* below
Can minister to weal or woe!—
195 I feel that when the Body dies
Its memories and feelings die;
That they from earth shall never rise,
As it in earth shall ever lie:
I know that Mortal eyes incline,
200 Whenever aught remains unseen,
With phantoms dreadful or divine
To people the mysterious scene;
That Human life revolts to think
It ever stands on nothing's brink;
205 That Human pride recoils to see
The Heap of dust 'tis doomed to be!—
I know that if I staid till night
Alone in this unlighted Hall
My mind would fill with many a sight
210 The vacuum of the midnight wall;
But—when the Morning light shall rise
The *real* would banish phantasies.
So, when the shadow of TO COME
Surrounds the Heart with boding gloom,
215 Nature abhors to look at naught

And frames, for ease, a world of thought.
So—when the sick man lies to die
He gasps for Hope in Agony;
And as the Earth yields none to save
220 He makes a Hope beyond the grave!—
Thus Heaven is but an earthly dream:
'Tis Man makes God—not God makes him!

'But why should I of others speak,
As if all minds but mine were weak?—
225 We are all the same and each one tries
To cheat his sense with phantasies—
Weak as the weakest—now, even now
When conquest almost crowns my brow,
When with a word I cheer or check
230 The crowd that follows at my beck,
When those I hated fear my name
And those I feared are bowed with shame,
When, though I tread on Hostile laws,
Am welcomed with the world's applause—
235 Yet, all avails not!—There is still
A sickening sense of future ill;
Of what I love about to be
A part of what has ceased to be!—
For, I may rise to sovereign sway,
240 But—MARAH must descend to clay.
To-morrow night must bring me power,
But—*this may* bring her dying hour.
To me a Throne—To her a Tomb—
Fleeting light—And fixed gloom!
245 Well, so arise, through each one's life,
From laughter, tears—from feasting, strife;
And Earth is not—as some have said—
From Chaos but *to* Chaos made.

'Sometimes I think this inward pain
250 Is but the ferment of the brain,
Which on this eve of mighty things,

While all is doubt, vain phantoms brings
To fill the void—But comes anon
Death, the real phantom, striding on,
255   Which, if with wine I drive away,
From merry night comes mournful day.
At night I drive the tumult on,
Pledging healths to lose my own;
Or bask in light from beauties' eyes,
260   Which I enjoy—and then despise!
At morn, I rise with head confused
To work neglected, food refused,
Until my mind reverts on schemes
To realize a traitor's dreams;
265   Until the day brings forth again
The evil thoughts of restless men,
Who me their leader hurry on
Towards the deed that *must* be done;
And while their minds my own employ
270   My heart can feel a troubled joy;
But, if my thoughts a moment roam
Towards what should be my happy home,
Then, oh, my Marah, comes the shade
Of hopes beclouded, joys decayed!
275   Then I feel that I must be
Soon—how soon!—deprived of Thee!'

There Azrael stopped with bated breath
As if he saw the face of death;
But while he stood there—on his sight,
280   Between him and the darkened wall,
Behold! a Lady clothed in white
     With frighted haste swept through the hall.
Her face and lips were pale as death—
     Her glassy eyes were fixed on him—
285   She strove to speak but gasped for breath
     Like one oppressed with goblin dream;
But Azrael cried—'Good God! Is't THOU?—

Marah, my love! *what ails thee now?*'
She answered—but he scarce *might* hear
290 Her words, so faint and chilled they were—
She said—'I've risen, who never thought to rise—
Death has unclasped—a little space—
The strictness of his cold embrace,
That I may warn thee ere this body dies—
295 I've seen—Oh Azrael!'
         There her gaze
Went wildly round, while Azrael caught
Her almost falling in the maze
Of some strange scene or stunning thought,
300 And back his clasp her senses brought;
For, once more wildly gazing round,
She said, with awed and solemn sound,
'I've seen God rise from His Eternal Throne
And say—"Bring Mercy *back*—be Vengeance done!"'
305 Then every Angel stooped his golden wing
Before that voice divine
That utter darkness seemed to bring,
Even over Heaven's unutterable shine!
Azrael—I lay alone in bed,
310 Composing, in my silent room,
My mind to meet its coming doom,
When, lo! a Holy Angel came
And opened to my dimming sight
That scene terrifically bright—
315 All Heaven—revealed like a wide world of flame.
Oh! Then I heard that dread command,
Which bowed with awe that shining band;
While wide the Angel of Destruction spread
His midnight wings and from the Presence sped
320 Bent on the deed of doom—
         All, all is o'er!
And this wide world will never brighten more,
Nor joy be seen again!
A thousand Storms are waiting for the word,

325 And when its deep, commencing peal is heard,
       Over this heedless Earth they'll spread a shore-
          less main!
     My mourning Angel told me I must go
     Before begins the march of woe;
     Called where the blest in glory reign:
330 The *last* on earth who may to Heaven attain!
     So I must bid farewell to thee,
       Doomed to so dread—
                      Oh God! I cannot speak!
     This miserable heart will break
335 For—NONE WILL HEAR!'

     She sickened in his arms—
       On his broad breast declined her head,
          And strayed her hair;
       All sense of feeling fled,
340 And blighted all her charms!
     'She raves,' Lord Azrael said, 'Her brain
     Is dizzied with her dying pain.'
     So, on a couch her form he laid,
     And called her servants—all dismayed
345 To find their Lady—when, so nigh
     All knew the hour when she should die—
     Arisen unhelped, and lying there,
     They knew not how—but whispers fraught with
          fear
     Passed as they bore her to the bed
350 Where, decked for death, she erst had laid.

     They left Lord Azrael wrapt in thought—
     His restless schemes for once forgot,
     For once declined his haughty brow,
     His haughty hopes for once laid low;
355 For though he strove to scoff away
     All he had just heard Marah say,
     It would not go—Methuselah's tomb,
       And aged Noah's warning cry,

And that strange night of utter gloom,
360   Those gathering clouds, that boding sky,
That mournful wind bewailing by,
All fell upon him in that hour
With Nightmare-weight and stunning power.
But, while in sorrows lost, his mind
365   Was wandering into years behind,
A hand was placed upon his arm
And he turned round with vague alarm
Of some new ill—But, at his back,
Lo, Moloch!—with a treacherous eye
370   Glinting with false hilarity
Beneath his eyebrows broad and black—
Ah, Tiger heart! that jesting mien
Hides naught but bitterness and sin:
Then each of Hell a worthy brother,
375   Azrael and Moloch face each other.
'Ha, Azrael! sure that dotard's preaching
Has waked, at last, thy erring heart;
And, softened by his heavenly teaching,
Thou hast ta'en the better part:
380   Nonsense! leave your saintly sighs;
Fill that goblet—and, be wise!'

'But Marah's dying!'—
'Tell me not so,
When crowns and thrones are waiting on her:
385   A Crown will cheat both death and woe,
And women best love pomp and honour.
But, what *is* sighing—what is death?
Why, too much or too little breath!
I laugh to think what fools we are
390   To pull unmeasured jaws at care,
When just a simple glass of wine
Will drive the demon power of evil
To his and our good lord, the Devil!
Come, drink this draught and—feel divine!'

395 Lord Azrael, at his *fiend's* command,
The goblet seized with shaking hand,
And while at heart the tempter laughed
Deep and devotedly he quaffed;
And with more flushed but brighter brow
400 Said grimly—'To our *business* now!
To-morrow night must pleasure gay
From all but us drive care away;
But, oh! *with us* to-morrow night
Come counsel black and genius bright.
405 Then let our stateliest beauties bloom
Like roses round an open tomb;
Then let our Monarch think his power
Stands firmest in its latest hour,
Let MIDNIGHT end his dream!—Let night bring
morn
410 To us brave hearts! from darkness born!
Remember—That to-morrow night
　　Our Hate, our Tyrant means to join,
With *Thy* dear SARA's looks of light,
　　His faltering form and soul supine.
415 Remember—All his nobles' eyes
Will gaze upon the sacrifice,
When she must say, with voice divine,
To that old Dotard, 'I am thine!'
Remember—To the Royal Court
420 His sycophants will all resort,
While Cain and Haman mean to vie
'Neath their proud roofs with Majesty,
And all the citizens prepare
To feast beneath the midnight air,
425 But—the dark lanes—the alleys vile—
On what will *they* be bent the while?
Will their grim brows shine bright with joy?
Yes—with the longing to destroy!
Yes—they *will* join the festival!
430 Yes—they *will* visit each proud hall!

Here's to their health! Soon may I see
   Their naked arms and matted hair,
Tossing aside festivity—
   Frighting the rose from faces fair—
435   Stunning the music-laden air;
   And—where they gather—We'll be there!'

He ceased—Each drained another draught,
And Moloch smiled and Azrael laughed;
For laughter waits at trouble's side,
440   And shouts through cities ta'en by storm—
So—when Lord Azrael saw the wide
   Commencing waste assume its form,
Grim gladness buoyed his heart—He took
   His comrade's hand and pledged him well,
445 And spoke a word, and gave a look
   That seemed of blood to tell.
They ran o'er many a haughty name,
   Marked who should 'scape and who should fall....

                                              [1842.]

The first forty-eight lines of this poem were printed by F. A. Ley-
land in *The Brontë Family*, Vol. II, pp. 26–28, under the title of 'Noah's
Warning over Methuselah's Grave.'

THE CALLOUSNESS PRODUCED
BY CARE

WHY hold young eyes the fullest fount of tears
　　And why do youthful breasts the oftenest sigh
When fancied friends forsake, or lovers fly,
Or fancied woes and dangers waken fears:
5　Ah! He who asks has seen but springtide years,
　　Or Time's rough voice had long since told him why!
Increase of days increases misery,
And misery brings selfishness, which sears
The heart's first feelings—mid the battle's roar
10　In Death's dread grasp the soldier's eyes are blind
To other's pains—so he whose hopes are o'er
Turns coldly from the sufferings of mankind.
A bleeding spirit will delight in gore—
A tortured heart will make a Tyrant mind.

PEACEFUL DEATH AND PAINFUL LIFE

WHY dost thou sorrow for the happy dead?
　　For if their life be lost, their toils are o'er
And woe and want shall trouble them no more,
Nor ever slept they in an earthly bed
5　So sound as now they sleep while, dreamless, laid
　　In the dark chambers of that unknown shore
　　Where Night and Silence seal each guarded door:
So, turn from such as these thy drooping head
And mourn the 'Dead alive' whose spirit flies—
10　Whose life departs before his death has come—
Who finds no Heaven beyond Life's gloomy skies,
　　Who sees no Hope to brighten up that gloom,
'Tis HE who feels the worm that never dies—
The REAL death and darkness of the tomb.

THE EMIGRANT. I

WHEN sink from sight the landmarks of our Home,
  And—all the bitterness of farewells o'er—
We yield our spirit unto Ocean's foam,
  And in the newborn life which lies before,
5   On far Columbian or Australian shore
Strive to exchange time past for time to come,
  How melancholy then—if morn restore
  (Less welcome than the night's forgetful gloom)
  Old England's blue hills to our sight again,
10 While we, our thoughts seemed weaning from her sky
  The *pang*—that wakes an almost silenced pain.
Thus, when the sick man lies resigned to die,
  A well-loved voice, a well-remembered strain,
Lets Time break harshly on Eternity.

May 28, 1845.

One of the only two compositions of Patrick Branwell Brontë dur-
ing the time that he was a tutor at Thorp Green, the first being dated
March 30, 1843, a little more than two months after his duties com-
menced, the above, two months before they ended.

THE EMIGRANT. II

WHEN, after his long day, consumed in toil,
  'Neath the scarce welcome shade of unknown trees,
Upturning thanklessly a foreign soil,
  The lonely exile seeks his evening ease,—
5   'Tis not those tropic woods his spirit sees;
Nor calms, to him, that heaven, this world's turmoil;
  Nor cools his burning brow that spicy breeze.
Ah no! the gusty clouds of England's isle
  Bring music wafted on their stormy wind,
10 And on its verdant meads, night's shadows lower,
  While 'Auld Lang Syne' the darkness calls to mind.
Thus, when the demon Thirst, beneath his power
  The wanderer bows,—to feverish sleep consigned,
He hears the rushing rill, and feels the cooling shower.

I SAW a picture yesterday
  Of him who died for me
Which vainly struggled to display
  His mortal agony.
5 And, though the painter's name was old,
  And high his meed of fame,
I scarce could guess the tale he told,
  Or deem him worth acclaim.

To-day I saw a picture too,
10   With lighter pencil drawn,
Which, to its subject not more true,
  Gave midnight hues to morn;
And, if I blame Pietro's skill
  In painting features gone,
15 I must believe her feebler still
  Who could not paint her own!

Her effort shows a picture made
  To contradict its meaning:
Where should be sunshine, painting shade,
20   And smiles with sadness screening;
Where God has given a cheerful view,
  A gloomy vista showing;
Where heart and face are fair and true,
  A shade of doubt bestowing.

25 Ah, Lady, if to me you give
  The power your sketch to adorn,
How little of it shall I leave
  Save smiles that shine like morn.
I'd keep the hue of happy light
30   That shines from summer skies;
I'd drive the shades from smiles so bright
  And dry such shining eyes.

I'd give a calm to one whose heart
Has banished calm from mine;
35 I'd brighten up God's work of art
Where thou hast dimmed its shine,
And all the wages I should ask
For such a happy toil—
I'll name them—far beyond my task—
40 THY PRESENCE AND THY SMILE.

JUAN FERNANDEZ

A LONELY speck in ocean's waste
Fernandez' rocks our Anson saw,
Yet English parks by beauty graced
Could ne'er so much his eyesight draw,
5 Or steal from that old hero's eyes
The gleam with which he viewed it rise.
For him, 'twas hope of rest to come
To worn out men who knew their doom—
If separate from it—must be
10 A burial 'neath a boiling sea.
To him, 'twas hope that Fortune still
On valour's hand would deign to smile;
That Fame their greeting cup would fill.
Worn out with tracing league and mile
15 His seamen, while the hand of Death
Composed each shrunk and fevered limb,
Felt in each gale Hope's whispers breathe,
And Paradise before them swim.
So sweet a wind blew off that shore,
20 The bitterness of death seemed o'er.

But Oh, as whatsoe'er we do,
What joy through life we fondest woo,
Will, though it seems like happiness,
Unnoticed drift us toward Despair,

25 And prove the bane of our distress,
    And not the balm of our despair,
  That very gale they loved so well
    Blows *from*—not *to* Fernandez' groves,
  And every flowered and leafy dell
30   Which sends them scents the sailor loves,
  Still but the farther o'er the foam
  Removes them from a happy home.
  The salt wind from the prisoning main
  Had given them all they longed t'obtain;
35 The sweet wind from the healing shore
  Denies them what would health restore.

  Oh for the melancholy blast
    That howled round desolate Cape Horn,
  When comrade barks were parting fast
40   Through rain and wind and thunder borne,
  While nought could close the ocean tomb
  Though they had given their hecatomb!
  It would have borne them howsoe'er
  Through whitened breakers fraught with fear—
45 It would have borne them to that sand,
    Whose grains to them worth more than gold
  Had power to nerve each helpless hand,
    Each parting spirit to uphold.

  No, Fate that loves man's grief defied them,
50 The wished-for haven of hope denied them,
  And hour by hour, and day by day,
  As Manhood childlike sunk away,
  The sunshine from those thunder-hills
    That frowned o'er Chile's hostile shore
55 Gilt fairy-like the thousand rills
    In salt waves lost—those eyes, before
  Whom from death's films they might restore
  Again to gaze on Spanish war,
    Unblinkingly as eagle's eye,

60　Again to do—again to dare,
　　And not at least so meanly die
　　Like aged hound in corner lying,
　　Weak, sore and unattended dying.

　　Their chief had bade his fancy wake
65　To thoughts—how world-surrounding Drake,
　　And Raleigh—day-star of the sea—
　　The last bright beam of chivalry,
　　Might greet him when, from battle's plain,
　　War's clouds should bear him up to heaven,
70　And that green crown he wished to gain
　　Should by their English hands be given.
　　But now a north-west wind must doom
　　To him, forgetfulness—to his, a tomb.

　　Oh, when we feel that high emprize
75　In melancholy weakness fades,
　　That pulse beats faint and vigour dies
　　As woe our every thought invades,
　　We can perchance the sorrow feel
　　Of that brave heart who o'er the wave
80　But led his sailors to their grave,
　　When, with red fire and flashing steel,
　　He thought to have made his foemen reel,
　　New realms to explore and show his world
　　The portrait of herself unfurled.
85　Now every hour the white wave roared
　　For victims still to be devoured,
　　And still those sweet scents filled the air—
　　Fernandez' forests still waved there—

　　And when we see our Anson reach
90　At last yon tantalizing shore,
　　What lands he on the welcome beach?
　　The wretched wreck of those no more!
　　How like ourselves whose years of toil

Are spent life's hour of ease to gain,
95 And yet when reached through long turmoil,
To the rich feast of gathered spoil
No guests can sit but aches and pain!
Instead of some beloved bride
Disease and Death are placed beside
100 The table where our feast is spread,
And 'To the memory of the dead'
Must be our toast mid all our pride.

Anson—upon the sea of life
The worn and wasted soul like thee,
105 Mid winds and waves of care and strife
A rest like Juan's Isle may see—
May to its woodlands wish to roam,
Forgetting in that happy home
The rough Cape Horn of agony.

110 I'd long been tossed like withered leaf
That eddying blasts whirl round and round,
And born through many a gust of grief
While to the port of pleasure bound.
I saw at last Fernandez' Isle—
115 I saw a heart that beat for me,
A look that gave not friendship's smile
Or kindness of affinity—
The intercourse 'twixt man and man,
The kindnesses by kindred shewn,
120 Though not extinguished, were outshone
When Nature's deeper power began
To point the mental sight afar
To love's own sun from friendship's star.
Sunlike, my own Fernandez shines,
125 While early eve o'er me declines,
Laid like a log with—deep beneath—
The scarce unwelcome gulph of Death.

Tossed overboard, my perished crew
Of Hopes and Joys sink, one by one,
130   To where their fellow-thoughts have gone
When past gales breathed or tempests blew
Each last fond look ere sight declines
To where my own Fernandez shines,
Without one hope that they may e'er
135   Storm-worn, recline in sunshine there.

Alongside the last stanza of this poem, is written the name Λυδια (Lydia) in Greek characters, and a pen-and-ink sketch of a tombstone.

In July, 1845, Branwell Brontë was dismissed from his position at Thorp Green, because of his relations with Mrs Lydia Robinson, the wife of his employer, with whom the young tutor was desperately in love. (See *The Brontës: Their Lives, Friendships and Correspondence.* Shakespeare Head Press, Vol. II, pp. 63–65.)

In 1739, on the outbreak of war with Spain, George, Lord Anson, was given the command of a Pacific squadron of six vessels, with instructions to inflict whatever injury he could on the Spanish commerce and colonies. He sailed from England in September, 1740, and arrived in the neighbourhood of Cape Horn in the stormy season. The ships were severely buffeted; two were driven back and never got round the Cape at all; one, the *Wager*, was driven ashore and totally lost; the *Centurion* narrowly escaped a similar fate, and it was not until June 11, 1741 that she arrived at Juan Fernandez, with no more than thirty men, officers included, fit for duty. The two remaining ships arrived in still worse plight, and the surviving crew were transferred to the *Centurion*, where many died of scurvy. In spite of these misfortunes Anson, with one ship and less than 200 of his original followers, managed to destroy the Spanish commerce and to capture an enormous amount of treasure. He returned home via the Cape of Good Hope, arriving in England on June 15, 1744, having sailed round the world in three years and nine months.

PENMÆNMAWR

THESE winds, these clouds, this chill November storm
  Bring back again thy tempest-beaten form
To eyes that look upon yon dreary sky
As late they looked on thy sublimity;
5 When I, more troubled than thy restless sea,
Found, in its waves, companionship with thee.
'Mid mists thou frownedst over Arvon's shore,
'Mid tears I watched thee over ocean's roar,
And thy blue front, by thousand storms laid bare,
10 Claimed kindred with a heart worn down by care.
No smile had'st thou, o'er smiling fields aspiring,
And none had I, from smiling fields retiring;
Blackness, 'mid sunlight, tinged thy slaty brow,
I, 'mid sweet music, looked as dark as thou;
15 Old Scotland's song, o'er murmuring surges borne,
Of 'times departed,—never to return,'
Was echoed back in mournful tones from thee,
And found an echo, quite as sad, in me;
Waves, clouds, and shadows moved in restless change,
20 Around, above, and on thy rocky range,
But seldom saw that sovereign front of thine
Changes more quick than those which passed o'er mine.
And as wild winds and human hands, at length,
Have turned to scattered stones the mighty strength
25 Of that old fort, whose belt of boulders grey
Roman or Saxon legions held at bay;
So had, methought, the young, unshaken nerve—
That, when WILL wished, no doubt could cause to swerve,
That on its vigour ever placed reliance,
30 That to its sorrows sometimes bade defiance—
Now left my spirit, like thyself, old hill,
With head defenceless against human ill;
And, as thou long hast looked upon the wave
That takes, but gives not, like a churchyard grave,

35   I, like life's course, through ether's weary range,
     Never know rest from ceaseless strife and change.

     But, PENMÆNMAWR! a better fate was thine,
     Through all its shades, than that which darkened mine;
     No quick thoughts thrilled through thy gigantic mass
40   Of woe for what might be, or is, or was;
     Thou hadst no memory of the glorious hour
     When Britain rested on thy giant power;
     Thou hadst no feeling for the verdant slope
     That leant on thee as man's heart leans on hope;
45   The pastures, chequered o'er with cot and tree,
     Though thou wert guardian, got no smile from thee;
     Old ocean's wrath their charm might overwhelm,
     But thou could'st still keep thy unshaken realm—
     While I felt flashes of an inward feeling
50   As fierce as those thy craggy form revealing
     In nights of blinding gleams, when deafening roar
     Hurls back thy echo to old Mona's shore.
     I knew a flower, whose leaves were meant to bloom
     Till Death should snatch it to adorn a tomb,
55   Now, blanching 'neath the blight of hopeless grief,
     With never blooming, and yet living leaf;
     A flower on which my mind would wish to shine,
     If but one beam could break from mind like mine.
     I had an ear which could on accents dwell
60   That might as well say 'perish!' as 'farewell!'
     An eye which saw, far off, a tender form,
     Beaten, unsheltered, by affliction's storm;
     An arm—a lip—that trembled to embrace
     My angel's gentle breast and sorrowing face,
65   A mind that clung to Ouse's fertile side
     While tossing—objectless—on Menai's tide!

     Oh, Soul! that draw'st yon mighty hill and me
     Into communion of vague unity,
     Tell me, can I obtain the stony brow
70   That fronts the storm, as much unbroken now

As when it once upheld the fortress proud,
Now gone, like its own morning cap of cloud?
Its breast is stone. Can I have one of steel,
To endure—inflict—defend—yet never feel?
75   It stood as firm when haughty Edward's word
Gave hill and dale to England's fire and sword,
As when white sails and steam-smoke tracked the sea,
And all the world breathed peace, but waves and me.

Let me, like it, arise o'er mortal care,
80   All woes sustain, yet never know despair;
Unshrinking face the grief I now deplore,
And stand, through storm and shine, like moveless
      PENMÆNMAWR!

[*November*, 1845.]

Towards the end of July, 1845, Branwell Brontë visited North
Wales. He sent the above poem to J. B. Leyland on November 25,
1845, with a request that he would have it printed in the *Halifax
Guardian*. (See *The Brontës: Their Lives, Friendships and Correspondence*.
Shakespeare Head edition, Vol. II, p. 72.)

REAL REST

I SEE a corpse upon the waters lie,
With eyes turned, swelled and sightless, to the sky,
And arms outstretched to move, as wave on wave
Upbears it in its boundless billowy grave.
5 Not time, but ocean, thins its flowing hair;
Decay, not sorrow, lays its forehead bare;
Its members move, but not in thankless toil,
For seas are milder than this world's turmoil;
Corruption robs its lips and cheeks of red,
10 But wounded vanity grieves not the dead;
And, though these members hasten to decay,
No pang of suffering takes their strength away.
With untormented eye, and heart and brain,
Through calm and storm it floats across the main;
15 Though love and joy have perished long ago,
Its bosom suffers not one pang of woe;
Though weeds and worms its cherished beauty hide,
It feels not wounded vanity nor pride;
Though journeying towards some far-off shore,
20 It needs no care nor gold to float it o'er;
Though launched in voyage for eternity,
It need not think upon what is to be;
Though naked, helpless, and companionless
It feels not poverty, nor knows distress.

25 Ah, corpse! if thou could'st tell my aching mind
What scenes of sorrow thou hast left behind,
How sad the life which, breathing, thou hast led,
How free from strife thy sojourn with the dead;
I would assume thy place—would long to be
30 A world-wide wanderer o'er the waves with thee!
I have a misery, where thou hast none;
My heart beats, bursting, whilst thine lies like stone;
My veins throb wild, whilst thine are dead and dry;
And woes, not waters, dim my restless eye;

35 Thou longest not with one well loved to be,
    And absence does not break a chain with thee;
    No sudden agonies dart through thy breast;
    Thou hast what all men covet—REAL REST.
    I have an outward frame, unlike to thine,
40 Warm with young life—not cold in death's decline;
    An eye that sees the sunny light of Heaven—
    A heart by pleasure thrilled, by anguish riven—
    But, in exchange for thy untroubled calm,
    Thy gift of cold oblivion's healing balm,
45 I'd give my youth, my health, my life to come,
    And share thy slumbers in thy ocean tomb.

                                   [1845–1846.]

'Here the poet, his soul longing for freedom from mortality, his crushed and wounded spirit hovering above the salt and restless wave, contemplates the pale and ghastly body that floats thereon, and, holding communion with it, touches in melancholy and beautiful words its isolation and oblivion. Accompanying the dead in its watery wanderings, he sees, with keen sympathy, its utter disseverance from the world it has left, and contrasts with its condition the hopeless sorrow of his own disappointed youth. He delineates, in words of singular power and felicity, this weird and lonely picture; and, as an artist and a poet, paints wildly, but beautifully, the decay of the drowned in the ocean, and of the living, through the effects of long-continued woe. . . . There was a tendency to gloom and despondency implanted in his very nature, a disposition of mind in which his sister Emily largely resembled him. To such an extent was this the case that, in her poem of "The Philosopher," written in the October of 1845, she not only gives expression to similar weird thoughts and desires, but one might think there had been some interchange of ideas between the two. . . . It is noteworthy that Charlotte, also, in the second part of her poem "Gilbert," has used the incident of a corpse floating upon the waters, which is seen by the unhappy man in his vision, not, indeed, to give him the calm of oblivion, but rather, in contrast to Branwell's poem, to wake in him the pains of sorrow and remorse.' F. A. Leyland, in *The Brontë Family*, Vol. II, pp. 97–99.

EPISTLE FROM A FATHER TO A
CHILD IN HER GRAVE

FROM Earth,—whose life-reviving April showers
 Hide withered grass 'neath Springtide's herald
    flowers,
And give, in each soft wind that drives her rain,
Promise of fields and forests rich again,—
5   I write to thee, the aspect of whose face
Can never change with altered time or place;
Whose eyes could look on India's fiercest wars
Less shrinking than the boldest son of Mars;
Whose lips, more firm than Stoic's long ago,
10 Would neither smile with joy nor blanch with woe;
Whose limbs could sufferings far more firmly bear
Than mightiest heroes in the storms of war;
Whose frame, nor wishes good, nor shrinks from ill,
Nor feels distraction's throb, nor pleasure's thrill.

15   I write to thee what thou wilt never read,
For heed me thou *wilt not*, howe'er may bleed
The heart that many think a worthless stone,
But which oft aches for some belovèd one;
Nor, if that life, mysterious, from on high,
20 Once more gave feeling to thy stony eye,
Could'st thou thy father know, or feel that he
Gave life and lineaments and thoughts to thee;
For when thou died'st, thy day was in its dawn,
And night still struggled with Life's opening morn;
25 The twilight star of childhood, thy young days
Alone illumined, with its twinkling rays,
So sweet, yet feeble, given from those dusk skies,
Whose kindling, coming noontide prophesies,
But tells us not that Summer's noon can shroud
30 Our sunshine with a veil of thundercloud.

If, when thou freely gave the life, that ne'er
To thee had given either hope or fear,
But quietly had shone; nor asked if joy
Thy future course should cheer, or grief annoy;

35 If then thoud'st seen, upon a summer sea,
One, once in features, as in blood, like thee,
On skies of azure blue and waters green,
Melting to mist amid the summer sheen,
In trouble gazing—ever hesitating
40 'Twixt miseries each hour new dread creating,
And joys—whate'er they cost—still doubly dear,
Those 'troubled pleasures soon chastised by fear;'
If thou *had'st* seen him, thou would'st ne'er believe
That thou had'st yet known what it was to live!

45 Thine eyes could only see thy mother's breast;
Thy feelings only wished on that to rest;
That was thy world;—thy food and sleep it gave,
And slight the change 'twixt it and childhood's grave.
Thou saw'st this world like one who, prone, reposes,
50 Upon a plain, and in a bed of roses,
With nought in sight save marbled skies above,
Nought heard but breezes whispering in the grove:
I—thy life's source—was like a wanderer breasting
Keen mountain winds, and on a summit resting,
55 Whose rough rocks rose above the grassy mead,
With sleet and north winds howling overhead,
And Nature, like a map, beneath him spread;
Far winding river, tree, and tower, and town,
Shadow and sunlight, 'neath his gaze marked down
60 By that mysterious hand which graves the plan
Of that drear country called 'The Life of Man.'

If seen, men's eyes would loathing shrink from thee,
And turn, perhaps, with no disgust to me;
Yet thou had'st beauty, innocence, and smiles,
65 And now hast rest from this world's woes and wiles,

While I have restlessness and worrying care,
So sure, thy lot is brighter, happier far.

So let it be; and though thy ears may never
Hear these lines read beyond Death's darksome river,
70 Not vainly from the borders of despair
May rise a sound of joy that thou art freed from care!

April 3, 1846.

SONNET

WHEN all our cheerful hours seem gone for ever,
    All lost that caused the body or the mind
To nourish love or friendship for our kind,
And Charon's boat, prepared, o'er Lethe's river
5 Our souls to waft, and all our thoughts to sever
From what was once life's Light; still there may be
Some well-loved bosom to whose pillow we
Could heartily our utter self deliver;
And if, toward her grave—Death's dreary road—
10 Our Darling's feet should tread, each step by her
Would draw our own steps to the same abode,
And make a festival of sepulture;
For what gave joy, and joy to us had owed,
Should Death affright us from, when he would her
    restore?

April, 1846.

WHILE fabled scenes and fancied forms
    And leanings upon thoughts laid by,
With visionary calms or storms,
    May strive to cheat my memory,
5   Still, still before my inward eye
Thou, my life's sunbeam, shinest afar,
    And 'mid a drear December sky
Giv'st comfort to thy wanderer;

Yet, hardly *comfort*, for that word
10   Speaks too much of security
And peace—two names too long unheard
To own acquaintanceship with me.
They would be mine were I with thee,
But while dissevered I'm resigned,
15   If thy far light can let me see
One glimpse, where life would keep me blind.

MORLEY HALL

Leigh, Lancashire

WHEN Life's youth, overcast by gathering clouds
Of cares, that come like funeral-following
crowds,
Weary of that which is, and cannot see
A sunbeam burst upon futurity,
5   It tries to cast away the woes that are
And borrow brighter joys from times afar.
For what our feet tread may have been a road
By horses' hoofs pressed, 'neath a camel's load,
But, what we ran across in childhood's hours
10   Were fields, presenting June with May-day flowers:
So what was done, and borne, if long ago,
Will satisfy our heart though stained by tears of woe.

When present sorrows every thought employ
Our father's woes may take the garb of joy,
15   And, knowing what our sires have undergone,
Ourselves can smile, though weary, wandering on.
For, if, our youth a thunder-cloud o'ershadows,
Changing to barren swamps life's flowering meadows,
We know that fiery flash and bursting peal
20   Others, like us, were forced to hear and feel,

And while they moulder in a quiet grave,
Robbed of all havings—worthless all they have—
We still with face erect behold the sun—
Have bright examples in what has been done
25 By head or hand—and in the times to come
May tread bright pathways to our gate of doom.

So, if we gaze from our snug villa's door,
By vines or honeysuckles covered o'er,
Though we have saddening thoughts, we still can smile
30 In thinking our hut supersedes the pile
Whose turrets totter 'mid the woods before us,
And whose proud owners used to trample o'er us;
All now by weeds and ivy overgrown
And touched by Time, that hurls down stone from stone—
35 We gaze with scorn on what is worn away,
And never dream about our own decay.
Thus while this May day cheers each flower and tree,
Enlivening Earth and almost cheering me,
I half forget the mouldering moats of Leigh.

40 Wide Lancashire has changed its babyhood,
As time makes saplings spring to timber wood,
But as grown men their childhood still remember
And think of summer in their dark December,
So Manchester and Liverpool may wonder
45 And bow to old halls over which they ponder
Unknowing that man's spirit yearns to all
Which once lost—prayers can never more recall:
The storied piles of mortar, brick and stone,
Where trade bids noise and gain to struggle on
50 Competing for the prize that Mammon gives—
Youth killed by toil and profits bought with lives—
Will not prevent the quiet, thinking mind
From looking back to years when summer wind
Sang, not o'er mills, but round ancestral Halls,
55 And, 'stead of engine's steam, gave dew from water-falls.

He, who by brick-built houses closely pent
That show nought beautiful to sight or scent
Pines for green fields, will cherish in his room
Some pining plant bereft of natural bloom,
60° And, like the crowds which yonder factories hold,
Withering 'mid warmth, and in their springtide old,
So Lancashire may fondly look upon
Her wrecks fast vanishing, of ages gone,
And while encroaching railroad, street, or mill
65 On every side the smoky prospect fill,
She yet may smile to see some tottering wall
Bring old times back like ancient Morley Hall.
But towers that Leyland[1] saw in times of yore,
Are now, like Leyland's works, almost no more—
70 The Antiquarian's pages, cobweb-bound—
The antique mansion levelled with the ground.

When all is gone that once gave food to pride
Man little cares for what time leaves beside,
And when an orchard and a moat half dry
75 Remain, sole relics of a power past by,
Should we not think of what ourselves shall be
And view our coffins in the stones of Leigh.
For what within yon space was once the abode
Of peace or war to man, and fear of God,
80 Is now the daily sport of shower or wind,
And no acquaintance holds with human kind.
Some who can be loved, and love can give,
While brain thinks, pulses beat and bodies live,
Must in death's helplessness, lie down with those
85 Who find, like us, the grave their last repose,
When death draws down the veil and night bids even-
        ing close.

King Charles who fortune falling, would not fall,
Might glance with saddened eyes on Morley Hall,

[1] John Leyland or Leland, the noted antiquary, when on his great tour about 1537, visited his kinsman, Sir William Leyland at Morley Hall.

And while his own corse glides into the grave
90 Remember Tyldesley died his throne to save.

.   .   .   .   .

[1846–1847.]

These lines were designed by Branwell as an Introduction to a long
epic poem relating to the family of Leyland of Morley Hall, Leigh,
Lancashire. (See *The Brontë Family*, by F. A. Leyland, Vol. II, p. 242.)
Branwell makes frequent references to this poem in his letters to J. B.
Leyland. (See *The Brontës: Their Lives, Friendships and Correspondence*,
Vol. II, pp. 91, 95, 100, 113.)

THE END OF ALL

IN that unpitying Winter's night,
When my own wife—my Mary—died,
I, by my fire's declining light,
    Sat comfortless, and silent sighed,
5   While burst unchecked grief's bitter tide,
As I, methought, when she was gone,
    Not hours, but years, like this must bide,
And wake, and weep, and watch alone.

All earthly hope had passed away,
10   And each clock-stroke brought Death more nigh
To the still-chamber where she lay,
    With soul and body calmed to die;
But *mine* was not her heavenward eye
When hot tears scorched me, as her doom
15   Made my sick heart throb heavily
To give impatient anguish room.

'Oh now,' methought, 'a little while,
    And this great house will hold no more
Her whose fond love the gloom could while
20   Of many a long night gone before!'
Oh! all those happy hours were o'er

When, seated by our own fireside,
   I'd smile to hear the wild winds roar,
And turn to clasp my beauteous bride.

25 I could not bear the thoughts which rose
   Of what *had* been, and what *must* be,
And still the dark night would disclose
   Its sorrow-pictured prophecy;
   Still saw I—miserable me—
30 Long, long nights else, in lonely gloom,
   With time-bleached locks and trembling knee—
Walk aidless, hopeless, to my tomb.

Still, still that tomb's eternal shade
   Oppressed my heart with sickening fear,
35 When I could see its shadow spread
   Over each dreary future year,
   Whose vale of tears woke such despair
That, with the sweat-drops on my brow,
   I wildly raised my hands in prayer
40 That Death would come and take me now;

Then stopped to hear an answer given—
   So much had madness warped my mind—
When, sudden, through the midnight heaven,
   With long howl woke the Winter's wind;
45   And roused in me, though undefined,
A rushing thought of tumbling seas
   Whose wild waves wandered unconfined,
And, far-off, surging, whispered, 'Peace.'

I cannot speak the feeling strange,
50   Which showed that vast December sea,
Nor tell whence came that sudden change
   From aidless, hopeless misery;
   But somehow it revealed to me
A life—when things I loved were gone—
55   Whose solitary liberty
Might suit me wandering tombward on.

'Twas not that I forgot my love—
    That night departing evermore—
'Twas hopeless grief for her that drove
60   My soul from all it prized before;
    That misery called me to explore
A new-born life, whose stony joy
    Might calm the pangs of sorrow o'er,
Might *shrine* their memory, not destroy.

65   I rose, and drew the curtains back
    To gaze upon the starless waste,
And image on that midnight wrack
    The path on which I longed to haste,
    From storm to storm continual cast,
70   And not one moment given to view;
    O'er mind's wild winds the memories passed
Of hearts I loved—of scenes I knew.

My mind anticipated all
    The things my eyes have seen since then;
75   I heard the trumpet's battle-call,
    I rode o'er ranks of bleeding men,
    I swept the waves of Norway's main,
I tracked the sands of Syria's shore,
    I felt that such strange strife and pain
80   Might me from living death restore.

Ambition I would make my bride,
    And joy to see her robed in red,
For none through blood so wildly ride
    As those whose hearts before have bled;
85   Yes, even though *thou* should'st long have laid
Pressed coldly down by churchyard clay,
    And though I knew thee thus decayed,
I *might* smile grimly when away;

Might give an opiate to my breast,
90   Might dream:—but oh! that heart-wrung groan
Forced from me with the thought confessed
    That all would go if *she* were gone;

I turned, and wept, and wandered on
All restlessly—from room to room—
95   To that still chamber, where alone
A sick-light glimmered through the gloom.

The all-unnoticed time flew o'er me,
    While my breast bent above her bed,
And that drear life which loomed before me
100   Choked up my voice—bowed down my head.
Sweet holy words to me she said,
Of that bright heaven which shone so near,
And oft and fervently she prayed
That I might some time meet her there;

105 But, soon enough, all words were over,
    When this world passed, and Paradise,
Through deadly darkness, seemed to hover
    O'er her half-dull, half-brightening eyes;
One last dear glance she gives her lover,
110 One last embrace before she dies;
    And then, while he seems bowed above her,
His *Mary* sees him from the skies.

PERCY HALL

THE westering sunbeams smiled on Percy Hall,
    And green leaves glittered o'er the ancient wall
Where Mary sat, to feel the summer breeze,
And hear its music mingling 'mid the trees.
5 There she had rested in her quiet bower
Through June's long afternoon, while hour on hour
Stole, sweetly shining past her, till the shades,
Scarce noticed, lengthened o'er the grassy glades;
But yet she sat, as if she knew not how
10 Her time wore on, with Heaven-directed brow,
And eyes that only seemed awake, whene'er
Her face was fanned by summer evening's air.
All day her limbs a weariness would feel,
As if a slumber o'er her frame would steal;
15 Nor could she wake her drowsy thoughts to care

For day, or hour, or what she was, or where:
Thus—lost in dreams, although debarred from sleep,
While through her limbs a feverish heat would creep,
A weariness, a listlessness, that hung
20 About her vigour, and Life's powers unstrung—
She did not feel the iron gripe of pain,
But *thought* felt irksome to her heated brain;
Sometimes the stately woods would float before her,
Commingled with the cloud-piles brightening o'er her,
25 Then change to scenes for ever lost to view,
Or mock with phantoms which she never knew:
Sometimes her soul seemed brooding on to-day,
And then it wildly wandered far away,
Snatching short glimpses of her infancy,
30 Or lost in day-dreams of what yet might be.

Yes—through the labyrinth-like course of thought—
Whate'er might be remembered or forgot,
Howe'er diseased the dream might be, or dim,
Still seemed the *Future* through each change to swim,
35 All indefinable, but pointing on
To what should welcome her when Life was gone;
She felt as if—to all she knew so well—
Its voice was whispering her to say 'farewell';
Was bidding her forget her happy home;
40 Was farther fleeting still—still beckoning her to come.
She felt as one might feel who, laid at rest,
With cold hands folded on a panting breast,
Has just received a husband's last embrace,
Has kissed a child, and turned a pallid face
45 From this world—with its feelings all laid by—
To one unknown, yet hovering—oh! how nigh!
And yet—unlike that image of decay—
There hovered round her, as she silent lay
A holy sunlight, an angelic bloom,
50 That brightened up the terrors of the tomb,
And, as it showed Heaven's glorious world beyond,
Forbade her heart to throb, her spirit to despond.

But, who steps forward, o'er the glowing green,
With silent tread, these stately groves between?
55 To watch his fragile flower, who sees him not,
Yet keeps his image blended with each thought,
Since but for *him* stole down that single tear
From her blue eyes, to think how very near
Their farewell hour might be!
60   With silent tread
Percy bent o'er his wife his golden head;
And, while he smiled to see how calm she slept,
A gentle feeling o'er his spirit crept,
Which made him turn toward the shining sky
65 With heart expanding to its majesty,
While he bethought him how more blest *its* glow
Than *that* he left one single hour ago,
Where proud rooms, heated by a feverish light,
Forced vice and villainy upon his sight;
70 Where snared himself, or snaring into crime,
His soul had drowned its hour, and lost its count of time.

The syren-sighs and smiles were banished now,
The cares of 'play' had vanished from his brow;
He took his Mary's hot hand in his own,
75 She raised her eyes, and—oh, how soft they shone!
Kindling to fondness through their mist of tears,
Wakening afresh the light of fading years!—
He knew not why she turned those shining eyes
With such a mute submission to the skies;
80 He knew not why her arm embraced him so,
As if she *must* depart, yet *could not* let him go!

With death-like voice, but angel-smile, she said,
'My love, they need not care, when I am dead,
To deck with flowers my capped and coffined head;
85 For all the flowers which I should love to see
Are blooming now, and will have died with me:
The same sun bids us all revive to-day,
And the same winds will bid us to decay;
When Winter comes we all shall be no more—

90 Departed into dust—next, covered o'er
    By Spring's reviving green. See, Percy, now
    How red my cheek—how red my roses blow!
    But come again when blasts of Autumn come;
    Then mark their changing leaves, their blighted bloom;
95 Then come to my bedside, then look at *me*,
    How changed in all—*except my love for thee!*'

    She spoke, and laid her hot hand on his own;
    But he nought answered, save a heart-wrung groan;
    For oh! too sure, her voice prophetic sounded
100 Too clear the proofs that in her face abounded
    Of swift Consumption's power! Although each day
    He'd seen her airy lightness fail away,
    And gleams unnatural glisten in her eye;
    He had not dared to dream that she could die,
105 But only fancied his a causeless fear
    Of losing something which he held so dear;
    Yet—now—when, startled at her prophet-cries,
    To hers he turned his stricken, stone-like eyes,
    And o'er her cheek declined his blighted head.
110 He saw Death write on it the *fatal red*—
    He saw, and straightway sank his spirit's light
    Into the sunless twilight of the starless night!

    While he sat, shaken by his sudden shock,
    Again—and with an earnestness—she spoke,
115 As if the world of her Creator shone
    Through all the cloudy shadows of her own:
    'Come, grieve not—darling—o'er my early doom;
    'Tis well that Death no drearier shape assume
    Than this he comes in—well that widowed age
120 Will not extend my friendless pilgrimage
    Through Life's dim vale of tears—'tis well that Pain
    Wields not its lash nor binds its burning chain,
    But leaves my death-bed to a mild decline,
    Soothed and supported by a love like thine!'

    According to F. A. Leyland 'Percy Hall' was the last poem Bran-
    well Brontë ever wrote. He sent the first draft of it to J. B. Leyland in
    July, 1847, but never lived to complete it.

2

POEMS IN BRANWELL BRONTË'S
1837 NOTEBOOK

THE VISION OF VELINO

I SEE through Heaven with raven wings
   A Funeral Angel fly,
The Trumpet in his dusky hands
   Wails wild and mournfully.

5   Beside him on her midnight path
      The Moon glides through the sky,
   And far beneath her chilly face
      The silent waters lie.

   Around me—not the accustomed sight
10   Of Hill and Vale I view
   With meadows bathed in cheerless light
      And woods in midnight hue.

   No! All these Moors around me here
      Seem one wide waste of graves,
15   And round each trench so dark and drear
      The black earth stands like waves.

   These are not common graves of men
      With Yew Trees waving by,
   Where when their life's short hour is gone
20   They slumber peacefully.

   These seem as if a torrent's force
      Had rent its sudden way,
   And they the channels of its course
      Towards some tremendous sea.

25   These are the graves of Armies, where
      Together must consume
   Foeman and friend and sword and spear
      Within their bloody tomb.

Oh God! And what shall this betide?
30   Why does that Angel fly?
Why does that Moon so solemn glide
Across that stormy sky?

Why does my Spirit cold and chill,
Though winter roars around,
35   In visioned wonders linger still
On this mysterious ground?

Behold upon the midnight Heath
A mighty Army lie,
In slumber hushed each warrior's breath
40   And closed each eagle eye.

The Moon from heaven upon each face
With saddest lustre shines,
And glitters on the untrampled grass
Between the longdrawn lines.

45   Are *They* the Tenants of the Tomb?
And did those trenches yawn
To hide them in eternal gloom
Before tomorrow's dawn?

Avert my God the avenging sword
50   And turn thy wrath away;
Or if battle come with midnight gloom
Let *Victory* come with day!

THE CXXXVIIth PSALM

BY the still streams of Babylon
We sat in sorrowing sadness down,
All weeping when we thought upon
Our Zion's holy dome;

5   There hung our harps, unheeded now,
From the dark willow's bending bough,
Where mourning o'er the waves below
    They cast their evening gloom.

There round us stood that Iron band
10   Who tore us from our home;
And in their far off stranger land
    Compelled our feet to roam.

They turned them to our native west
    And laughed with victor tongue;
15 Now sing—they said in stern behest—
    Your Zion's holiest song!—

How can we name Jehovah's name
So far away from Jordan's stream?

Jerusalem! Jerusalem!
20   May hand and heart decay
If I forget thy diadem
    And sceptre passed away!
If 'mid my brightest smiles of joy
    I do not think of thee,
25 Or cease one hour my thoughts to employ
    On Salem's slavery,
Let this false tongue forget to speak,
And this torn heart with anguish break!

Remember, God, how Edom's sons
30   In Zion's darkest day
Rejoiced above her prostrate wall
    Like Lions o'er their prey;
How ruthlessly they shouted then
    As dark they gathered round,
35 'Down with it! Yea, Down with it
    Even to the very ground!'

Daughter of Babel, worn with woe
  And struck with misery,
As thou hast served God's people—so
40 Shall thy destruction be!
And in thine own dark hour of death,
  When foemen gather round,
Happy be they who on thy stones
Of ruin take thy little ones
45 And dash them to the ground!

SONG

I SAW Her in the Crowded hall
  When plumes were waving there,
But 'mid the mazes of the Ball
  Seemed none like her so fair!

5 I saw the circlet round her brow,
  The diamonds in her hair,
But her hazel eyes with Angel glow
  Outshone their borrowed glare!

Yet call her from that glittering crowd,
10 For Fate o'ershades her brow,
And the neck which sorrow never bowed
  Must bend to anguish now!

Oh Loftiest of the Lofty
  And fairest of the fair,
15 Must the spectre's shade pass o'er thee,
  Must *thou* shake hands with care!

Then where in Heaven or where in Earth
Can our eyes find tearless mirth?
Alike the man of stormy life,
20 Unwed to battle blood and strife,

Alike that beauteous Queen of May
  Their perished hopes must mourn,
In a single glimpse of gladness gone,
  Never to return!

25 Then cease, my Lyre, thy wailing cease,
    Lingering, quivering, die in peace!

THE ROVER

SAIL fast, sail fast, my gallant ship! Thy Ocean thunders
    round thee,
At length thou'rt in thy paradise, thy own wide heaven
    around thee.
The morning flashes up in light and strikes its beams before,
Where those wide streaks of lustre bright lie like a fairy
    shore.
5 The day presages storm and strife. But what need Percy
    care?
The deck that braved the blast of heaven can brave the fires
    of war.
The thundering winds are swelling up and whistle through
    thy shrouds,
Though over head in the Iron sky sleep sullenly the clouds.
So that first blast hath swept the seas and covered them with
    foam,
10 Yet it shall bear thee o'er the deep where e'er thou mayest
    roam.
Though the rich and puny merchant ship may quiver in this
    gale,
For it toward such a destined prey shall speed thy swelling
    sail.
  When Night and tempest gather up to shroud the stormy
    sky,
The timid sheep will look to heaven with an imploring eye,

15 And while they flock with frightened haste and crowd the
   narrow way,
   What cares the Lordly Lion then who pounces on his prey?
   The storm has but his reaper been to gather in his grain,
   And thus to thee my ship shall be this hoarse resounding
   main.
   Oh look beneath those thick black clouds on yon dark line
   of water
20 A home returning merchant fleet just gathered for the
   slaughter;
   See how their spread sails glimmer white as scudding far
   before
   They steering in unsteady line o'erpass the watery roar.
     Now rouse ye then, my gallant men, rouse up with
     hearty cheer!
   Quick clear your deck and crowd your sail and bring your
   guns to bear.
25 Ho Connor! Gordon!—steer ye right; the winds confuse
   them now
   And, as 'mid the swans an eagle's flight, so 'mid them drive
   my prow.
   I stand upon my steady deck; around me flies the foam,
   And my Rover skims before the blast across her ocean
   home.
   The Merchant Convoy still before with furled or shivered
   sail
30 Like helpless geese together crowd and tremble in the
   gale.
   Now light your Matches!—From that smoke bursts up one
   crash of thunder
   Rebellowing from the clouds above and from the surges
   under.
   They know that voice, they hear my call, but dread hath
   paled each brow.
   So canvas furl and grapplers cast, for we're upon them now
35 And fastened by our trusty hooks one proud Galleon lies,
   Whose hesitating broadside burst uncertain to the skies.

We heed it not, and I'm the first upon her shaking deck,
While all my band of gallant hearts have followed at my
    back.
Now 'mid the thickening smoke and sleet one mighty
    tumult reigns
40 And sparkles flash before our eyes and blood boils through
    our veins.
Men dashed on men in trampled blood strew thick each
    groaning plank,
And all unseen the sabres clash amid each gory rank.
Where am I—? dashed into the hold upon a dying foe,
All stir and smoke and shouts above—that writhing wretch
    below.
45 He dies—I rise and grasp a rope—am on the deck once
    more,
And Percy's arm and Percy's sword bathe all that deck with
    gore.
An hour of tempest passes by—the Galleon blazes now,
And smoke and slaughter crowd her deck and heap her
    bending prow.
Our swords are grown into our hands, our eyes glance
    fiery light
50 As faint we stagger o'er the wrecks of that impetuous fight.
We have done your work most gallantly. That precious
    merchandise
Convey upon our Rover's deck—to be our well earned
    prize.
Then fire the ship and follow me to our own deck again
To chase the coward wanderers across the stormy main.
55   The evening sinks in sullen light behind the heaving
    sea
And sees the Rover o'er its waves plough on her gallant
    way,
While far behind across the surge a blaze of blood red
    light
Drifts on to windward shrouding round the relics of that
    fight.

I see afar the blackened masts stand 'gainst the flaring
   flame,
60 While high in heaven the heavey smoke curls o'er its
   blazing frame.
Whose fires discharge its cannonry with sullen sounding
   boom
Till like a blood red moon it sets behind its watery tomb.

AUGUSTA

AUGUSTA! Though I'm far away
   Across the dark blue sea,
Still eve and morn and night and day
   Will I remember Thee!

5 And, though I cannot see thee nigh
   Or hear thee speak to me,
Thy look and voice and memory
   Shall not forgotten be.

I stand upon this Island shore,
10   A single hour alone,
And see the Atlantic swell before
   With sullen surging tone,

While high in heaven the full Moon glides
   Above the breezy deep,
15 Unmoved by waves or winds or tides
   That far beneath her sweep.

She marches through this midnight air,
   So silent and divine,
With not a wreath of vapour there
20   To dim her silver shine.

For every cloud through ether driven
   Has settled far below,

And round the unmeasured skirts of heaven
  Their whitened fleeces glow.

25 They join and part and pass away
      Beyond the heaving sea,
    So mutable and restless they,
      So still and changeless she.

    Those clouds have melted into air,
30   Those waves have sunk to sleep,
    But clouds renewed are rising there,
      And fresh waves crowd the deep.

    How like the chaos of my soul,
      Where visions ever rise,
35 And thoughts and passions ceaseless roll,
      And tumult never dies.

    Each fancy but the former's grave
      And germ of that to come,
    While all are fleeting as the wave
40   That chafes itself to foam.

    I said that full Moon glides on high,
      Howe'er the world repines,
    And in its own untroubled sky
      For ever smiles and shines.

45 So dark'ning o'er my anxious brow,
      Though thicken cares and pain,
    Within my Heart Augusta thou
      For ever shalt remain.

    And Thou art not that wintry moon
50   With its melancholy ray,
    But where thou shinest is summer noon
      And bright and perfect day.

The Moon sinks down as sinks the night,
But Thou beam'st brightly on.
55 She only shines with borrowed light,
But Thine is all Thine Own!

SOUND THE LOUD TRUMPET

SOUND the loud Trumpet o'er Africa's bright sea!
Zamorna has triumphed, the Angrians are free.
Sound that loud Trump and let winds waft its story!
Sound! For our Day Star hath risen in its glory.
5 Sing! For the Sunbeams have burst forth to brighten,
   A Reign such as never through age or in clime
The pages of History has deigned to enlighten,
   Alone in its glory and proud in its prime,
   Never to darken and never decline.
10 Tempests may threaten and storms may assail us,
Friends may forsake us and Fortune may fail us,
   Angria thy full sun unshadowed shall shine!
Sing, for the power of our Foemen has flown,
Quenched in the sunbeams that smile round thy throne!
15 Raise higher and louder your voices to sing
Angria our Country and Adrian our King!
River, whose waves through the wide desert winding
   Hurry their floods toward the home of thy pride,
Each weary waste of our glory reminding,
20 Rise and spread round thee thy life-giving tide!
All ye proud Mountains, that shadowing afar
Crown your blue brows with the wandering star,
Tell you each summit and valley and plain
Adrian has triumphed o'er Angria to reign.
25 Tell ye the North with its tempests and snow,
Tell ye the South where the ocean's gales blow,
Tell ye the West where the suns ever glow
   Angria and Arthur are shining again!
   Midnight and tempest may darken in vain,

30 Foes may arise and Fate may surprise—
Dust on the Mountains and drops in the main!

Sing, for the Sun has arisen on Creation,
Sound ye the Trumpet to herald his dawn,
Rise Man and Monarch and City and Nation,
35 Away with your Midnight and Hail to your morn!
Sound the Loud Trumpet o'er land and o'er sea,
Join Hearts and Voices rejoicing to sing,
Afric arising hath sworn to be free,
And Glory to Angria and God save our King!

THE ANGRIAN HYMN

SHINE on us, God of Angria, shine,
And round us pour thy light divine,
For sailing o'er a stormy sea
Through life to death we look to Thee!

5 Do Thou with Thine Almighty power,
Shield us in Battle's darkest hour,
If dying, take our souls to Thee,
If living, grant us victory!

And Oh, *should* Foemen threaten round,
10 Let not amid our ranks be found
One Traitor Craven who would fly
His country's Flag of Liberty!

And ever may that Flag remain
As we received it, free from stain,
15 And never may its watchword shine
In fields unblessed by beams of thine.

Yet may it wave through years afar
O'er glorious fields of conquering war

POEMS

To free the world from Error's chain
20 And bring thy kingdom back again!

May future ages thus proclaim
Our noble Adrian's deathless name,
Look back on what his arm has done
And press with him to conquest on.

25 And may he long, as life to him
Shall spare his own bright diadem,
Think on the prow its glories shade
As not for Kin but Kingdom made.

Oh let not care that circlet hide,
30 Nor crime nor sorrow stain its pride,
And when in Death he lays it down
Give him an Everlasting Crown.

And when his subjects meet their doom
Following their Monarch to the Tomb
35 Be theirs an endless paradise
When the last Trumpet sounds ARISE!

THE ANGRIAN WELCOME

WELCOME, Heroes, to the War,
    Welcome to your glory.
Will you seize your swords and dare
    To be renowned in story?
5 What though Fame be distant far
Flashing from her upper air,
Though the path which leads you there
    Be long and rough and gory?
Still that path is straight and wide,
10 Open to receive the tide,
Youth's first flush, and manhood's pride,

Age all stiff and hoary.
Sire and son may enter in,
Son and sire alike may win,
15 So rouse ye then and all begin
To seek the glory o'er ye.

Angrians, when your morning rose
Before your Monarch's eye,
He swore that ere its evening's close
20 All your foes should fly.
He knew that Adrian's very name
Would force those foes to fly.
He saw the brightest star of fame
Was flashing forth on high.
25 So down from heaven ZAMORNA came
To guide you to the sky,
And shook his sword of quenchless flame
And shouted Victory!

Angrians, if your Noble King
30 Rides foremost in the fight,
Up in glorious gathering
Around that Helmet bright!
Angrians, if you wield your sword,
Every stroke shall be
35 Fixed as one undying word
In Afric's History.

Angrians, if in fight you die,
The clouds that o'er you rise
Shall waft your spirits to a sky
40 Of everlasting joy.

Angrians, when that fight is o'er,
Heaven and earth and sea
Shall echo in the Cannon's roar
Your shout of victory.

45   So now, if all your bosoms beat
       To reach your native star,
       Shake the shackles from your feet
       And Welcome to the War!

NORTHANGERLAND'S NAME

HISTORY sat by her pillar of fame
    With a shade on her brow and a tear in her eye,
And, Oh, must she blot her Northangerland's name
    From its own glorious chapter of victory?

5   She held o'er that chapter the pencil of fate,
       But her white arm drew back from the page as it lay,
    So in sorrow and silence she mournfully sat
       Oppressed with the shades of her Hero's decay.

    She raised her dark eye and she gazed on the sea,
10   Where all its black billows were whitened with foam,
    And she thought of the 'Rover' unconquered and free,
       Her noble Northangerland's Empire and Home.

    'Oh, for the hours of that Ocean to come,
       When shall I write of such sunshine and storm?
15   When shall a pirate so gallantly roam
       As unconquered in heart and as glorious in form?'

    She looked to the South and she looked to the North
       And she looked to the East where the twilight's
          decline
    Had melted from morning who joyously forth
20   Was rising in glory o'er Angria to shine.

    She thought of that Empire so bright and divine,
       She thought of the Monarch its ruler in War,
    And 'Angria' she cried, then '*Two* leaders like thine
       Has Fate then denied to *one* empire's share?

25 And must He, whose bidding has roused up a Land,
       From midnight to morning to life from the tomb,
      Oh must his great name now be traced by my hand
       In pages of darkness and letters of gloom?'

      She paused and she pondered, but Freedom drew
          nigh
30 With pride in her port and with fire in her eye.
      She looked to the shore and she looked to the sea
      And she vowed that eternal his memory should be.
      'From all my wide empire through ages to come
      From palace to cottage, from cradle to tomb
35 Shall the name of my Saviour through ages endure
      Vast as that Ocean and firm as this shore!'
         So History seizes her pencil of light,
      And again with rejoicing she bends to indite,
      While high on the top of her column of Fame
40 She blends with ZAMORNA'S NORTHANGERLAND'S
          name!

                    MORNING

      MORN comes and with it all the stir of morn,
          New light new life upon its sunbeams borne.
      The Magic dreams of Midnight fade away,
      And Iron Labour rouses with the day.
5   He who has seen before his sleeping eye
      The times and smiles of childhood wandering by,
      The memory of years, gone long ago
      And sunk and vanished now in clouds of woe,
      He who, still young, in dreams of days to come
10 Has lost all memory of his native home,
      Whose untracked future opening far before
      Shews him a smiling heaven and happy shore,

While things that are frown dark and drearily
And sunshine only beams on things to be:
15 To such as these night is not all a night,
For one in eve beholds his morning bright,
The other basking in his earliest morn
Feels noontide summer o'er his feelings dawn.
But that worn wretch who tosses night away,
20 And counts each moment to returning day,
Whose only hope is dull and dreamless sleep,
Whose only choice to wake and watch and weep,
Whose present pains of body and of mind
Shut out all glimpse of happiness behind,
25 Whose present darkness hides the faintest light
Which yet might struggle through a milder night,
And He like *one* whom present cares engage
Without the glare of youth or gloom of age,
Who must not sleep upon his idle oar
30 Lest life's wild Tempests dash him to the shore,
Whom high Ambition calls aloud to awake,
Glory his goal, and death or life his stake,
And long and rugged his rough race to run
Ere he can stop to enjoy his Laurels won,
35 To these the night is weariness and pain
And blest the hour when day shall rise again!
'Mid visions of the Future or the past
Others may wish the shades of night to last,
Round these alone the *present* ever lies,
40 And these will first awake when morning calls Arise!

LINES

WE leave our bodies in the Tomb,
Like dust to moulder and decay,
But, while they waste in coffined gloom,
Our parted spirits, where are they?
5 In endless night or endless day?

POEMS 199

Buried as our bodies are
Beyond all earthly hope or fear?
Like them no more to reappear,
  But festering fast away?
10 For future's but the shadow thrown
From present and, the substance gone,
  Its shadow cannot stay!

AN HOUR'S MUSINGS
ON THE ATLANTIC

BLOW, ye wild winds, wilder blow,
Flow, ye waters, faster flow,
Spread around my weary eye
One wide waving sea and sky!

5 Aloft the breezes fill my sail
And bend its canvass to the gale
In its own ethereal dwelling,
O'er the Ocean proudly swelling.
    See the billows round me now
10 Dash against my cleaving prow.
Far and wide they sweep away
O'er the rough and roaring sea.
By heaven! my heart beats high today,
Lord of such a realm to be,
15 Monarch of the fierce and free!

But I'll turn my eyes toward the skies
    And view the prospect there,
Where broad and bright the noonday light
    Sheds glory through the air.
20 I'll gaze upon that dome of heaven
    With its deep, cerulean hue,
The white clouds o'er its concave driven
    Till lost amid the blue.

Then I'll turn my forehead to the blast
25   And think upon the sea,
That chainless boundless restless waste
    Which shines so gloriously,
That only Lethe for the past
    Or Freedom for the free!

30   The winds are whistling in my hair,
    As I gaze upon the main,
And view the Atlantic from his Lair,
    Aroused to rage again.
And view the horizon stretched afar,
35   Wide around that Ambient air,
One weary water welt'ring there
    Where I gaze for rest in vain!

Well! Here I am, and Afric's shore
Has sunk beneath the Atlantic roar,
40   Yet seems to me as but even now
Had set Leone's glittering brow,
That hardly yet that azure line
Conceals fair Gambia's shores divine!
Not so!—a thousand miles away
45   I ride upon this raging sea,
And long long Leagues of Ocean roar
Between me and my native shore.
    Oh all the scenes of a lifetime past
    Far far behind me lie,
50   And tossing on this stormy waste
    Oh who so lone as I?
I heard that wind. It sighed to me
    Like memory of feelings gone.
Bleak Blast, my heart responds to thee
55   With mourning bitterer than thine own,
And my own voice with stronger tone
Now strikes upon my startled ear.
    It seems 'mid these wild waves unknown

A Thing I should not hear;
60 'Tis the voice of my morning fresh and
      free,
The very voice of my Infancy,
But what has that voice to do with me
    A wearied wanderer here?

Oh Afric, Afric, where art thou?
65 Even I can sorrow o'er thee now
Though, ere I left thy smiling shore,
I knew my joy in life was o'er.
Yes! I had seen my evening sun,
    Sink in a sullen sea of tears,
70 Had seen his race of daylight run,
    Gone lights and shadows, hopes and fears.
Yes I had seen my day decline,
Never again to rise and shine,
And it was not pleasure blighted,
75   It was not hope destroyed,
Nor love nor friendship slighted
    That made the dreary void.
And yet my pleasures all had flown,
All my hopes were dashed and gone,
80 And though none scorned the love I gave
Yet—Thou, the loved, wert in thy grave,
'Twas that despair of heart which can
Nor joy nor sorrow yield to man,
'Twas that decay of spirit, when
85 'Twill neither wake to joy or pain,
When heard no more Ambition's call
Can wile the soul to rise or fall,
When seen no longer beauty's beam
Can wrap it in an Eden dream,
90 When not even rage can rouse the mind
To leave its apathy behind.
    Ah, power and peace were lost to me,
And beauty brought satiety,

And who would quarrel with a worm,
95   Because it writhed in human form?
I *could* not love, when all the charms
I clasped so madly in my arms
Were sure that day to pass away
From youthful death to dark decay.
100   I would not hear Ambition's voice
Delude me to its visioned joys,
When, while I stood the chief 'mong men,
I sought, but found no pleasure then.
Why should I hate an enemy
105   When firmest friends had turned on me?
Why think on lover, foe, or friend
When all so soon in death must end?
    Nor this the worst—for ever gone
The mind had lost its native tone.
110   Here is the Ocean—but to me
Its mighty waste has ceased to be!
There is the Heaven—but now no more
My eyes its glorious paths explore,
I'm only yearning for the tomb
115   And that last refuge will not come.

Oh! When I was a little child
    Upon my mother's knee,
With what a burst of pleasure wild
    I gazed upon the sea.
120   I stretched my arms toward its face
And wept to meet its proud embrace!
    And when amid youth's earliest day
    I paced the foam white shore,
    I smiled to see the wild waves play
125   And joyed to hear them roar.
And now where am I?—On that sea
Where I so often longed to be,
But it is like all human joys;
One single touch their bloom destroys.

130   The waves around my vessel sweep
        And cover her with foam,
Yet, though they shake the shattered ship,
They still shall bear her home.
The sleep which shuts the watcher's eye
135   'Mid dangers threatening near,
Though helplessly the sleeper lie,
     Still quiets all his care.
The night that darkens o'er the earth
     'Mid daylight's deep decline,
140   Shall give a glorious morrow birth
     In morning's light divine.
But thou, stern midnight of my soul,
     With thy dread darkness closing round,
Ye storms of strife which o'er me roll,
145   Where have ye hope or rest or bound?
Well roll ye, waves of ocean, roll!
And close ye sorrows o'er my soul.
I care not, though your fatal blight
Should cloud this mind with lasting night.
150   But, while one streak of daylight lies
Behind the far off twilight skies,
Permit the wanderer's weary gaze
To fix upon its fading rays.
The wretch, whom naught from Death can save,
155   Still grasps the grass around his grave;
The Lion in the Hunter's toils
     Glares madness from his eye,
And nets and dogs and lances foils
     Though lost to Liberty;
160   The prisoner bound with iron chains
His wearied load of life sustains
By gazing on the vanished days
That beamed like heaven with freedom's rays.
And strange it is, when we look back,
165   We still see sunshine on our track,

For false they speak who say we spy
Nothing but joys *before* our eye.
No! all the future path to me
Seems beat by storms of misery
170 And scenes alone long past away
Can glimmer through life's dark decay,
For through his short and narrow span
Pleasure can only *follow* man.
And yet when wearily he dies
175 He dreams before him in the skies
He sees its happy paradise!

What is MAN? A wretched being,
    Tossed upon the tide of time,
All its rocks and whirlpools seeing,
180 Yet denied the power of fleeing
    Waves and gulfs of woe and crime;
Foredoomed from life's first bitter breath
To launch upon a sea of death
Without a hope, without a stay
185 To guide him on his weary way.

See that wrecked and shattered bark
    Drifting through the storm;
O'er the ocean drear and dark
    Sweeps its shattered form.
190 Where those sails which late on high
Swelled amid the smiling sky?
Where those masts which braved the gale
Towering o'er the swelling sail?
Where the glasslike deck below?
195 Where the gilt and glorious prow?
    Where are they? Sunk beneath the sea
Or shattered tossing far away;
Where are they? Saw'st the shrieking gale
Tear from the arms the swelling sail?

200 Saw'st thou the mast beneath the storm
Bend to the surge its stately form?
And Hark that Crash!—as foam and spray
Force o'er the deck a boiling sea.
So there—! Its gallant glories gone,
205 There the wild Tempests drive it on!
And now as round the shivered mast,
As shrinking from the screaming blast,
How do the hopeless sailors brave
The heaven and ocean, wind and wave?
210 Aye, how have all the hopes of life
Stood 'gainst its fears and storms and strife?
And what thinks MAN, when—danger o'er—
Stranded he lies on Death's dark shore?
Oh view him, sickened, palsied, lone,
215 Where is his strength, his beauty gone?

I am a MAN. Yes, I have seen
Each change upon life's changing scene,
And I am on the track which thou
And thine and mine are following now!
220 Well, when I first launched from Eternity
Upon this undiscovered sea,
Hope shone forth with glorious ray
Blazing round my dawning day.
Expectation's eager gale
225 Swelled and sounded in my sail.
Ambition's world impelling power
Urged me on in morning's hour.
And, Love, thy wide and welcome light
Beamed and brightened on my sight.
230 Beauty, strength and youth divine
With all the heaven of Mind were mine.
And when I saw the expanse before me,
When I knew the glory o'er me,
Oh how little did I dream
235 Heaven and glory all a dream,

Life alone with its midnight sea,
The Terrible Reality!

Sleeper awake, thy dream is flown
And thou'rt on Ocean all alone.

240   I am awake and round the sky
        Wild I cast my wandering eye.
        Where is the love and hope and light?
        Vanished for ever from thy sight!
        And now I am on the wild wide sea
245   Without a hope to shine on me.
        The winds arise, and the stormy skies
        Snatch my daylight from my eyes.
        Ambition's sails that bore me on
        Shiver in the blast they seemed to have won;
250   And Glory!—Aye, thou welcome wave,
        Dash *that* illusion to its grave!
        But spare, wild Ocean, spare me Love!
        That only power that can above
        Like one mild star from out the sky
255   Beam comfort on my misery!
        Oh! Life, though all its oceans roll,
        Thee ne'er shall sunder from my soul,
        For thou within this heart shalt lie,
        With this heart alone to die!
260   Will it be so?—the pealing blast
        Howls wilder round the quivering mast!
        With what a sweep the surge and spray
        Thunder above the whitening sea.
        A gloomier tempest darkens down.
265   Love survives—but the Loved is gone!
        Gone! and one unfathomed ocean
        O'er me bears its vast commotion.
        Sails and masts and cordage gone
        All unaided! all ALONE!

270   O MARY! when I closed thy eye,
      When I beheld thee slowly die,
      When thou before me silent lay,
      A loveless lifeless form of clay,
      When I saw thy coffined form
275   Decked out to feast the gnawing worm,
      When the dull sod o'er thee thrown
          Hid thee from my tearless eye,
        'Twas then my Mary, then alone,
          I felt what 'twas to Die!

280   Oh! long long years may lie before me,
      A thousand woes may darken o'er me,
      And ere I lay me down to die
      Old age may dim this anguished eye.
      Yet through that wide wide waste of years,
285   That channeled gulf of burning tears,
      Aye if I live till Earth's decay
      Is crumbling to its latest day,
      If thousand winters' winteriest snow
      Fall withering on my blighted brow,
290   Still through that vast Eternity
      I know that Thou *has ceased* to be.
      Lost! For ever Lost to me!
      That all thy woes and joys are o'er,
      That thou art dead!—gone long before!
295   That I shall never, never see thee more!

                THERMOPYLAE

      THERMOPYLAE'S tremendous Height
      Has lost the evening's latest light.
      And each huge mountain girding round
      Stands black'ning in the shade profound.
  5   Alike wild waste and ocean wild,
      Dark as those clouds above them piled

Lie gloomy as they ne'er had worn
The sunshine of a summer's morn.
Above the moonbeam's fitful light
10 Breaks shivering through the darksome night,
And as the stormy wrack sweeps by
Fades—lost amid the troubled sky.
    At times that moonlight sadly shines,
Where yon vast hill its steep declines,
15 Where bloody grass and trampled heath
Lie soaked beneath their loads of death,
Where scattered rocks with mossy head
Form many a warrior's dying bed,
Where many a dim and dark'ning eye
20 Up gazes toward that stormy sky!
    'Tis o'er!—No sighs, no anguished cries
From the wild wreck of battle rise.
No murmured moan of misery.
No sudden shout of victory.
25 The senseless corpse on earth reclining
Nor feels defeat nor knows repining.
For death has stretched his dreary wing
O'er that wide waste of suffering.
    Sleep, Noble Soldiers, sleep alone!
30 The whistling winds your burial moan,
The bloody rocks your bed of death,
Your shrouds grey grass and trampled heath,
While that vast rock Thermopylae
Your monument and grave may be!
35   O Glorious Dead, unconquered lie,
Your very death your victory.
By you your country saved from chains.
Still free, unconquered, Greece remains,
And not a drop of all that blood
40 Which curdles now in Peneus's flood,
No, not one drop is spent in vain,
For every drop dissolves a chain!

And each cold hand and nerveless arm
Which never more that blood shall warm
45   Have while they struck their meanest foe
Given Susa's domes a fatal blow,
And though long past the flight of time
In distant age and different clime,
Still may your memory wake a flame
50   Which, once aroused, no power can tame,
Still when infuriate factions rise
Their native land to sacrifice,
Not like the Mede a foreign band,
But fighting 'gainst their fatherland,
55   Still to oppose their impious war
Their pride to crush, their power to dare,
May once again Thermopylae
Rise o'er the storms of Albion's sea!
Still may *Three Hundred** once again
60   'Gainst that mad march their fight maintain.
And while they stay the troubled tide
From its dire deluge wild and wide,
Another Mightier Marathon
Complete the victory thus begun!
65   And if, two thousand years ago
'Gainst Greece a Monarch struck the blow
And Freedom saved her from the foe,
Here through this Island of the Free
Our Foemen shout for Liberty,
70   Our Throne is our Thermopylae!

* The Conservative party in the Commons being 300 in number

SONG

S ON of Heaven, in heavenly musing
  Gaze beyond the clouds of time,
Future glory rather choosing
    Than a present world of crime.

5   Thou whose heart that world caressing
      Bows, its bubbles to adore,
    On and hunt each fleeting blessing,
      Still in sight but still before!

    Christian, Worldling, hence and leave me,
10   Here with thee, my love, alone;
    Things to come shall ne'er deceive me
      While I hold Thee now my own!
    Earth of bliss shall ne'er bereave me,
      While we two continue one!

THE DOUBTER'S HYMN

LIFE is a passing sleep,
  Its deeds a troubled dream,
And death the dread awakening
  To daylight's dawning beam.

5   We sleep without a thought
      Of what is past and o'er,
    Without a glimpse of consciousness
      Of aught that lies before.

    We dream, and on our sight
10   A thousand visions rise,
    Some dark as Hell, some heavenly bright,
      But all are phantasies.

    We wake, and, oh, how fast
      These mortal visions fly,
15   Forgot amid the wonders vast
      Of immortality!

    And oh! when we arise,
      With 'wildered gaze to see
    The aspect of those morning skies,
20   Where will that waking be?

How will that Future seem?
What is Eternity?
Is Death the sleep?—Is Heaven the Dream?
Life the reality?

SONG

THOU art gone, but I am here,
Left behind and mourning on,
Doomed in Dreams to deem thee near,
But to awake and find thee gone!
5 Ever parted! Broken hearted!
Weary, wandering all alone!

Looks and smiles that once were thine
Rise before me night and day,
Telling me that thou *wert* mine,
10 But *art* dead and passed away.
Beauty banished—Feelings vanished
From thy dark and dull decay,
No returning! Naught but mourning,
O'er thy cold and coffined clay!

SONG

FROZEN fast is my heart at last,
And unmoved by thy beams divine,
For wild o'er the waste the wintery blast
Has withered and weakened thy shine.

5 The pulse that once beat to each look, each word
Is congealed by the frosts of care.
And thine eyes are ungazed on, thy voice is unheard,
For love ever flies from despair.

Farewell then, farewell then, for parted for ever
10   The blooming and blighted should be,
So soon shall the Ocean eternally sever
    My Heart from my country and thee.

LINES

NOW then I am alone,
    And there's none to trouble me,
So I will hasten on
    From present scenes to flee.

5   The Land where I have lived,
    The Hall where I was born,
Whatever hath survived
    Through my wild life unworn.

The outline of those Mountains
10   Which still have towered the same,
The brooks whose rushing fountains
    Can still supply their stream.

Each token and each trace
    Of life time passed away,
15   I'll from my spirit chase
    Through every future day.

The waters of the Ocean
    Shall drown that life gone by,
Shall give a Lethean potion
20   To banish memory.

THE SPIRIT OF POETRY

LIST to the sound that swells alone
    Shrilly and sweet with trembling tone!
Why should such music strike my ear
In thoughtful silence seated here?

5   The sky is ebon black tonight,
       But the stars are fixed on high,
    Each glorious planet twinkling bright
       Or smiling silently.
    Dreary and dark the mountains rise,
10   All underneath those starlit skies.

    And far beyond the gloomy moor
    Hear how the Loch's low waters roar,
    While wearied with his wandering wide
    The Goodman by his ingle side
15   Stirs up the fire that glows afar
    In yonder reddened mountain star.

    The midnight hills are passing by,
    And gone the black and starlight sky
    That music thrills in the rising morn
20   Upon the blasts of Ocean born.
    It mixes its notes with the rising gale,
    And sounds in the cords of the flowing sail.
    It rises and falls as the waters flow.
    Oh, why does that Music haunt me so?

25   It is not the night on the Highland moor,
    It is not the Cot on Loch Maris's shore,
    It is not the Ocean so boundless and drear
    That wakens around me the notes that I hear,
    For gone is the cot and the moor and the main,
30   Yet I hear those wild notes and they're rising again.
    Vanished those visions of skies unknown,
    But present that changing Eolian tone!

'Tis a chord of the Heart, 'Tis the music of mind
From Earth and its cares for a moment refined,
35　'Tis a sound caught by it as it soars toward the sky
Wafted down from the Heaven of bright Poetry!

AN ANGRIAN BATTLE SONG

STORMS are waking to inspire us,
Storms upon our morning sky.
Wildly wailing tempests fire us
　　With their loud and God given cry.
5　Winds our trumpets howling come,
Thundering waves our deeper drum.
　　Wild woods o'er us
　　Swell the chorus,
Bursting through the stormy gloom.
10　What's their Omen? Whence its doom?

Loud those voices, stern their pealing,
　　Yet what is it those voices say?
Well we feel, when, God revealing
　　All his wrath, their powers display,
15　Trembles every child of clay.
　　Still we know
　　That blow on blow
O'er us bursting day by day
Shews that wrath as well as they.

20　But 'tis not a common call
　　That wakes such mighty melody.
Crowns and kingdoms rise or fall,
　　Man and nations chained or free,
　　Living death or liberty,
25　Such their terrible decree.
　　And yonder skies
　　Whose voices rise

In that unearthly harmony,
Through Angria round
30   Shall wake a sound,
A voice of victory,
A thundering o'er the sea,
Whose swelling waves
And howling caves
35   Shall hear the prophecy.
Storms are waking,
Earth is shaking,
Banners wave and bugles wail.
While beneath the tempest breaking
40 Some must quench and some must quail.
Hark the artillery's iron hail
Battles through the ranks of war,
Who beneath its force shall fail.
Must the sun of Angria pale
45 Upon the Calabar?
Or yonder bloody star
O'er Afric' main
With fiery train
That wanders from afar?

50 No, O God! our sun its brightness
Draws from thine eternal throne,
And come what will, through good or ill,
We know that thou wilt guard thine own!
'Tis not 'gainst us that thunder's tone
55   But, risen from hell
With radiance fell,
'Tis the wanderer of the west whose powers shall be
o'erthrown!

Tempest, blow thy mightiest blast,
Wild wind, wail thy wildest strain.
60   From God's right hand
O'er his chosen land

Your music shall waken its fires again.
And over the earth now and over the ocean,
    Wherever shall shadow these storm covered
        skies,
65 The louder through battle may burst your
        commotion,
    'Twill only sound stronger, *O Angria Arise!*

THE BATTLE EVE

ALONE upon Zamorna's plain,
    With twilight o'er me falling,
And once again the bugle's strain
    To troubled slumber calling.

5   Alone with thousands round me laid
        In dizzy torments dying,
    All stretched upon their bloody bed
        In sleep eternal lying.

    So not alone, yet all alone,
10   For these sad wrecks of slaughter
    Are senseless thrown as forms of stone
        Or dead to all but torture.

    I stand, and see the silent Moon
        Drive wildly through the sky
15 'Mong clouds that, gathering up since noon,
        Commence their march on high.

    It is not night—it is not day,
        So she can hardly shine,
    And dull and dead and cold and grey
20   Behold the eve decline.

A *Battle Eve*, a victory,
   A day of deathless fame,
For which the Muse of history
   Must seek a noble name.

25   A Monarch's and a Nation's fall,
   The Grave of Glories cherished,
That Hope proclaimed with trumpet call,
   Now silent sunk and perished,

A Day of far extended power,
30   Which changes smiles to tears,
But from this lonely twilight hour
   O'erlooks a hundred years!

That casts its shadows o'er the things,
   Which lately seemed to shine,
35   As night to gloom and darkness brings
   The evening skies divine.

Oh soon again this natural night
   In happy morn shall rise,
But never more returning light
40   May gladden *Adrian*'s eyes.

That *Sun of Angria* rose in *red*
   To chase the clouds away,
That sun has sunk, his light has fled,
   His power has passed for aye.

45   How like a Star from upper air
   I see *Zamorna* fall,
Archangel once and throned so far
   Above this earthly ball.

But vast thine hopes and high thy pride,
50   Thou man of shining crime,
Till Pride has perished, Hope has died,
   All withering ere their time.

Come, listen to the distant gun
That thunders on the wind,
55　The awful voice of Victory won
That seems to say Thy race is run
And vanished out of mind.

Better for thee that thou hadst died
Than thus to see thy new born pride
60　In this wild warfare scattered wide
And *Thou* a wretched Captive left alone behind!

ASHWORTH'S HYMN

BEFORE Jehovah's awful Throne
Now let us trembling kneel in prayer,
And Mercy ask and Justice own,
For we must pray that he may hear.

5　And deep, O Lord, be our despair,
And clear our consciousness of sin,
Lest from thine eyes our outside fair
Should strive to hide the crimes within.

We know that we are formed in crime,
10　And through our lives that crimes we form,
Yet madly dreaming all the time
Thy Mercy shields us from the storm.

Or, as long since in Shinar's plain
Rebellious men their tower of pride
15　Raised up in hope, by labours vain,
That thus thy power might be defied,

So we by impious moral code,
And creeds of ever changing faith,
Think we may climb the heavenly road
20　And shun thine arm and vanquish death.

But, oh, when once we reach thy gate
    In hopes the eternal crown to win,
Long must we knock and lingering wait
    Ere yon bright Spirit lets us in.

25 'Hast thou repented of thy sin?'
    And who, O God, can answer then?
'Go back, thy path again begin,
    And weep and watch and wait again!'

But, if returning be denied,
30   By *Death's* grim portal closed behind,
Where flies our Heaven and hope and pride?
    Vanished like chaff before the wind!

Lord, may we know our treacherous mind,
    Even though that knowledge bring despair,
35 Since wandering thus, accursed and blind,
    We cannot hope that THOU wilt hear!

LUCIFER

STAR of the West, whose beams arise
    To brighten up o'er Afric's shore,
While coming clouds and changing skies
    Bring on the shades of twilight's hour;

5 Who, as our day sinks fast away,
    While flowers of pleasure close their bloom,
Send'st down from Heaven thy flashing ray
    And shinest to dazzle—not to illume;

Who, as upon our sunken sun
10   The storm clouds gather from the sea,
So far above goest wandering on,
    As if our hopes were naught to thee.

And gathering glory while the night
Comes deeper, darker, drearier down,
15   And shining still with brighter light
When every beam save thine is gone.

Star of the West, we see thee shine,
We know thy glory from afar,
But we have seen our sun decline,
20   As if it sunk for thee to appear.

We have seen our sun of happiness
'Mid coming clouds of conflict fall,
Nor can thy lustre beam in place
Of that which blessed and brightened all.

25   We know that in our time of pride
'Mid summer suns and noonday skies
Though Heaven were cloudless, calm and wide,
Such lights as thine dared never rise.

We know thou art an Orb divine
30   Within thine own celestial sphere,
But still a storm-portending sign
To us who gaze in wonder here.

Star of the West, though storm and night
Gave birth and beauty to thy blaze,
35   Still that which kindled up thy light
May in a moment quench its rays.

As darker grow the clouds of woe,
As day declines, as empires fall,
Brighter and brighter bursts thy glow,
40   Till thou seem'st soaring lord of all.

But westward clouds are rolling on,
And louder thunders swell the wind.
The tempest comes, and thou art gone
Past like the sunshine out of mind.

45   *Percy*—amid the coming hour,
        When peace and pleasures disappear,
     Those storms and strifes which gave thee power
     May darken Afric's '*Western Star*'!

LINES

NOW heavily in clouds comes on the day,
     The great, the important day,
That gathering all its gloom shall roll our foes away.

Come life, come death, or conquest or defeat,
5   I who am called my Judgement here must meet,
With my own arm must carve my road to power,
With my own deeds must fill my fated hour,
With my own lips proclaim what is to be,
And then in my own self meet my own destiny.
10   'Tis man must struggle—man must fight
And stigmatise his wrong and name his right,
But fate or chance the question will decide,
His hopes and fears and plans all scattering far and wide.

     Here I will crown a life of war
15   With power which long has lured me from afar,
With vengeance taken on my slaughtered foes,
Contempt repaid with hate and hatred soothed with
        blows,
Kings, crowns and armies fallen and all to be
A bloody footstool of ascent for me,
20   The wings of conquest folded o'er my head,
Supporters kneeling on opponents dead,
What I hate lowest—next what I despise,
So who dare speak to me of miseries?
Chance will—or fate, with still small voice it cries
25   'Man, though thou hast *seized* the lamp, its *light* is gone
And blindly still thy steps must wander on!
She is gone! The last bright link which bound thy mind,
To years of paradise left long behind,

Treasure of hopes stored up in happier years,
30 To feed thy famine in this vale of tears!
And she is gone whom in thy worst distress
Thou found'st, a fountain in the wilderness!
And He is gone who glorious used to shine
With radiance steadier, brighter far than thine,
35 Yet such as shewed on earth there still might be
Communion with a soul so like to thee.
All these are gone whom thou hast left to gain,
A flying hope, a meteor light and vain!
Thy sun has sunk and left the darkening air
40 To seek enlightening from that wandering star.
Thy flower deprived of warmth will withering die,
Thy store is squandered and thy well run dry,
While HE whose glory chased the clouds of woe,
Thy Dearest friend, thou'st made thy Deadliest foe!'

PERCY'S MUSINGS UPON THE BATTLE OF EDWARDSTON

THROUGH the hoarse howlings of the storm
I saw—but did I truly see—
One glimpse of that unearthly form,
Whose very name was—VICTORY.
5 'Twas but a glimpse—and all seems past,
For cares like clouds again return,
And I'll forget him till the blast
For ever from my soul has torn
That vision of a Mighty Man
10 Crushed into dust!

Forget him!—Lo, the cannon's smoke,
How dense it thickens, till on high
By the wild storm blast roughly broke
It parts in volumes through the sky,
15 With dying thunder drifting by,

Till the dread burst breaks forth once more,
　　And loud and louder peals the cry,
Sent up with that tremendous roar
Where—as it lightens broad before
20　　The thick of battle rends in twain
With roughened ranks of bristling steel,
　　Flashing afar while armed men
In mighty masses bend and reel
Like the wild waters of the main
25　　Lashed into foam!—Where, there again
Behold him! as with sudden wheel.
At bay, against a thousand foes,
He turns upon their serried rows,
All heedless round him though they close,
30　　With such a bloodhound glare.
That eye with inward fires so bright
Pierces the tempest of the fight,
And lightens with the joyless light
　　Of terrible despair!
35　He sees his soldiers round him falling
In vain to heaven for vengeance calling,
He sees those noble friends whom he
　　Had called from happy, happy Home
For a vain prize of victory
40　　Over the eastern world to roam.
He sees them lie with glaring eye,
　　Turned up to him, that wandering star,
Who led them still from good to ill
　　In hopes of power to meet with war,
45　And fall from noontide dreams of glory
To this strange rest so grim and gory!—
When rolling on those friends o'erthrown
War's wildest wrack breaks thundering down.
Zamorna's pale and ghastly brow
50　　Darkens with anguish—all in vain
To stem the tide of battle now,
　　For every rood of that wide plain

Is heaped with thousands of his dead,
Or shakes beneath the approaching tread
55   Of foes who conquer o'er the slain.
No! never must he hope again,
Though still abroad that banner streams
On whose proud folds the sun of glory beams,
   Though still, unslaughtered, round their lord
60 His chosen chiefs may grasp the unvanquished
   sword,
Still, all is Hopeless!—and he knows it so,
   Else would not anguish cloud his brow,
   Else would not such a withering smile
Break o'er his hueless face—the while
65 Some friend of years falls hopelessly,
And yet upon that Eagle eye
Gazing with dying ecstacy!
That Eagle eye! the Beacon light
Through all the changes of the fight,
70 Whose glorious glance spoke victory,
And fired his men to do or die,
On the red roar of battle bent
As if its own wild element,
And glancing o'er each thundering gun
75 As he were war's unconquered son.
That Eye! Oh I have seen it shine
   'Mid scenes that differed far from these,
As Gambia's woods and skies divine
   From Greenland's icy seas;
80 I've seen its lustre bent on me
   To old adventure gone,
With beam as bright and glance as free
   As His own Angria's sun;
When o'er those mighty wastes of Heath
85   Around Elymbos' brow
As side by side we used to ride,
   I smiled to mark its glow.
I smiled to see him, how he threw

His feelings into mine,
90   Till my cold spirit almost grew
     Like his a thing divine.
I saw him in his beauty's pride,
     With Manhood on his brow,
The falcon-eyed with heart of pride
95   And spirit stern—for many a shade
     Had crossed his youthful way,
And clouds of care began to mar
     The dawning of his day.
I knew him and I marked him then
100 For one remote, as far
From Earth's surrounding crowds of men
     As Heaven's remotest star.
I saw him in the battle's hour,
     And conquered by his side,
105 I was with him in his height of power
     And triumph of his pride.
'Tis past!—but I am with him now,
     Where he spurs fiercely through the fight,
His pride and power and crown laid low,
110 His glorious future wrapt from sight,
'Mid clouds like those which frown on high
     Over the plains in purpled gloom,
With rain and thunder driving by
     To shroud a nation's bloody tomb;
115 And in the cannon's ceaseless boom,
     The toll which wafts the parting soul,
     While Heaven's bright flashes serve to
         illume
Like torches its funereal stole,
     Its horrid funeral—Far and wide
120 I see them—falling in the storm
'Mid ranks of horse that wildly ride
     Above each gashed and trampled form,
His charger shot, Zamorna down,
'Mid foes and friends alike o'erthrown!

125 Yet never may that desperate soul
Betray the thoughts which o'er it roll;
Teeth clenched, cheeks blenched and eyes that
  dart
A Lion fierceness from his heart
As all the world were naught beside
130 The saving of his iron pride.
For every one on earth might die,
And not a tear should stain that eye,
Or force a single sob or sigh
  From him who cannot yield.
135 Yet stay—one moment—'tis but one,
A single glance to heaven is thrown,
One frenzied burst of grief—!—'Tis gone,
  Again that Heart is steeled!
That was a burst of anguish—there
140 Blazed all the fierceness of despair.
It said—Oh all is lost for ever!
  All he loves to him is dead,
  All his hopes of glory fled,
  All the past is vanished
145   Save what naught can sever,
  Ever living memories
That shall haunt him till he dies
  With what he can realise
  Never Never Never!

150 I said I saw his anguished glance.
  Say did it fall on me?
Incendiary of rebel France,
  Parrot of liberty!

The wretched Traitor who let in
155   On Afric's opened land
Deceit and craft and hate and sin
  In an united band.

Who raised the Standard of Reform,
  And shouted Earth be free
160 To whelm his country 'neath the storm
  Of rebel Tyranny

Who called himself the good right hand
  And Father of our King,
  Only on his adopted land
165 A double curse to bring.

Aye it was I and only I
  That hurled Zamorna down,
From power and glory placed on high
  This day to be o'erthrown.

170 I barbed the arrow which has sped
  To pierce my sovereign's breast,
And only on my guilty head
  May all his sufferings rest!

QUEEN MARY'S GRAVE

I STAND beside Queen Mary's grave, 'neath Alnwick's
  holy dome,
With sacred silence resting o'er the marble of her tomb,
The organ's thunders hushed to sleep, the mourners past
    away,
All left to her the sepulchre, the coffin and the clay.
5 The vault is closed, the stone is placed, the inscription only
    tells
Within that dark and narrow house whose corpse
    corrupting dwells,
Last one with those who passed from earth forgotten years
    ago;
From theirs around by sight or sound her tombstone none
    may know,

So I may stand to think awhile on things for ever gone,
10 And drop a tear to memory dear above her funeral stone.
    What seek my eyes—they rest not on the columns
        arching o'er me,
    Nor the storied windows shimmering round or sculptures
        piled before me.

M AN thinks too often that the ills of life—
     Its fruitless labour—its unceasing stife—
   With all its train of want, disease and care
   Must wage 'gainst spirit a successful war:
5   That faint indeed must prove the shackled soul
   Struggling with waves that ever round it roll—
   That it can never triumph or feel free,
   While pain its body binds, or poverty.
   Nor will Man hear me if I prove how high
10   His soul may soar o'er body's misery,
   For if I bid him rise and point the way
   He points in answer to his bonds of clay.
   But, where orations, eloquent and loud
   Prove weak as air to move the listening crowd,
15   A single word just then if timely spoken
   The Mass inert has roused—their silence broken
   And driven them shouting for revenge or Fame,
   Trampling on fear and death led by a single name.
        So now—to him whose worn out soul decays
20   'Neath nights of sleepless pain and toilsome
        days,
   Who thinks his feeble frame in vain may long
   To tread the footsteps of the bold and strong,
   Who thinks that, born beneath a lowly star,
   He cannot climb those heights he sees from afar
25   To him I speak one word—it needs but one—
   NELSON—a world's defence—a Kingdom's noblest
        son!

    Ah! Little child, torn early from thy home
Over a desolate waste of waves to roam,
I see thy fair hair streaming in the wind,
30   Wafted from green hills left so far behind
Like one lamb seen upon a gloomy moor,
Or one flower floating leagues away from shore,
Thou hast given thy farewell to thine English
      home
And hot tears dim thy views of fame to come.
35   Thou then, perhaps, wert clinging to the mast
Rocked high above the Northern Ocean's waste.
Stern accents only shouted from beneath—
Above the keen wind's bitter biting breath—
While thy young eyes were straining to descry
40   The ice blink gleaming 'neath a Greenland sky.

    Each change thy frame endured might meetly be
The total round of common destiny,
For next upon the wild Mosquito shore
San Juan's guns their deadly vollies pour,
45   Though deadlier far that pestilential sky
Whose hot wind only whispered who should die.
And while—forgotten all their honours won—
Strong frames lay rotting 'neath a tropic sun,
While mighty breasts heaved in death's agony,
50   Death only left the feeble Nelson free
Left him—to dare his darts through many a year
Of storm tossed life unbowed by pain or fear.
    Death saw him laid on rocky Tenereiffe
Where sailors bore away their bleeding chief
55   Struck down by shot and beaten back by fate,
Yet keeping front unblenched and soul elate.
    Death saw him calm, off Copenhagen's shore
Amid a thousand guns' heaven-shaking roar,
Triumphant riding o'er a fallen foe
60 With arm prepared to strike, but heart to spare the
     blow

    Death saw him, conqueror, where a tide of blood
Stained the swollen waves of Egypt's ancient flood,
Where clouds first dimmed Napoleon's destiny,
When mighty L'Orient fired the midnight sky,
65   When in its blaze flashed redly sea and shore,
And sudden silence stilled the battle's roar,
As fell on all one mighty pause of dread,
As though wide heaven were shattered overhead.
But—from his pallet—where the Hero *lay*,
70   His forehead laced with blood and pale as clay,
He rose—revived by that tremendous call—
Forgot the blow which lately made him fall,
And bade the affrighted battle hurry on,
Nor thought of pain or rest till he the victory won.

75   I see him sit—his coffin by his chair—
With pain worn cheek and wind dishevelled hair,
A little shattered wreck from many a day
Of Ocean storm and battle passed away,
Prepared at any hour God bade to die,
80   But not to stop or rest or strike or fly,
While like a burning reed his spirit's flame
Brightened while it consumed his mortal frame.

He knew his lightning course would soon be o'er,
That Death was tapping at his cabin door,
85   That he must meet the grim yet welcome guest,
Not on a palace bed of downy rest,
But where the stormy waters rolled below,
While pealed above the thunders of the foe,
That no calm sleep should soothe a slow decay,
90   Till scarce the watchers knew life passed away,
But stifling agony and gushing gore
Should fill the moments of his parting hour.
He knew—but smiled—for, as that polar star
A thousand years as then had shone from far,
95   While all had changed beneath its changeless sky—
So—what to earth belonged—on earth should die,

While he—all soul—should only take his flight
Like yon, through time a still and steady light,
Like yon, to England's sailors given to be
100 The guardian of their fleet, the pole star of the free.

A vessel lies in England's proudest port,
Where venerating Britons oft resort,
And though ships round her anchor bold and gay,
They seek her only in her grim decay,
105 They tread her decks all tenantless, with eyes
Of awestruck musing, not of vague surprise,
They enter 'neath a cabin dark and low,
And o'er its time-stained floor in reverence bow.
There's naught to see but rafters worn and old—
110 No mirrored walls, no cornice bright with gold.
Yon packet steaming through its smoky haze
Seems fitter far to suit the wonderer's gaze
But—'Tis not present times they look on now—
They look on six and thirty years ago.
115 They look where fell the 'thunderbolt of war'
On the storm swollen waves of Trafalgar!
They see the spot where sank a star of glory:
The 'Finis' to one page of England's story.
They read a tale to wake their pain and pride
120 In that brass plate engraved—'HERE NELSON DIED'!

A FRAGMENT

THE Clouds are rolled away—the light
Breaks suddenly upon my sight,
And feelings that no words can tell
Have utterance in that Funeral bell!

5   My heart, my Soul, was full of feeling,
Yet nothing clear to me revealing,
Sensations strong but undefined,
The Eolian music of the mind!

Then strikes that Chord—and all subsides
10   Into a harmony that glides,
Tuneful but solemn like the dream
Of some remembered burial Hymn.

This scene was that Mysterious glass,
Which bore upon its changing face
15   Strange shadows that deceived the eye
With forms defined uncertainly.

That bell the Enchanter's stern command
Which parts the clouds on either hand,
And shews the pictured forms of doom,
30   One moment bright'ning through the gloom.

It shews a scene of bygone years,
It opes a fount of sealed up tears,
It wakens in my memory
An hour by time borne far from me.

25   A Day like this—a summer's day,
Shining its hours in peace away,
With hills as blue and groves as green,
Clouds piled as bright, skies as serene!

Oh! well I recollect the Hour,
30   Seated alone as I sit now,
And gazing toward that very Tower
O'er these wild flowers which wave below!

No—not *these* flowers!—They're long since dead,
And flowers have come and flowers have gone
35   Since those which wither round the head,
Laid low beneath that churchyard stone.

I stretched to pluck a rose that grew,
Close by this window waving then,
But back again my hand withdrew
40   With a strange sense of inward pain.

For she who loved it was not there
   To check me with her dove-like eye,
And something bid my heart forbear
   Her favoured floweret to destroy.

45 Was it the bell—the funeral bell
   So sudden sounding on the wind?
Yes—'twas that melancholy knell
   Which woke to woe my infant mind.

I looked upon my mourning dress
50   Till my heart beat with childish fear,
When—startled at my loneliness
   I bent some distant sound to hear.

But all without was silent in
   The sunny hush of afternoon,
55 And only muffled steps within
   Paced slow afar and soon were gone!

Well do I recollect the awe
   With which I hasted to depart,
And—hurrying from the room—the start
60 With which my Mother's form I saw,
All robed in black with pallid face,
   And hood, and kerchief wet with tears,
Who stooped to kiss my infant face
   And hush my childish fears!

65 She led me on with muffled sound
   Through galleries vast to one high room,
'Neath whose black hangings crowded round
   With funeral dress and looks of gloom
Stood Lords and Ladies—And with head
70 Bent sadly o'er that gilded bed
My awful Father dropt a tear
In the dark coffin rested there.

My Mother raised me to survey
What 'twas which in that coffin lay,
75   But to this moment I can feel
The voiceless gasp, the shuddering chill,
Wherewith I hid my whitening face,
Within the folds of her embrace.
I dared not even turn my head,
80   Lest it should glance toward that bed!
     'But—will you not, my child,' said she,
'Your sister's form one moment see?
One moment—ere that form be hid
For ever 'neath its coffin lid?'
85   I heard the appeal and answered too,
I turned to look that last adieu,
And hushed at once my aimless fright
Into a trance of calm delight!

There lay she then—as *now* she lies,
90   For not a limb has moved since then;
In dreamless slumber closed those eyes
     That never more should wake again.

She lay as I had seen her lie
     On many a moonlight night before,
95   When I perhaps was kneeling by
     The Almighty to adore.

Oh! Just as when by her I prayed,
     While she was listening to my prayer,
She lay, with wild flowers round her head
100   And lilies in her hair.

Still did her lips their smile retain—
     The smile with which she died—
Still was her brow as smooth from pain
     As in its beauty's pride.

105 Though strange and narrow looked her bed,
     In slumber sweet she seemed,
     And, as I bent above her head,
     I thought on Heaven she dreamed.

     And yet I felt—I knew not how—
110   A sudden chilld come o'er me,
     When my hand touched the marble brow
     Of that fair form before me.

     In fright I called on—'Caroline!',
     And bid her wake and rise,
115 But—answered not her voice to mine,
     Or oped her sleeping eyes.

     I turned toward my Mother then,
     And prayed of her to call,
     But, though she strove to hide her pain,
120   Full fast her tears did fall.

     She pressed me to her aching breast,
     As if her heart would break,
     And, silent, hung above the rest
     Which she could never wake.

125 The rest of Her, whose Infant years
     So long she'd watched in vain,
     The end of all a mother's fears
     That ne'er need brood again!

     They came—they pressed the coffin lid
130   Above my Caroline,
     And—then I felt—for *ever* hid
     My sister's face from mine!

     There was one moment's 'wildered start,
     One pang—remembered well!—
135 And—from the fountain of the heart
     My tears of anguish fell!

Seems all a blank the Mourning March,
  The proud parade of woe,
The passage 'neath the churchyard arch,
140   The crowd that met the show.

My place—my thoughts amid the train

*   *   *   *   *   *   *

And filled with thousand thoughts of grief,
  And sick with ghastly fear,
And longing—for a last relief—
145   That day would reappear,

And even praying that I might die,
  But thus the thought would come,
How—if I died—my corpse would lie
  In yonder awful Tomb!

150   It seemed as though I saw its stone
  By moonlight dim and drear,
While o'er it keeping watch alone
  Her spirit lingered there.

All white with Angel wings she seemed,
155   And weeping ceaselessly,
Yet, while her tears in silence streamed,
  She beckoned still to me,

And faded beckoning, while the wind
  Around that midnight wall
160   To me, thus lingering long behind,
  Seemed her departing call.

And thus it brought me back the hours
  When we would lie together,
Listening in silence to the showers
165   Of wild November's weather,

And sometimes as they woke in her
The chords of inward feeling,
She'd image on the midnight air
Scenes thick and fast revealing;

170 Or she would talk of distant Isles,
Our Father's far off shore,
Where seldom summer's sunshine smiles,
And ever Oceans roar,

And tell me of its moonlight lakes
175 And fairy-peopled bowers,
Or of that Banshee whose ghastly shrieks
Rung round the castle towers,

When, clasped within our Mother's arms,
She left that Ancient home
180 To join across Atlantic storms
A rising world to come.

Oh, for a while, methought again
I heard her silver tongue,
Rehearsing some remembered strain
185 Of Ages vanished long.

And, somehow, flashed across my sight
What she had often told me
When, laid awake on Christmas night
Her sheltering arms would fold me.

190 That midnight noon, that darksome day,
Whose gloom o'er Calvary thrown,
Shewed trembling Nature's deep dismay
At what her sons had done,

When all around the murky air
195 Was riven with one hoarse cry,
That told how wretched Mortals dare
Their Saviour crucify,

When those who sorrowing sat afar
  With dimmed and frighted eye,
200   Saw on His Cross extended there
  That Great Redeemer die.

When Mortal vigour fell and fled,
When thirst and faintness bowed His head,
When his pale limbs, all dark'ning o'er
205   With deathly dews and dropping gore,
Quivered as that last sickness came
Across his chill and stiffening frame,
When upward gazed his dying eyes
To the tremendous blackening skies,
210   When burst one cry of agony
  'My God, My God, hast Thou forgotten me?',
  I heard amid the darkness then
The mighty Temple rend in twain,
Horribly pealing on the ear,
215   With a deep Thunder note of fear,
And wrapping all the world in gloom
As it were Nature's general Tomb,
While sheeted ghosts before my gaze
Flitted across the murky maze,
220   Called from their graves on that dread day
When Death an hour o'er heaven had sway.
  In glistening charnel damps arrayed,
They came and gibbered round my head,
All pointing through the dark to me
225   Toward still and shrouded Calvary,
Where gleamed the Cross with steady shine
Around that thorn-crowned head divine,
A Fiery Cross, a Beacon light
To this world's universal night!
230   Still, still it shone with glorious glow
Into my spirit searching, so
That, panting first, I strove to cry
For help to Her who slumbered by,

And hid my face from that dread shine
235   In the embrace of Caroline
Awakening with the attempt—
                —'Twas day
The Troubled vision passed away—
'Twas day—and I *alone* was laid
240   In that great room and stately bed,
No Caroline beside me!—
             Wide
And deep and darksome rolled the tide
Of life 'twixt her and me!

MARY'S PRAYER

REMEMBER Me when Death's dark wing
  Has borne me far from Thee;
When, freed from all this suffering,
  My Grave shall cover me.

5 Remember me, and, if I die,
    To perish utterly,
Yet shrined within thy memory
  Thy Heart my Heaven shall be!

'Twas all I wished when first I gave
10   This hand unstained and free,
That I from thence might ever have
  A place, my Lord, with thee.

So, if from off my dying bed
  Thou'dst banish misery,
15 O say that when I'm cold and dead
  Thou wilt Remember Me!

UPON that dreary winter's night,
  Before my angel Mary died,
I, by the fire's declining light,
Sat comfortless, and silent sighed,
5 While burst unchecked the silent tide
For thoughts how I, when she was gone,
Through many an hour like that must bide
To wake and watch and weep alone.

   All earthly hope had passed away
10 And every hour brought death more nigh
In the still chamber where she lay
With looks and thoughts composed to die.
But mine was not her heavenward eye,
Whose hot tears gathered o'er her doom,
15 While my sick heart throbbed heavily
To give impatient anguish room.

   Oh now—I thought—a little while,
And that great house should hold no more
Her, whose fond love the gloom could wile
20 Of many a long night gone before!
Oh! all those happy hours were o'er
When seated by our own fireside,
I smiled to hear the loud wind's roar,
And turned to clasp my beauteous bride!

25 I could not bear the thoughts that rose
Of what had been and was to be,
But still the darkness would disclose
The sorrow-pictured prophecy,
Still saw I miserable me
30 Long long hence in lonely gloom,
With time-bleached locks and trembling knee
Go friendless, mourning, to my tomb.

Still—still the grove's eternal shade
Oppressed my heart with sickening fear,
35 When I behold its darkness spread
Over each desolate coming year,
Whose long vales filled me with despair
Till, with the sweat-drops on my brow,
I wildly raised my hands in prayer
40 That Death would come and take me now!

And stopped—to hear an answer given—
So much had madness warped my mind—
When sudden through the midnight Heaven
With long howl rose the winter wind,
45 And woke at once—all undefined—
A gushing thought of tumbling seas,
Whose wide waves wandering unconfined
Afar off surging whispered—peace!

I cannot speak the feeling strange
50   Which shewed that vast and stormswept sea,
Nor tell whence came such sudden change
   From endless hopeless misery,
   But somehow it revealed to me
A life when all I loved was gone,
55   Whose solitary liberty
Should suit me wandering tombward on.

'Twas not that I forgot my love,
   That night departing evermore,
'Twas hopeless grief for her that drove
60   My soul from all it praised before,
   Till that blast called it to explore
A new born life whose lonely joy
   Might calm the pangs of sorrow o'er,
Might shrine its memory—not destroy!

65 I rose and drew my curtains back
   To gaze upon the starless waste,
And image on that midnight wrack
   The path o'er which I longed to haste,
   From storm to storm continual cast,
70 And not a moment given to view
   O'er the far winds the memories past
Of hearts I loved and scenes I knew.

My mind anticipated all
   The things these eyes have seen since then.
75 I heard the trumpet's battle call,
   I rode o'er ranks of bleeding men,
   I swept the waves of Norway's main,
I tracked the sands of Syria's shore,
   I felt such danger's strife and pain
80 Might me from living death restore.

Ambition I would make my bride,
   And joy to see her robed in red,
For none through blood so wildly ride
   As those whose hearts before have bled.
85 Yes! Even though thou shoulds't long have laid
   All coldly pressed by churchyard clay,
   Though I know thee thus decayed
I might smile, to be away!

Might lull from grief my aching breast,
90   Might dream—But oh, that heart wrung groan
Forced from me with the thought confessed
   That all would go if she were gone!
I turned, and wept, and wandered on
   All restlessly from room to room
95 To the still chamber, where alone
   A sick light glimmered through the gloom.

There all unnoticed time flew o'er me,
  While I knelt beside the bed,
And the life which loomed before me
100   Choked my voice and bowed my head.
Many a word to me she said
  Of that bright heaven which shone so near,
And oft and fervently she prayed
  That I might sometime meet her there.

105 But, Oh, how soon all words were over
  When Earth passed, and Paradise
Through mortal darkness seemed to hover
  O'er her smiling Angel eyes:
One last look she gives her lover,
100   One embrace before she dies,
Then—while he is bowed above her—
  She beholds him from the skies.

SONG

THE present day's sorrow,
  Oh, why should we mourn,
Since every to-morrow
  Must rise o'er its Urn.
5   All that we think such pain
  Will have departed then.
Bear for a moment what cannot return.

For past Time has taken
  Each hour that it gave,
10 And *they* do not waken
  From yesterday's grave,
  So surely we may defy
  Shadows like Memory,
Feeble and fleeting as midsummer wave.

15 From the depths where they're falling,
    Both pleasure and pain,
    Despite its recalling
    Arise not again,
    Though we weep over them
20 Naught can recover them.
    There where they lie they shall never remain.

    Then seize we the present,
    And gather its flowers,
    For, mournful or pleasant,
25 'Tis all that is ours.
    While daylight we're wasting,
    The Evening is hasting,
    And night follows fast on the vanishing hours.

    Yes and we, when that night comes,
30 Whatever betide,
    Must die as our fate dooms
    And sleep by their side,
    For change is the only thing
    Always continuing,
55 And it sweeps Creation away with its tide.

SONNET

WHY hold young eyes the fullest fount of tears,
    And why will happiest hearts most sadly sigh
    When fancied friends forsake or lovers fly
Or Hearts of others throb beneath their cares?
5 Ah, questioner, thou at least art young in years,
    Or Time's rough voice had long since told thee why!
    Increase of days increases misery,
And misery brings selfishness which sears
    The Soul's best feelings.—'Mid the Battle's roar,
10 In Death's dread grasp, the soldier's eyes are blind

To others dying. And he whose Hopes are o'er
Smiles sternly at the sufferings of mankind.
A bleeding spirit most delights in gore,
A Tortured Heart will make a Tyrant mind.

AN ANALOGY

OF Earth beneath how small a space
  Our eyes at once descry,
But Heaven above us meets our gaze
  Like an Infinity.
5 On Earth we see our own abode,
A Smoky Town, a dusty road,
  A neighbouring hill or grove:
But worlds on worlds in legions bright
Are gliding over paths of light
10   Amid yon Heaven above!

While daylight shews this narrow earth,
  It hides that boundless Heaven,
And but by Night a visible birth
  To all its stars is given.
15 Yes, fast as fades departing day,
When silent marsh and Moorland grey
  To evening mists decline,
So slowly stealing star on star
As midnight hours draw softly near
20   More clear and countless shine.

I know how oft-times clouds obscure them,
  But *from earth* ascend
All such vapours drawn before them
  As *to* earth they tend,
25 But, when the storm has swept them by,
Upon the earth their ruins lie

Subsided down again,
While Heaven untouched more glorious glows
And every star more starlike shews
30   As 'shining after rain'.

Oh! Thus we view in mortal life
   So circumscribed a scene,
Where petty joys and cares and strife
   Alone are heard or seen,
35 But when beyond death's darksome tide
We let our minds a moment glide,
   How vast the prospect seems!
Not worlds of everlasting light,
But joy on joy celestial bright
40   O'er Heaven's dominion gleams.

'Tis day—The day of pomp and power
   That hides the world divine,
And few will heed in such an hour
   How bright its splendours shine.
45 But, when declines youth's summer sun,
When life's last vanities are gone,
   Our thoughts from earth are driven,
And as the shades of death descend
How truly seems its night our friend
50   Because it shews us Heaven!

3

OTHER POEMS OF BRANWELL BRONTË, NOT PREVIOUSLY PUBLISHED IN THE SHAKESPEARE HEAD EDITION

WHEN on the thorny bed of Death
      The wasted sick man quivering lies,
His breast scarce heaving with his breath,
And cold his brow and quenched his eyes,
5   Then, when as hopelessly he dies,
In that forlorn and dreary hour,
Oh what a host of feelings rise
To embitter death with darker power.
Then Death and darkness round him lower.
10 He sees his children round him stand
And cannot even lift that hand
Which gave them bread and strength and life,
While they in anguished hopeless strife
Pour out the unavailing shower.

WHEN on the thorny bed of death
      The wasted victim spent with pain,
His breast scarce heaving to his breath,
Still clings to bitter life in vain,
5   When moveless, powerless to complain,
All—hope and voice and eyesight—gone,
And dark and deep the livid stain
Leaves [?] each member cold and wan [?]
Then, as he turns his sightless eye
10 With bitter anguish to the sky,
And strives with hollow tone
One word—But now the gasping [?] tongue
But that death rattle can prolong.
It sinks and he is gone.

NOW the sweet hour of closing day
      Draws down from Heaven her latest smile,
And Evening's beams have ceased to play
      Round Scyros's lofty Isle.
5   Thermopylae's commanding height
Looks o'er the silent march of Night,

And wide beneath it Grecia lies
As still and silent as the skies.
A moveless shadow dim and blue
10   Spreads o'er her Hills one deathlike hue,
And wide Thessalia far away
Spreads her deep shadows cold and grey.

From far Euboea wild and lone
Why hear I not the shepherd's tone?
15   Why do his shrill notes dying afar
Cease to soothe the twilight air?
Where is the twinkling lamp of night,
Which used to flash on Phocia's height,
And down the Peneus's brawling stream
20   Glint the lone traveller's warning beam?

Where, dost thou ask, through smiling Greece
Have fled these signs of life and peace?
Where is the youth of the old man gone?
Why has the joy of the hapless flown?
25   Where is the light in the closing eye
Of the wretch in sickness stretched to die?
And why have the sweet sounds of Evening
      ringing
Sunk into silence through Hell as clinging?

I said that spent with Iron pain
30   The dying man may not complain.
I said that to the erring sight
Death's gloom may seem as beamy light.
A charnel vapour oft may shine
As fair as Anna's light divine.

35   Well now: All Grecia seems to sleep
In peaceful twilight dark and deep.
Where is the wild red fire of war?
No cries of Anguish fill the air.

No clash of arms, no battle cry,
40 And not one lightning from the sky.
Can thus a mighty Nation die?

HE rode across the moor at night
When starlight only shone,
But even those dim beams were bright
To that woe which weighed his spirit down.

5 He galloped as a fiend [?],
But could not fly from care.
He fearless faced the winter's wind,
But could not give his thoughts to air.

OUR hopes on earth seem wholly gone;
Each minute hastens the decline;
Yet, O my Mary, thou alone
Shall still through life seem only mine!
5 The burial of a darling wife
May not kill men so stern as me;
But only this world's storm and strife
Can aid my bosom's agony.

THE moon in glory mounts above
The darkness of the distant grove,
As if the skies were given to be
The palace of her majesty;
5 A silver grey is round her throne,
And far away the clouds are blown,
With all the lonely mountains [?] dying
In the pale haze [?] above them lying.

Now shines she silently and still
10 Over the brow of yonder hill,
In golden glory gazing down
On field and forest, tower and town;

But the dense trees that around him rise
Give earliest [?] prospects to his eyes
15   With far off cypresses whose gloom
In wood churchyard o'ershade a tomb,
And o'er the forests waving crest
That mild moon in her heavenly rest.

A BREEZE embued with rich perfumes
   Is waving yonder sea of plumes.

B EHOLD the waste of waving sea
   In stormy shadow lying,
As vast and shoreless stretched away
   As the clouds above it flying,
5   As rough as restless and as free
   As the wild winds o'er it sighing.
There, mingled with the ocean gale,
   I hear the sea-birds crying,
As through the unmeasured Heaven they sail,
10   Some far off rest descrying;
And oft their white wings glittering forth
Till lost amid the stormy North;
And still from out the Atlantic surge
   The heavy vapours rise,
15   Whence darkly gathering they diverge
   Around the gusty skies.
And is't the Heaven to Ocean speaks
   Or Ocean back replies,
That such a mournful music breaks
20   And swells and falls and dies?
For, as the wild winds wilder sound,
More hoarse the surges murmur round,
Till they are rolling o'er the deep,
   With such a thundering roar
25   As might arouse from fastest sleep
   The dwellers on the shore,

And waken many an anxious start
　　For those who never more
To some yet warm and yearning heart
30　　　Such tempests shall restore.
Each gust still calling it to mourn
For one who never can return;
Look how the tumbling ridges swell
　　And roll in restless agony:
35　The very burning lake of Hell
　　　Could scarce more rough and raging be!
Black billows ever rising round
Are hurried on toward Ocean's bound,
Till if a blast more strongly sweeps
40　It tears the waters from the deeps,
Whose boiling crests of tortured spray
Are torn and shivered o'er the sea,
While that white foam eternally
　　Brewed in the tempest's fiercest wrath—
45　As on the bit, steeds champ their froth—
Mounts on the broken blast, and scatters to the
　　　sky.
　　Yet—what is that which, 'mid the spray
　　Scuds like a mist-wreath o'er the sea,
　　Now bending downward through the surge,
50　　Then as its dripping sides emerge
Cast back upon the waves or forward borne away?

A ship! A ship! she bends her side
　　Rejoicing to the seas,
Beneath a cloud of canvas wide
55　　That stretches in the breeze.

The bristled poles which rise above
　　Are glancing through the rain,
And bow beneath the tempest's breath
　　With many a sudden strain.

60   So wild the blast, so dense the press
          Of canvas o'er her prow,
      That on her decks the tempest breaks
          Like flying clouds of snow.

      And yet—as if her desperate crew
65   Had maddened in the gale—
      Though driving past as whirlwinds fast
          Swells forth another sail!

      And yet another! Till she bends
          The boiling deeps below,
70   Where every dash the water sends
          In flashes from her bow.

      One moment slipping on her course
          As doubtful what to obey,
      And then with unresisted force
75   Borne forward o'er the sea.

      Her crew with dark locks o'er their brows
          Amid the tempest streaming,
      To each wild eye a spirit rouse
          That fires its fitful gleaming.

80   And brief words mixed with briefer smiles
          Are passed from man to man,
      As for a moment from their toils
          They pause their chief to scan.

      He stands upon the rocking prow
85   To see the surges boil below
      And mark his vessel plough her path
      Through heaven's and ocean's fiercest wrath;
      And then he lifts his wild blue eye
      To note the changes of the sky;

90 Then through the storm a glance he flings
   As if to search for unseen things,
   Since—failing even that eagle gaze
   To pierce the ever-varying maze—
   His seamen start to hear him hail,
95 'All hands aloft, and crowd all sail.'
      'Tis grand to view his noble brow
   Confront the breezes while they blow
   Aside his curls of auburn hair
   That forehead leaving free and fair
100 To change with the resistless light
      Which flashes from his azure eye,
   Now softened like the calm moonlight,
      Now troubled as that stormy sky,
      Now fiercely daring to defy
105 The deepest gulf those waves could form,
   The loudest piping of that storm;
   And loud that storm does pipe, and vast
   The foam-white waves are roaring past,
   And stands he on his streaming deck
110   As chiding even the flying gale,
   Till lo! the restless vapours break
      A wild wide waste of waves to unveil.
      There forward fleets a distant sail
   Tossed in distress—and eagerly
115 That storm-lost ship these sailors eye
   With such a shout as through the sky
      O'erpowers the tempest's wail:
   'Hurrah! she heaves in sight again;
   Now merrily haste we o'er the main;
120   Though from us she flew
      Like the fleet seamew
As like lightning we follow, her speed were in vain!'
   'Heave ho! my hearts,' the boatswain cries;
   'Now draw your lots and choose your prize!'
125 And back an ancient mariner
   His answer shouts with ruthless sneer,

'Let's leave 'em their sails their shroud to be,
Their ship their coffin, their grave the sea.'
That sailor was a hoary man
130   Tottering on life's remotest span,
But still his step was on the seas,
And still his grey locks faced the breeze:
Not one of all that desperate crew
With eye more quick or hand more true;
135   Not one with oaths more terrible
Could speak the mother tongue of Hell.
His ragged garments scarce might warm
His blighted carcase in the storm;
Yet those mean limbs had forced a way
140   Where thousands trembling stood at bay;
And though so rough his cursing tongue
His oaths had 'mid a palace rung;
Tutor and oracle in crime
To serf or lord who wished to climb;
145   And blithely now his wolfish eyes
Stretch to behold the promised prize,
While cool between his toothless jaws
A glittering knife he grimly draws,
Feels its keen edge and laughs to mind
150   The deeds it did in times behind,
And to his comrade, watching nigh,
Slowly he turns his tiger eye.
      That comrade was of statelier form,
As yet scarce battered by the storm;
155   Youth still o'er him her beams had flung,
If not in sins, in seasons young;
Wild rose the locks above his brow,
And brown his cheeks' unfading glow;
His eyes rolled ever fierce and free,
160   As fits a spoiler of the sea;
His pirate vest was dashed aside,
For that wild breast would scorn to hide
The beating of its lawless pride;

And loud and carelessly he sung
165   As reckless in the shrouds he hung:
Riot in peace and spoil in war
Were all O'Connor's hopes or care.
    But standing by a silent gun
Behold another, darker one:
170   A man of crime whose eyes had ne'er
Been clouded by a single tear;
Hard were those eyes and black the brow
That shadowed o'er their tiger glow;
Though scathed by storms, an age might pass
175   With all its winters o'er his face,
Yet never clear away the frown
Which called revenge in bloodshed down;
Now might his chieftain brook that scowl,
But that he trusted Gordon's soul;
180   However black the path he trod,
Would never bid him leave the road.

WHAT seek my eyes? They rest not on the columns
    arching o'er me,
Nor the storied windows shimmering round or sepulchres
    piled before me;
They are watching through its imprisoning tomb the cold
    corrupting clay;
They are wandering o'er the charnel gloom of death's
    unfathomed sea.
5   Not the wintry winds which moan without in such a
        mourning tone
Have so wild a path or so far a flight as the past of a spirit
    gone.
How strange seems now that vanished past reflected in my
    eye—
That pride of rank, that pomp of power, that wealth of
    royalty;

Collecting all their brightest beams around a single brow,
10 Yet paling all their borrowed light 'neath [?] native glow!
How strange to know that she to whom I bent my willing
    knee
Among a thousand round her throne who joined to kneel
    with me
Is now so near me all alone, with arms clasped on her breast,
Lying clothed in white in an endless night of an eternal rest;
15 Her lovely limbs stretched stiff and still, her eyelids closed
    for ever;
And her white lips in silence pressed, no more on earth to
    sever;
And her pale brow surrounded now with wild flowers
    withering:
She's to a long, long winter snatched from a short and
    sudden spring.
My mind reverted back to the path of this quenched and
    fallen star.
20 To that bright morn when first its light shone o'er the
    Calabar,
Companion of our country's Sun in his refulgent rise:
The chosen and the only one beside him in the skies!
And farther back upon her track to the hour remembered
    well
When Love's first word upon her heart like whispered
    thunder fell:
25 Her father's Palace roof above, its glorious Halls around,
When her cheek first flushed and her bosom beat to hear
    that awful sound!

CEASE, mourner, cease thy sorrowing for the dead,
   For, if their life be lost, its Toils are o'er,
And Woe and Want shall visit them no more.
Nor ever slept they so on earthly bed
5 Such sleep as that which lulls them, dreamless laid

In the long chambers of the eternal shore,
Where sacred silence seals each guarded door.
Oh, turn from tears for these thy bended head
And mourn the Dead Alive, whose pleasure flies
10 And Life departs before their death has come,
Who lose the Earth from their benighted eyes,
Yet see no Heaven gleam through the rayless gloom;
These only feel the worm that never dies
The Quenchless fire, the Horrors of a tomb.

DRINK to me only with thine eyes,
And I will pledge in wine!
For angels know of no such joys
As in this hour are mine!
5 O glorious glass! that givest to me
The sights that make my heaven,
Such forms as theirs could never be
By real mirror given!

FROM the thunder of the battle
That has laid a thousand low;
From the cannons' conquering rattle
That has stilled the sternest foe;

5 From Elva's far off water
That has dyed with blood the sea;
From Leyden's field of slaughter,
Thou hast risen to raise the free.

Again thy country meets thee
10 Who broke the captive's chain;
Again thy kingdom greets thee,
A conquering king again!

Thou hast given them power that love
   thee,
   And they shall give thee praise;
15 They shall pray to heaven above thee
   For a lengthened round of days;

For a brow unmarked by furrow,
   For a hand unstained by crime,
For a joy unchecked by sorrow
20   Beyond the bounds of time;

For laurels o'er thee, sleeping,
   Whose leaves shall ever bloom,
For a land like children weeping
   O'er a king's like a father's tomb!

FAR up in heaven I view the brightest star
  That ever blazed amid the storms of war—
The star that blazed o'er Persia's burning vale
When battle crushed the rose and scared the
   nightingale.

ROBERT BURNS

HE little knows—whose life has smoothly passed
  Unharmed by storm or strife, undimmed by care;
Who, clad in purple, laughs at every blast,
  Wrapped up contented in the joys that are—
5 He little knows the long and truceless war
Of one on poverty's rough waters cast,
  With eyes fixed forward on the glorious star
  That from Fame's temple beams, alas! how far—
Till backward buffeted o'er ocean's waste.

WHEN first old Time with me shook hands,
   And pointed out my way,
I little knew the unknown lands
   Through which life's journey lay.

WHEN side by side, at twilight, sitting,
   All our household group we see,
The shade and firelight o'er them flitting,
   The smiles and converse circling free;

5 Though winds within the chimney thunder
   And rain-showers shake each window-pane,
With one glance of awe or wonder
   Song or tale begins again.

Even when our house seems hushed and lonely,
10 Save whispers round a sick one's bed,
We find a pleasure were it only
   To soothe and still the throbbing head.

And, though our eyes seem moist with weeping,
   Hope is still our guest the while,
15 Our hearts but soothed if pain be sleeping,
   Satisfied if sickness smile.

Even—though far be such a sorrow!—
   Death takes back his 'clay to clay';
Though that face shall see no morrow
20 Which the coffin hides to-day;

Still a holy calm comes o'er us;
   All have loved, though one has died,—
As round our hearth shall death restore us
   'Neath one gravestone, side by side.

25 But oh! when eye to eye replying
       Glistens with the unbidden tear,
    As the storm through heaven is flying,
       As each dreary gust we hear,

    Of the well loved wanderer thinking—
30   Tempest tossed and torn from home—
    At his unknown perils shrinking,
       Doomed for years so far to roam,

    Still his fate the mind is painting
       As we see his vacant chair,
35 Perhaps 'mid wilds in famine fainting,
       Breathing for us some feeble prayer.

    And when we know that all is over,
       That he has died on foreign shores,
    Ne'er may our hearth its joys recover—
40   Toil may stun, but rest deplores.

THORP GREEN

I SIT, this evening, far away
   From all I used to know,
And nought reminds my soul to-day
   Of happy long ago.

5   Unwelcome cares, unthought-of fears,
       Around my room arise;
    I seek for suns of former years,
       But clouds o'ercast my skies.

    Yes—Memory, wherefore does thy voice
10   Bring old times back to view,
    As thou wouldst bid me not rejoice
       In thoughts and prospects new?

I'll thank thee, Memory, in the hour
   When troubled thoughts are mine—
15 For thou, like suns in April's shower,
   On shadowy scenes wilt shine.

I'll thank thee when approaching death
   Would quench life's feeble ember,
For thou wouldst even renew my breath
20   With thy sweet word 'Remember'!

BY Babel's waters Israel long ago
  Wept 'neath the willows o'er the overthrow
Of sacred Zion's hill, and o'er the dead
Whose brave breasts fronted those by whom they
    bled
5 When fighting 'neath their Salem's holy fane
For victory, but contented to be slain
If they could see, with death's deep sunken eye
Safety to His earth's home who rules on high.
   The Lord of Israel in his agony,
10 When laughed at, dying on the accursed tree,
Cried, 'Why, My God, hast thou forsaken me?'
   Stern Marius, gazing on the sullen flood
Which rolled where mighty Carthage once had
    stood,
Felt bitterly amind that lonely scene
15 That he was laid as low as it had been.
   Our Falkland on the field of fatal fight
That dashed to earth King Charles's hard held
    might
Told of his grief for times [?] his death ere night
   Anson, whom day on day the blast barred still
20 From shores that could have saved when waves
    would kill,
Felt like his sailor on the Cape Horn wave
Who fought for life till Ocean dug his grave.

Napoleon, when the Danube's flood he crossed
And murmured 'Oh world, world' as all seemed
    lost
25 'Mid Aspern's clouds of smoke and screams of
    blood,
Felt that life's joys on frail foundations stood.
And, when within a little town in France
He felt Despair's huge gun had checked the advance
Of earthly Hopes, he knew in spirit then
30 That Happiness could not live long with men.
    I scarce dare speak of HIM, whose heartfelt
        strain
Raised his own Scotland from her dust again,
Who died to prove the boldest manliest breast
Can neither conquer woe or live on rest.
35 BURNS has his grave and life has hid his tears,
But his bright soul is given to future years.
    And must I mention him whose glorious brow
In Hucknall Torkard's vault is mouldering now,
Sleeping from griefs that dimmed his living eye
40 Waking in souls that will not let him die.
For those whose blood and brain have power to
    feel
Joy's bright but fleeting flame, Woe's stabbing
    steel,
Our Byron's spirit can dissect and tell
Why 'twas his spirit bade this world farewell.
45 With them he dies not, though his faithful hound,
Were his loved master's wasted relics found,
And he himself could break death's well wrought
    chain,
With cold eyes only would behold again,
Wrecks of that vessel which like Cooke's begirt
    the main.

HOME thoughts are not with me
Bright, as of yore,
Joys are forgot by me
Taught to deplore.
5   My home has taken rest
In an afflicted breast
Which I have often pressed
But may no more.

MY soul is flown,
And clay alone
Has nought to do with joy or care.
So, if the light of life is gone,
5   There come no sorrows crowding on
And powerless lies despair.

SAY Dr Wheelhouse is a jewel
Or you and I must fight a duel—
Say that his skin is white as snow
Or down direct to Hell you go—
5   Say that his skin is rosy red
Or redder stains shall dye your head—
Say that his eyes seem formed of fat
I'll make yours blacker than my hat—
Say that his mouth seems sensual
10   I'll make yours seem no mouth at all—
Say that his neck wants drawing out
And soon I'll twist your own about—
Say that his belly is his God
And soon you'll feel God's chastening rod—
15   Say that his guts are all his riches
And I shall call you sons of bitches—
Say that his legs are walking sticks

And I'll walk into you like bricks—
Say that his temper is the devil
20 And with the floor your back is level—
Say the first word he learnt was 'Damn it'
And down your throat that word I'll cram it—
Say that he's not nor's been a maid
And your guts get my clasp-knife's blade—
25 Say that he longed like me for woman
And I and all will call you NO man—
Say that he isn't heaven's holiest son
Or by the Lord your work is done—
For listen to Lord Peter's prayer,
30 Who never knew what 'twas to swear.
If any man who says the womb
Must be first home, at last the tomb,
Or lives by bread or breathes by air,
Or knows he walks life's path of care,
35 Believes not that God never sent,
A form and soul more innocent,
More meek, more passionless, more calm,
More bright with all that heart can charm,
Than him whose name begins with wheel
40 And ends with House—Oh, may he feel
His addled brains like molten lead,
Antony's fire blaze in his head
St Vitus's dance distort each limb
His ears be dead, his eyes be dim,
45 His tongue more fit to curse his fate.

NOTES

Readers are referred back to the Textual introduction and the Abbreviations listed in the preliminary pages of this volume. In Sections 2 and 3 I have tried to establish a correct text by printing from the latest manuscript, or from the best attested printed version, recording in the notes occasional manuscript variations. Deletions are shown by †; corrections without deletion by *. In Section 1 the Shakespeare Head text is printed unaltered, but where it is incorrect this fact is indicated in the notes, using square brackets [ ]. So, for this section, the correct text taken from the latest manuscript or best attested printed version is to be found in the notes. Deletions and corrections are recorded in the same way as for Sections 2 and 3.

SECTION 1

pp. 3–5   *Ode to the Polar Star*   'Lord of the Northern fields of heaven'
Manuscript untraceable; though recorded by H as being in BPM, there is no catalogue entry for it. This poem shows Branwell's precocity and takes up several themes developed in later poems.

pp. 5–12   *Thermopylae*   'Now morning rises broad and bright'
Manuscript in BCH, 13 pp., 6″ × 4″, bound in morocco. At end signed PBB and dated August 9th 1834. In copperplate with fair punctuation and few corrections. First published in SHCBP, p. 257.

TEXT   l. 89   broad and high, to the sky, BCH†
　　　 l. 95   [sound], sounds, BCH
　　　 l. 129   [lord of glory], Lord of Glory, BCH
　　　 l. 179   [Persian], Persian's, BCH
　　　 l. 210   [yon], one, BCH
　　　 l. 213   hour, day, BCH†
　　　 l. 214   power, sway, BCH†

Branwell would have been interested in Thermopylae as a result of his classical studies and his reading of Glover's *Leonidas* in the Ponden House library. Byron's influence may also have contributed to this poem. There is an indecipherable poem on Greece in Branwell's handwriting in Mr Brontë's Greek prayer book and two more poems on Thermopylae in Sections 2 and 3, pp. 207 and 249.

pp. 12–22   (*Misery, Part I*)   'How fast that courser fleeted by'
Manuscript in BPM, pp. 2–8 of Notebook A. At end signed P. B. Brontë and dated December 18th, 1835. In minuscule with little punctuation and few corrections. Extract published in O, vol. II, p. 181. First published in full in SHCBP, p. 264. O had access to a manuscript in NLS, sent to Blackwood's, which was presumably

Branwell's fair copy, and these readings are recorded below. The titles in the Blackwood's manuscript of this and the next poem read *Misery, Scene 1st* and *Scene 2nd*. The manuscript in NLS of this and the next poem are in a very regular minuscule with good punctuation and few crossings out. Most of the t's are crossed, but the handwriting is probably Branwell's, though possibly Charlotte's. 9 pp., 10″ × 8″. Undated, but signed at end Northangerland.

TEXT	l. 2	[His], With, O, NLS
	l. 3	[His], And, O, NLS
	l. 4	[His], And, O, NLS
	l. 15	[see], view, O, NLS
	l. 19	[they], that, O, NLS
	l. 20	[To], And, O, NLS
	l. 24	[That], Which, O, NLS
	l. 25	[Well I hear], I can hear, O, NLS
	l. 52	[rough wrack of stormy], darksome veil of, NLS
	l. 59	[or], and, NLS
	l. 60	[must, must], may, may, BPM, NLS
	l. 63	[That], For that, NLS
	l. 69	[cherish], chain, NLS
	l. 73	[knew], thought, NLS
	l. 80	[to], of, BPM, NLS
	l. 87	[man], men, NLS
	l. 88	[NOW], *Now*, NLS
	l. 89	[thought], *thought*, NLS
	l. 92	[brighter], brightness, NLS
	l. 96	[could], would, NLS
	l. 98	[in], on, NLS
	l. 100	[bade my], made the, NLS
	l. 101	[But], Then, NLS
	l. 104	[THEE], Thee, NLS
	l. 105	[The moment that I gained], This moment as I gain, NLS
	l. 106	[began], begin, NLS
	l. 108	[THOU], Thou, NLS
	l. 112	[shall], may, NLS

TEXT l. 113 [should], could, NLS
l. 119 [hath], has, NLS
l. 129 [that], which, NLS
l. 131 [That], Which, NLS
l. 132 [I have ... heavenly], I've ... wished for, NLS
l. 136 [mad], wild, NLS
l. 139 [deep], steep, NLS
l. 144 [that], the, NLS
l. 149 [darkly], often, NLS
l. 152 [tales], fates, NLS
l. 154 [Had], Has, NLS
l. 160 [And], Had, NLS
l. 180 [gleam], beam, NLS
l. 181 [densest], deepest, NLS
l. 188 [around], amid, NLS
l. 189 that, the, NLS†
l. 194 [his], the, NLS
l. 196 [the], that, NLS
l. 205 [by], with, NLS
l. 211 [chequering o'er the floor], through the opened door, NLS
l. 213 [Towards the opened door], Across the chequered floor, NLS
l. 231 [impetuously], impatiently, NLS
l. 236 [cloud], shade, NLS
l. 227 [seems], seemed, NLS
l. 241 [it], him, NLS
l. 248 [now the], now in the, NLS
l. 253 [open], opened, NLS
l. 262 [That], which, NLS
l. 280 [near], there, NLS
l. 281 [surely, swiftly], swiftly, surely, NLS
l. 283 [dread], deep, NLS
l. 285 [native], happy, NLS
l. 286 [Parting], Parted, NLS
l. 293 [that], the, NLS
l. 294 [strikes], comes, NLS

TEXT   l. 298 [HIM], Him, NLS
        l. 303 [wrapt], swept, NLS
        l. 306 [and], a, NLS
        l. 315 [madness], wildness, NLS
        l. 321 [glittering], glistening, NLS
               [in], of, BPM, NLS
        l. 322 [And], As, NLS
        l. 338 [Thy spirit from the hideous grave], Thy sinking spirit from the grave, NLS
        l. 341 [me or], and naught, NLS
        l. 344 [the], a, BPM, NLS
        l. 347 [could], *could*, NLS
        l. 348 [frightful], fearful, NLS
        l. 349 [thou], *thou*, NLS
               [living], smiling, NLS
        l. 350 [In love and life], As once in love, NLS
        l. 356 [dying], flying, NLS
      ll. 361-2 these lines reversed, NLS
        l. 364 [the], their, NLS

G, pp. 113-17, 125-6 gives this poem a strong autobiographical emphasis, whereby Maria is Branwell's eldest sister, his guardian star in a world of sin and woe. Branwell's life was not all that full of sin and woe in 1835, and we must beware of pressing the autobiographical parallel too closely.

pp. 23-33 (*Misery, Part II*) 'Wide I hear the wild winds sighing' Manuscript in BCPML. Bound in calf by Riviere, pp. 9-17 of Notebook A. At end signed PBB and dated March 2nd, 1836. Minuscule handwriting, little punctuation and few corrections. Extract published in O, vol. II, p. 183. First published in full in SHCBP, p. 275. For Blackwood's version in NLS see note on *Misery, Part I*. Two variants in BPM are printed in Section 3, p. 249.

TEXT   l. 12   [Cleaved], Bleared, NLS
        l. 18   [Far away], Hark, far away, NLS
        l. 20   [ashgrove's], Ash tree's, NLS
        l. 25   [vales], voice, NLS
        l. 35   [rain], voice, BCPML, NLS
        l. 40   [foeman's], foeman's, NLS
        l. 44   ['Tis over, no sighs, no anguished cries], 'Tis over. No
                sighs, no anguished cries, NLS
        l. 50   [With... wandering], NLS† Their... wander, NLS
        l. 51   [look and seek], seek and see, NLS
        l. 52   [storm-tost], stormy, NLS
        l. 59   [these], those, BCPML, NLS
        l. 60   [There], Then, there, NLS
        l. 65   [advancing], careering, NLS
        l. 67   [in], to, NLS
        l. 82   his, that, NLS†
                [slashed], gashed, NLS
        l. 86   [Which], That, NLS
        l. 91   [streams], waves, BCPML**, NLS
        l. 93   [now], there, BCPML**, NLS
        l. 99   [stern], fresh, NLS
        l. 102 [lie], die, NLS
        l. 108 [my], our, NLS
        l. 132 [Oh], Now, NLS
        l. 133 [reward my], toward me, BCPML, NLS
        l. 136 [while], when, NLS
        l. 139 [my], our, NLS
        l. 142 [really], truly, BCPML, NLS
        l. 152 [hand], brow, NLS
        l. 158 [around], round, NLS
        l. 163 [When], Thus, NLS
ll. 174, 175, 176   [Ha], He, NLS
        l. 184 [seemed], seems, BCPML, NLS
        l. 185 [hope], light, NLS
        l. 186 [light], guide, NLS
        l. 189 [friendless], powerless, NLS
        l. 190 [thou], *thou*, NLS

TEXT   l. 192   [say not], said I, NLS
       l. 193   [Can], Could, NLS
       l. 194   [Oh No! Oh No! it is not so],
                This line replaced in NLS by:
                Oh No! For scenes gone long ago!
                and followed by:

                Make the main torrent of his woe.
                I meant, he thinks of pain alone;
                It skills (?) not whether come or gone;
                All dark alike to him and me,
                What has been, is, or is to be,
                And keen I feel much misery now.

       l. 195   [THOU], Thou, NLS
       l. 196   [O do], Lost, though, NLS
       l. 198   [Thy], And, NLS
       l. 199   [beaming], smiling, NLS
      ll. 200–2 NLS omits
       l. 203   [have thy . . . eyes], has that . . . eye, NLS
       l. 204   [shrine], shine, NLS
       l. 209   [Or], And, NLS
      ll. 211–17 NLS omits
       l. 222   [with], by, NLS
       l. 253   [left], here, BCPML, NLS
       l. 256   [in bliss], I know, NLS
       l. 257   [wondrous], Almighty, NLS
       l. 261   [nevermore], never made, NLS
       l. 262   [this site], its waves, NLS
       l. 263   [to], for, NLS
       l. 264   [vilest], rottenest, BCPML, NLS
       l. 265   [rushing . . . the], resting . . . its, NLS
  after l. 266 The omitted lines (not in NLS which has a line of asterisks
                after line 265, omitting line 266) are:

                O God, my fear lies there
                Without a hope to meet me there
                But howling in despair

       l. 267   [Why], But, Oh, NLS

TEXT l. 269 [be first], refuse, NLS

l. 272 [the], omitted in BCPML and NLS

l. 278 [Such], Of such, NLS

l. 284 [First with the angel and last with the worm],
If once with an angel, then now with a worm, NLS

l. 285 [doest thou point to the sea], NLS has:

sayest thou cares and annoy
Are probations on Earth to a heavenly joy,
Or next will thou point to the desolate sea,

l. 287 [desolate], vanishing, NLS

l. 291 [then, thou should ... joy], thou thus ... joys, NLS

l. 294 [tempest], tempests, NLS

l. 295 [safety], *safety*, NLS

l. 303 [View], See, NLS

l. 305 [the], that, NLS

l. 311 [that], which, NLS
Six lines follow in NLS:

And still as gloomier frowns that night,
Brighter it flashes on the sight,
And still—oh still—as time flies by,
While other things in shades may die,
'Tis but more present to my eye
My one sole star of memory!

l. 320 [NOTHINGNESS], nothingness, NLS

l. 321 [of], on, BCPML, NLS
[THEE], *Thee*, NLS

l. 325 [As then I'd feel my shivering breath],
As stern I'd feel my shortening breath, NLS

l. 326 [felt my life-blood flow], seen my power laid low, NLS

l. 330 [call], fall, BCPML, NLS

l. 331 [thine], thy, NLS

l. 332 [Oh], And, NLS

l. 336 [were there one ... were], If there is heaven ... is, NLS

l. 340 [nay], long, NLS

l. 344 [Thou art alone], Then thou art gone, NLS

l. 346 [state], shade, NLS

TEXT   l. 351   [All wild with pain and mad with fear],
                 All wildly mad with pain and fear, NLS, O
        l. 357   [cover], hide, Lord, NLS, O

G, pp. 117–18, with the same autobiographical work as *Misery, Part I*, perhaps justified by the new lines following l. 194; M, p. 59. Branwell's religious doubts are interesting; both Anne and Charlotte went through a religious crisis shortly after this time. Mrs Oliphant says that Branwell only sent a poem entitled *Misery, Scene 1st*, but quotes from both *Misery* poems, and Blackwood's clearly were sent a revised form of both poems. Branwell says that Blackwood's are not to think that he writes nothing but Miseries, as his day is too much in the morning.

pp. 33–4   (*Elrington*) 'The sunshine of a summer sun'
Manuscript in BCH, 1 p., 6½″ × 4½″. Bound in green levant by Riviere and attributed to Emily. Unsigned. Dated at beginning May 17th, 1836. In minuscule with little punctuation and a few illegible corrections. First published EBP, p. 309. Text as printed.

pp. 34–7   'My Ancient Ship upon my Ancient Sea'
Manuscript in BCH, 2 pp., 7½″ × 4½″. Bound in full morocco by Zaehnsdorf and attributed to Emily. Unsigned. Dated at beginning July, 1836. In minuscule with little punctuation and many illegible corrections. First published in EBP, p. 311.

TEXT   l. 19   [*present*], PRESENT, BCH
        l. 20   [But], And, BCH
        l. 75   [on their], oh, a, BCH

G, p. 119, pointing out that the sense of being adrift which this poem conveys is likely to derive from Branwell's sense of alienation after his London expedition, although it is Percy's travels which are here referred to.

p. 38 (*Memory*) 'Memory, how thy magic fingers'
Manuscript in BCH, 1 p., 7½"×4½". Bound in full morocco by
Zaehnsdorf and attributed to Emily. Unsigned and undated. In
minuscule with little punctuation and few corrections. First published
in SHCBP, p. 289.

TEXT   l. 18   [feelings], failings, BCH

There is an alternative version in the BCPML, 1 p., 4"×4¼". Bound
in green levant and attributed to Emily. Unsigned but dated at 2nd
July 1836, with the note to which Symington refers. In minuscule
with little punctuation and no corrections. It reads:

> Hours and days my heart has lain
> Through a scene of changeless pain,
> As it ne'er would rise again,
>   Sad and still and silently.
>
> Time has flown, but all unknown;
> Nothing could arouse a stone,
> Not a single string would answer
>   In replying sympathy.
>
> Memory, memory comes at last,
> Memory of failings past,
> And with an Eolian blast
>   Strikes the strings resistlessly.

G, p. 114. The agony arising from a feeling of lost opportunities may
be autobiographical, but seems a little strongly expressed.

pp. 39–48 'Still and bright, in twilight shining'
pp. 18–24 of Notebook A. 5 pp. in BCPML. Bound in brown sheep
by Riviere. 2 pp. in BPM, inserted in *Misery, Part I*. Signed at begin-
ning PBB, and at end P B Brontë. Dated at beginning August 8th,
1836, and at end August 13th, 1836, begun and finished in 5 days. In
minuscule with little punctuation, few corrections. Extracts published
in EBP, p. 317 and GCB, p. 165. First published in full in SHCBP, p.
291. There are fragments of earlier versions in BCH: A, 1 p., 7"×4",

bound in full morocco and attributed to Emily; B, another 2 pp.,
7″ × 4″, bound in full morocco; and C, 1 p., 7″ × 4″.

TEXT l. 60   [lone], blue, BCPML
　　　 l. 66   [soul to], course of, BCPML
　　　 l. 69   [*are*], are, BCPML
　　　　　　 [*what are*], *what* are, BCPML
after l. 103 The missing line is: But dimly is revealed below
　　　 l. 110 [hallowed], haloed, BCPML
　　　 l. 113 [rolling], falling, BCPML
　　　 l. 131 [Moon... Moon], MOON ... MOON, BCPML
　　　 l. 135 [shining...], glinting, BCPML
　　　 l. 140 BCH (A) begins here
　　　 l. 142 light, sight, BCH
　　　 l. 148 shining, golden, BCH
　　　 l. 152 BCPML fragment ends here as does BCH (A) variant
　　　 l. 153 BPM fragment begins as does the BCH version; the former is
　　　　　　　 much better transcribed than the BCPML, the BCH contains
　　　　　　　 many variants
　　　 l. 166 with, by, BCH
　　　 l. 168 till its mysterious, all its heavenly, BCH
　　　 l. 169 unnoticed, trembling, BCH
　　　 l. 180 huge concave stretched, great arch spread wide, BCH
　　　 l. 181 But-Every star is hung, But every star all hung, BCH
　　　 l. 184 [well], with, BPM, BCH
　　　 l. 185 cannot, care not to, BCH
　　　 l. 188 Those wondrous times, So many things, BCH
　　　 l. 190 happy, wondrous, BCH
　　 ll. 191–5 BCH omits
　　　 l. 196 this, that, BCH
　　　 l. 197 gazed, beamed, BCH
　　　 l. 203 [lit], it's, BCH and possibly the correct reading
　　　 l. 208 hills, rocks, BCH
　　　 l. 211 BCH continues:

　　　　　　　 As if across an Ocean wide
　　　　　　　 Breasting the dark unfathomed tide
　　　　　　　　 Far far away from home

TEXT   l. 213   A vessel's, It were a vessel's, BCH
        l. 214   O'er, Over, BCH
after l. 215   BCH (B) manuscript concludes with the insertion of the lines:
                He is but a child, so all his dreams
                    Are wanderings of the mind,
                Where all before in glory teems,
                    And little lies behind,
                Formless as any child might be.
                Yet he who looks in them may see
                    In glowing light defined
                The first formed feelings of a soul
                Destined a nation to control.
        l. 229   GCB quotes the next twenty-four lines
        l. 232   might, may, GCB
        l. 236   he, He, GCB
        l. 252   Yon, The, GCB
        l. 267   BCPML manuscript begins here
        l. 283   [sad], and, BCPML
        l. 289   BCH (C) fragment begins here
        l. 290   To spend, So spends, BCH
        l. 291   native . . . gone, dear loved . . . flown, BCH
        l. 294   pleasure glimmering on thy sight,
                  all that fascinates thy sight, BCH
        l. 295   As soon as, The moment, BCH
       ll. 296-7 BCH omits
        l. 297   [willows], meteors, BCPML
        l. 299   Hell, hate, BCH
       ll. 300-3 BCH omits
        l. 305   rapid, quickly, BCH
        l. 308   But farther, The further, BCH
        l. 309   Than those around, Those spirits round, BCH
        l. 319   And, See, BCH
        l. 320   young, soft, BCH
        l. 322   in, with, BCH
        l. 326   in, of, BCH
        l. 327   Yon is the image of a man,
                  'Tis the forehead of a mighty man, BCH

TEXT   l. 328   to lead the foremost, on earth to lead, BCH
        The BCH manuscript continues:

> Of onward minds, a man whose soul
> Nor Death nor Danger shall control,
> One whom no mortal power shall tame,
> One who shall set the world aflame.

GCB, p. 165; G, pp. 114, 126; M, pp. 65–7. GCB says she is quoting the first six stanzas of the poem sent to Wordsworth and that this was about a third of the poem. It would seem that he only received part of this poem. As it stands the poem is full of obvious imitations of Wordsworth's *Immortality Ode* and Coleridge's *Kubla Khan* as well as of the hymn 'While shepherds watched their flocks by night', and, as H points out, a hymn by Isaac Watts copied on p. 45 in the portion quoted by Mrs Gaskell. The hymn runs:

> When I can read my title clear
> To mansions in the skies,
> I bid farewell to every fear
> And wipe my weeping eyes.

Such plagiarism is hardly likely to have impressed Wordsworth. It is also worth remembering that Percy is the hero of this poem, and Wordsworth, though knowing nothing of Percy, may have disliked the dark hints of woe and sin that lay ahead for the infant child.

pp. 48–51   'Sleep, mourner, sleep!—I cannot sleep'
Manuscript in BCH, pp. 29–30 of Notebook A. Unsigned, said to be unfinished, dated at beginning January 13th, 1837. In minuscule with little punctuation, few corrections. First published in EBP, p. 236.

TEXT   l. 20   [to be], be—to, BCH
        ll. 21–2   [to live in Lethe every thought; What I have seen], to live in
                    Lethe, every thought Of what I have seen, BCH
        l. 25   [not], *not*, BCH

The variant mentioned by Symington is in BPM, 3 pp., $7\frac{1}{2}'' \times 4\frac{1}{2}''$, Undated, but signed Northangerland, and said to be unfinished.

Normal large handwriting. Well punctuated with no corrections. For this and other reasons it is probably safe to conclude that it was written at the time of Branwell's disgrace after Thorp Green.

'Poor mourner, sleep.' 'I cannot sleep—
My mind though wearied wanders on.'
'Then, mourner, weep.' 'I cannot weep,
For eyes and tears are turned to stone.'

Oh, might my footsteps find some rest.
Oh, might my eyes with tears run o'er.
Oh, might my life-thoughts leave my breast,
Could they my life's sweet love restore!

But if I might in silence mourn,
Apart from canting sympathy,
From man's sour scoff and bitter scorn,
From woman's heartless flattery.

Then, nothing nearer Paradise
Need, as a heritage be mine;
For I've survived unreal joys,
And cannot bear their dreamlike shine.

I have been given o'er to grief,
Nor could I live were sorrow gone;
So all my solace or relief
Must be, to drop my tears alone.

To live in pleasure would be now
To live forgetful—every thought
Of all that I have known below
Must be forsaken or forgot—

And oh, can I departed years
Forget, as though they had not been!
Though, if I must remember, tears
Will dim the storm and sunshine scene.

I have no choice; however bright
May beat the blaze of July's sun,
'Twill only give a far off sight
Like breaks in clouds, of pleasures gone.

However young and lovely round
Fresh forms may court my frozen eye,
They'll only desecrate the ground
Where fairer far, corrupting lie.

And voices sweet as music's thrill,
And laughter light as marriage strain
Will only wake a ghastly chill,
As if the buried spoke again.

All, all is over—friend or lover
Need never seek for refuge here;
Though they may sweep my heart strings over,
No music will awake the air.

I'm dying away in dull decay,
I feel and find the sands are down;
That evening's latest lingering ray
At last from my wild heaven has flown.

I feel and find that I am cast
From hope and peace and power and pride,
A withered leaf on autumn's blast,
A scattered wreck on ocean's tide.

G, p. 133 (1st version); M, p. 70 (2nd version). G comments on the intense wretchedness of this poem, but does not see the strong influence of Byron which might cast some doubt on Branwell's sincerity.

pp. 51–8 'Well! I will lift up my eyes once more'
Manuscript in BPM with two fragments in BCNY (1 p., 2″ × 3½″; 1 p., 2″ × 3½″), one in HRT (1 p., 1½″ × 3½″) and two fragments in BCPML

(1 p., 4½″×3½″; 1 p., 4¾″×3½″), bound in green levant as Emily's.
Originally pp. 31-6 of Notebook A. At end signed P B B–te and dated
February 9th 1837. Minuscule handwriting with some punctuation
and no corrections. First published in SHCBP, p. 303.

TEXT   l. 2   [wonder], wander, BPM
           l. 40 [And all], All fleeting and all, BPM
           l. 96 1st BCNY fragment begins here
           l. 112 1st BCNY fragment ends here, and I have not been able to
                 trace the next 14 lines in manuscript
           l. 126 1st BCPML fragment begins here
           l. 145 1st BCPML fragment ends here and the 2nd BCNY fragment
                 begins l. 146
           l. 161 [disturbed], distorted, BCNY
                 2nd BCNY fragment ends here; HRT fragment begins l. 163
           l. 163 [lifelike], lifeless, HRT
           l. 175 HRT fragment ends here; 2nd BCPML fragment begins
                 l. 176
           l. 195 2nd BCPML fragment ends here and the remainder of the
                 manuscript is in BPM

G, p. 125. The dying person is assumed to be Mary Percy, wife of
Zamorna and daughter of Northangerland. Branwell in his *History of
Angria* VIII Sept. 19th 1836 had killed off the Duchess and G com-
pares the prose version to this poem. Confusingly there is another
Mary, the wife of Northangerland, about whose death Branwell wrote
several poems, of which this may be one.

pp. 58-64 'Alone she paced her ancient Hall'
Manuscript in BPM, pp. 37-41 of Notebook A. Signed on 1st page
PBB and dated March 1st 1837. In minuscule with little punctuation
and few corrections. First published in SHCBP, p. 310.

TEXT   l. 16 [a Grecian], an unseen, BPM
           l. 20 [siezed], fraught, BPM
           l. 24 [tears], fears, BPM

TEXT   l. 27   [sun], scene, BPM
        l. 37   The missing word is: instead
        l. 42   [All...], A home, BPM
        l. 107   [seemed], deemed, BPM
        l. 148   [now], NOW, BPM
        l. 176   There is a note here: Append this to Harriet's death
        l. 229   Blackbird's, Skylark's, BPM*

G, p. 114. This poem with a female sinner trying to recapture her lost innocence would seem to foreshadow the Harriet poems and the note at l. 176 appears to make the link certain.

p. 65   (*On Caroline*)   'The light of thy ancestral hall'
Manuscript untraceable. First published in L, vol. I, p. 212. Leyland publishes this, the next poem and a portion of *Sir Henry Tunstall*, mentioning Caroline, together, although apart from the name there is no particular connection. The titles are his.

pp. 66–76   (*Caroline*)   'Calm and clear the day declining'
Manuscript of first 24 lines in BPM, 1 p., 7″ × 4½″. Well punctuated, one correction. Normal large handwriting. Undated and unsigned. An early revision of this poem is in Notebook B, and is printed in full in Section 2, p. 231. This was written May 4th to June 15th 1837, and transcribed June 16th 1837. First published in L, vol. I, p. 214. L presumably had access to a later version, since we find Branwell asking for *Caroline* back as late as 1848.

TEXT   l. 23   [seas], sea's, BPM

L, vol. I, pp. 211–27; G, pp. 12–16; M, pp. 26–7. All three attribute the memories of a dead sister to memories of Maria Brontë. I. Holgate in 'The Key to Caroline', BST, 68 (1958), pp. 251–9, makes Caroline Dearden, cousin of Branwell's friend William Dearden whom he met at Luddenden Foot, the eponymous heroine, but though Caroline Dearden died in 1828 and her memorial is in Luddenden church, Branwell would not have heard of her until 1840.

pp. 76–90   (*Harriet I*)   'How Edenlike seem Palace Halls'
Manuscript in BPM, pp. 42–52 of Notebook A. In minuscule with
little punctuation and few corrections. At beginning signed PBB and
dated August 27th, 1837; at end signed P. B. Brontë and dated November, 1837. First published in SHCBP, p. 328.

TEXT   l. 1   There is a fragment in the BCH, 1 p., 4¾″ × 4½″, undated and
unsigned, in minuscule with little punctuation and few
corrections. It reads:

> How Edenlike seem palace walls,
>   When youth and beauty join,
> To waken up their lighted Halls
>   With looks and smiles divine.
>
> How free from care the perfumed air
>   About them seems to play!
> How glad and bright appears each sight,
>   Each sound how soft and gay.
>
> 'Tis like the heavens which parting days
>   In summer's pride imbue
> With beams of such impartial blaze,
>   And yet so tender too.
>
> Ah, memory brings a scene to mind,
>   Beneath whose noble dome
> Rank, beauty, wealth, and power combined
>   To light their lordly home.
>
> Yet parting day, however bright,
>   It still is parting day!
> The herald of approaching night,
>   The trappings of decay.

l. 58   There is a fragment in the BCH, 1 p., 4½″ × 4½″, undated and
unsigned, in minuscule with little punctuation and many
illegible corrections, representing an alternative version. It
reads:

There's something in this glorious hour
That fills the soul with heavenly power,
And dims our eyes with sudden tears
That centre all the joys of years,
For we feel alone that there lingers still,
Like evening sunshine o'er a hill,
A Glory round Life's pinnacle.
And we know, though we be yet below,
That we may not always linger so.
For still ambition beckons on
To this a height that may be won,
And hope still whispers in our ear
'Others have been—thou may'st be there.'

l. 258 A variant of the song was sent by Branwell to Leyland in
1842, and published in HG, 11 June 1842. It reads:

Should life's first feelings be forgot
  As Time leaves years behind?
Should Man's forever changing lot
  Work changes on the mind?

Should space that severs heart from heart
  The heart's best thoughts destroy?
Should years that bid our youth depart
  Bid youthful Memories die?

Oh! say not that these coming years
  Will warmer friendships bring,
For friendship's joys and hopes and fears
  From deeper fountains spring.

Its feelings to the *heart* belong
  Its sign the glistening eye,
While new affections on the *tongue*
  Arise and live and die.

So passing crowds may smiles awake
The passing hour to cheer,
But only old Acquaintance's sake
Can ever wake a tear.

l. 299   ['Tis], The (?), BPM
l. 315   [heart], *heart*, BPM
l. 374   [ought], aught, BPM
l. 417   [ills], woes, BPM

L, vol. I, p. 24; G, p. 226; M, p. 63. M explains well the Angrian background, whereby Harriet O'Connor, later Harriet Montmorency, deserts her husband for Percy, whom she has loved in her youth, but who later abandons her. Although both Percy and Harriet receive a certain amount of sympathy, adultery is treated fairly severely. There is no known adultery in Branwell's life at this time, and this poem can hardly be seen in an autobiographical light, although it is interesting to observe that there is a note of hope struck on p. 78.

pp. 90–100   (*Harriet II*)   'At dead of Midnight, drearily'
Manuscript in BPM, pp. 53–60 of Notebook A. In minuscule handwriting with some punctuation and few corrections. At end signed PBB and dated May 14th, 1838. Alternative version 1 p., $7\frac{1}{4}'' \times 4\frac{1}{2}''$ in BPM (referred to as X). Undated and unsigned. In minuscule with little punctuation and many illegible corrections. First published in SHCBP, p. 342.

TEXT   l. 1   At dead of Midnight, drearily, at dead midnight
                affrightedly,† pantingly,*
        l. 6   an, chill, X
        l. 7   While, And, X
        l. 8   Repressed with sudden fear,
                Sudden and short as checked by fear, X
        l. 9   As she gasped faintly, While faint she murmured, X
        l. 11 no one, no, naught, X
       ll. 11–14 Repeated twice in X, and then the manuscript concludes
                with:

NOTES TO PAGES 91-101

O God, she murmured, take from me
This awful night of agony.
'Twas but a dream, yet such a one
As might my dying spirit dim.
Oppressed with horror, chilled with fear,
And lying alone and death so near,
I feel amid this spectral gloom
      As if my outcast soul was hurled
      To some void space without the world
*   *   *   *   *
(3 illegible lines)

l. 48   chills, strikes, BPM†
l. 115   [the], that, BPM
l. 122   [was], saw, BPM
l. 126   [her], *Her*, BPM
l. 174   The date May 2nd, 1841 is written here, presumably as a
          result of Branwell looking over his manuscript again
l. 265   [IT], *it*, BPM

G, pp. 117–19; M, pp. 64–5. M suggests some collaboration with
Emily during this period, although the name Augusta, one of the
names of the chief heroines in Gondal is hardly evidence for this. It
might equally well have come from a knowledge of Byron's life, and
there is a poem addressed to Augusta in Section 2, p. 190, composed
in 1835, Augusta being the name of Percy's first love.

p. 101   'Now—but one moment, let me stay'
Manuscript in BCH, 1 p., 4¾″ × 3¾″. Unsigned and undated. In minu-
scule handwriting, with some punctuation, no corrections. First pub-
lished in EBP, p. 241.

TEXT   l. 8   [sullen], far off, BCH
         l. 11   [I standing], I, standing, BCH
         l. 22   [yet], though, BCH

There is a variant in BCH, 1 p., 2″ × 4″, bound in morocco, attributed to Emily. Unsigned and undated. In minuscule handwriting with little punctuation and many illegible corrections. It reads as follows:

> Now one moment, let me stay:
> One moment ere I go,
> To join the ranks whose Bugles play
> On Westwood's waving brow.
>
> One calm hour on the brink of life,
> Before it breaks in headlong strife
> Upon its downward road;
> One insight through the waters clear,
> Before their pictures disappear
> In the fierce foaming flood.
>
> Here I am standing underneath
> The shade of quiet trees,
> Whose leaves can hardly catch a breath
> Of this sweet evening breeze.

This is presumably a poem about some Angrian battle.

pp. 101-2   'Oh all our cares these noontide airs'
Manuscript in BCPML, 1 p., 3½″ × 4½″. Bound in green levant as Emily's. Unsigned and undated. In minuscule handwriting with little punctuation and no corrections. Text as printed. First published in EBP, p. 233.

p. 102   (*Fragment*)   'As if heartsick at scenes of death, the day'
Manuscript in BCH, 1 p., 9¼″ × 7¼″. Unsigned and undated. Normal large handwriting, little punctuation and some corrections. First published in SHCBP, p. 354.

TEXT   l. 3   its customed gift, the peaceful smile, BCH†

pp. 102-3   'There's many a grief to shade the scene'
Manuscript untraceable. First published in L, vol. I, p. 205. Leyland

states that it is the conclusion to a poem of sixty lines and draws attention to the spirit of Christian optimism in the poem.

pp. 103–4 (*Death triumphant*) 'Oh! on this first bright Mayday morn'
Manuscript untraceable. First published in L, vol. I, p. 206 with the date May, 1838. Leyland says he is only printing a fragment and points out the return in this fragment from melancholy to happy memories of the past.

pp. 104–19 (*Sir Henry Tunstall*) ' 'Tis only afternoon—but midnight's gloom'
There are three manuscripts of this poem. In BL a manuscript entitled *The Wanderer*, alleged falsely to be in Emily's handwriting. 12 pp., 7¾" × 5", bound by Riviere. Dated at beginning July 31st, 1838, unsigned and written in Bradford. In minuscule with some punctuation and some corrections. In HLH, 13 pp., 10½" × 8". At end signed PBB and dated April 15th, 1840. In normal small handwriting with good punctuation and some corrections. In NLS, 16 pp., 9" × 7½". Signed at end Northangerland and undated. In normal small handwriting with good punctuation and few corrections. First published in full in Q, vol. II, p. 212. Extracts in HG, 4 June 1842, L, vol. I, p. 211 and O, vol. II, p. 189 who dates the last version September 1842. The SHCBP version would seem to rely on these printed texts. The NLS version would seem to be the most recent, and it is that I have accepted as the definitive text, while recording the variants.

TEXT   l. 1   but, yet, BL
   l. 4   cares, light, O
   l. 6   Sounds, Stands, O, BL
   ll. 20–1   BL reverses lines
   l. 24   Earnest, Steadfast, O, Q, HLH, BL
   ll. 27–8   O omits; HLH has the SHCBP reading as has Q with the substitution of too bright for too long; BL has:

So sick from long hope, bursting into morn
Too bright for her with longer pining worn
NLS reads:
Sickened with joy, impatient to be born
Too bright for her, with long repining worn.
l. 31   through, o'er, O, BL
ll. 33–41 Erased in HLH, omitted by Q
l. 35   sigh at, sighing o'er, BL
l. 36   it, that, BL
        [well-beloved warrior's], well-loved warrior's, O, NLS
        wanderer's far off, HLH, far off wanderer's, BL
l. 38   or, and, HLH
l. 40   [wander ... wastes], O, linger ... wastes, BL,
        wander ... wrecks, HLH, NLS
l. 43   [childhood's], Q, HLH, BL, boyhoods, NLS
l. 44   NLS omits
l. 49   [drooped and died], Q, HLH, bloomed and died, BL,
        budded, bloomed, NLS
l. 50   tempestuous seas, the weary waves, BL†
l. 52   have, had, BL
l. 53   [voiceless farewells of], Q, HLH, BL, last long look upon,
        NLS
l. 55   as now, so new, BL
l. 57   The, Our, BL
l. 58   arm ... raised, drum ... urged, BL
l. 59   [o'er], on, BL, NLS
l. 63   [weeping Mother ... his sunny], Q, BL, HLH, Mother
        weeping ... her soldier's, NLS
l. 64   Our, My, BL
l. 66   on, to, BL
l. 69   [o'er], Q, HLH, BL, on, NLS
l. 70   scarce seemed, seemed not, BL
        [so long as we beheld], Q, HLH, while yet our eyes beheld,
        BL, NLS
l. 71   [The chequered sunshine and the open field], Q, HLH
        The shadowy woodland and the open field, BL,
        The shadowy avenue and open field, NLS

TEXT   l. 73   Heaven, vision, BL
        l. 74   [never more those], Q, HLH, ne'er these, BL,
                 ne'er those, NLS
        l. 75   [never more his step], Q, HLH, ne'er his rapid step, BL, NLS
        l. 77   [all the world to us seemed gone], Q, HLH,
                 all the world seemed passed away, BL, NLS
        l. 78   but, yet, BL
        l. 79   [that o'er], Q, HLH, BL, which round, NLS
        l. 80   home, bright, BL
        l. 82   [will wander], Q, HLH, have wandered, BL, NLS
        ll. 83–4 BL reverses the lines
        l. 86   twilight, starlight, BL†
        l. 87   Silently ... of, Intently ... on, BL
        l. 88   [shining], BL, Q, HLH, radiance, NLS
        l. 90   Because it seemed to link those lands,
                 Dreams seemed to link those distant lands, BL
        l. 94   While, Where, BL
        l. 96   that ... through his boyhood's, which ... in his bygone, BL
        l. 97   [Is], BL, Q, HLH, was, NLS
        l. 98   [and], BL, Q, HLH, the, NLS
                 [burning], Q, HLH, torrid, BL, tropic, NLS
        l. 101   [greet], BL, Q, HLH, NLS†, meet, NLS
        l. 102   [made], BL, Q, HLH, formed, NLS
        l. 103   [Heart ... is], Q, HLH, Hearts ... are, BL, NLS
        l. 104   [She ... she], Q, HLH, They ... they, BL, NLS
        l. 105   [she said nothing], Q, HLH, so she spake not, BL, so she
                 spoke not, NLS
        l. 107   [dull], Q, HLH, cold, BL, NLS
        l. 108   [clear], Q, HLH, close, BL, chase, NLS
        l. 109   worn, when, BL, Q, HLH
        l. 110   [of feverish], Q, HLH, it favoured, BL, of fevered, NLS
        l. 116   [his aged Father's frame], Q, HLH, his father's aged frame,
                 BL, his father's failing frame, NLS
        l. 123   [the], BL, Q, HLH, and, NLS
        l. 124   neglect, BL, Q, HLH, suspense, NLS but wrongly
        l. 127   mighty, very, BL, expectant, NLS†
        l. 128   should, must, BL

TEXT l. 131   are, is, BL
after l. 134   Q omits, and HLH crosses out, but BL and NLS include
four rather flat lines:

Advances hastily a stranger's tread.
The children shrink behind with sudden dread.
All rise together—open flies the door,
And steps that stranger on the parlour floor.

l. 135   [I cannot paint], Q, HLH, My pen might paint, BL, NLS
l. 138   [ever could give vent], Q, HLH, could find their vent, BL,
might find a vent, NLS
l. 139   [look], Q, HLH, BL, eyes, BL†, gaze, NLS
l. 142   Her, That, BL
l. 143   o'erflow, soft glow, BL
l. 145   [With whom], Q, HLH, BL, Through which, NLS
l. 147   [With whom], Q, HLH, BL, Through which, NLS
l. 148   [Since where it darkened Hope seemed shining by], Q, HLH
For where it comes Hope ever hovers by, BL,
Since where it broods Hope ever hovers by, NLS
l. 149   [His], Q, HLH, that, BL, his, NLS
l. 154   used, wed, BL
l. 156   [the], Q, HLH, BL, each, NLS
l. 158   [strove], Q, HLH, BL, sought, NLS
ll. 159–60   BL and NLS omit
l. 162   [behind the cloud], Q, HLH, BL, amid the haze, NLS
l. 165   [Their innocence destroyed], Q, HLH, The golden locks
were gone, BL, Those golden locks were gone, NLS
l. 166   [him], Q, HLH, BL, them, NLS
l. 168   [Can sometimes bring], Q, HLH, Brought back, BL, NLS
l. 170   [his], Q, HLH, a, BL, NLS
l. 173   [the], Q, HLH, BL, their, NLS
l. 179   [hide ... smiles], Q, HLH, hide ... curls, BL, deck ...
smiles, NLS
l. 182   [words], Q, HLH, robes, BL, garb, NLS
l. 186   [fast], Q, HLH, BL, strict, NLS
l. 192   lurked, peeped, BL, lurked, BL†
l. 201   back, o'er, BL

TEXT l. 203   [To mark], Q, HLH, And mark, BL, And note, NLS

l. 205   [erewhile enshrined in], Q, HLH, so lately constant to, BL, NLS

l. 207   *like* a vision, dim and distant, BL**

l. 209   [never], ever, Q, HLH, BL, NLS

l. 210   old-thus, old star, BL

l. 219   breeze, wind, BL

l. 221   [cheat], Q, HLH, BL, light, NLS

l. 225   [through], Q, HLH, BL, in, NLS

l. 227   [infant], Q, HLH, BL, youthful, NLS

l. 230   [wherewith], Q, HLH, BL, with which, NLS

l. 232   [And], Q, HLH, BL, Or, NLS

l. 242   [commingling], Q, HLH, the mingling, BL, those mingling, NLS

l. 243   immortal, the immortal, BL†

l. 244   [over Indian seas], Q, HLH, fixed his destinies, BL, NLS

l. 245   [First . . . fixed his destinies], Q, HLH, And . . . over Indian seas, BL, NLS

l. 246   chief, best, BL

l. 247   [his], Q, HLH, BL, its, NLS

l. 248   old print, grief, BL

[does the *old mind* remain], BL, Q, HLH, *does the old mind remain*, NLS

l. 251   [really], *really*, Q, HLH, BL, NLS

l. 254   [now . . . I've], Q, HLH, BL, I . . . have, NLS

l. 255   [all], Q, HLH, BL, those, NLS

l. 259   [saw], Q, left, HLH, BL, NLS

l. 262   [I have], Q, HLH, BL, I've, NLS

[those], those eyes, Q, HLH, BL. NLS

l. 263   [I have], Q, HLH, BL, I've, NLS

l. 264   [I have], Q, HLH, BL, I've, NLS

l. 267   [with blessings], Q, HLH, BL, in blessing, NLS

l. 268   [I have], Q, HLH, BL, I've, NLS

l. 269   [they have], Q, HLH, BL, they've, NLS

l. 272   [Yet], Q, HLH, BL, But, NLS

l. 273   [this], Q, HLH, BL, such, NLS

l. 278   these, my, BL

after l. 279   HLH (crossed out), BL and NLS insert:

But well I used to love the things I see.
Now if I lost them 'twould be naught to me;
And once my sire's or sister's voice to us was dear,
Now—if they perished,[1] friends are everywhere.
Once naught could tear me from my own dear home,
Now—every roof's the same where'er I roam.
Once when I saw that picture, every vein
Beat, fame like that, even with that death to gain.
Now I have looked on many a bloody[2] field.
But oh, how different are the thoughts they yield
They bend my brain[3] to calculate their plan
But wake[4] no wishes wild to combat in their van.

[1] if I lost them, NLS*   [3] brow, BL, HLH
[2] battle, BL, HLH   [4] rouse, BL, HLH

l. 280   [saw], Q, HLH, knew, BL, NLS
l. 283   [could], Q, HLH, BL, would, NLS
l. 285   [or], Q, HLH, BL, and, NLS
l. 288   [had perhaps left an associate], Q, HLH, was leaving a
          companion, BL, NLS
l. 291   broken, shaken, BL
l. 292   [hastening], Q, HLH, fading, BL, NLS
l. 297   [that we loved remains], Q, HLH, that we love remains, BL,
          loved or loving keeps, NLS
l. 299   that, which, BL
          gave, gives, BL†
l. 303   their, our, BL
l. 304   [scarce], Q, HLH, not, BL, NLS
l. 307   dart after, love often, BL
l. 308   [it—], Q, HLH, —'Tis, BL, NLS
l. 309   [sickman's tortured], Q, HLH, BL, tortured sick man's,
          NLS
l. 310   [but], Q, HLH, BL, and, NLS
after l. 315   HLH (crossed out), BL and NLS insert:

Ah, Rover—wert thou here and could'st thou feel
The utter change this spirit would reveal

Thoud'st rather keep thy long neglected grave
Than kiss again the hand that¹ would not have
One welcoming stroke to give—My Dog—they say
That when I left thou pined'st fast away
Till death restored thee to thy humble clay,
And ceased there² at last to think of me
Who then afar was fast forgetting thee.
Yes—'twas forgetting—Memory lingered yet,
But lost affection makes the word forget.

¹ Which, BL, HLH
² And there forgot, HLH, And hast then ceased, BL

TEXT l. 321   [in which], Q, HLH, from which, BL, from whence, NLS
      l. 323   [known], Q, HLH, BL, seen, NLS
      l. 324   [And on one], Q, HLH, BL, on whose first, NLS
      l. 325   effaced, defaced, BL
      l. 326   L prints the next 20 lines, but they were first published in HG, 4 June 1842
      l. 332   [still], Q, HLH, BL, HG, Thou, L, NLS
      l. 333   And calm my breast, and clear my brow,
            Soothe at once my weary brow, BL†
      l. 334   I am, I'm, BL, L
            guileless, little, L, BL†
      l. 335   Thine angel, Thy mighty, L
      l. 336   [For even my . . . are], Q, HLH, BL, My very . . . are, L, NLS, My very . . . seem, HG
      l. 339   [hopes], Q, HLH, BL, HG, hope, L, NLS
      l. 340   [ancient . . . forms], Q, HLH, BL, HG, former . . . shapes, L, NLS
      l. 341   or, and, BL
      l. 343   [fare ye well lost shores], Q, HLH, fare ye well lost times, BL, farewell childhood's shores, L, NLS, HG
      l. 344   [O], Oh
      l. 345   [its wild], Q, HLH, the wild, BL, the rough, BL†, these wide, L, NLS, HG
      l. 348   [Yet], Q, HLH, BL, Though, NLS
      l. 353   [were], Q, HLH, BL, seemed, NLS

TEXT   l. 363   [scarce . . . would], Q, HLH, not . . . could, BL, NLS

        l. 367   victorious, in victory, BL

        l. 375   [that], Q, HLH, BL, what, NLS

        l. 391   [Remember Me], Q, HLH, *remember me*, BL, NLS

        l. 410   [that], Q, HLH, BL, of, NLS

        l. 411   [Was], Q, HLH, BL, As, NLS

        l. 412   [*bends*], Q, HLH, bends, BL, NLS

        l. 413   [shall], Q, HLH, BL, will, NLS

               [*break*], Q, HLH, break, BL, NLS

        l. 417   rough, plain, BL

        l. 418   [my . . . thine], Q, HLH, BL, Thy . . . mine, NLS

        l. 420   [speak], Q, HLH, BL, say, NLS

        l. 421   [dreariness], Q, HLH, BL, weariness, NLS

        l. 425   [*once* was], Q, HLH, BL, once gave, NLS, BL†

        l. 429   [when], Q, HLH, BL, if, NLS

        l. 439   But, And, BL

        l. 441   [A seat in council or command in Spain], Q, HLH, A future power or present to maintain, BL, NLS

        l. 444   [Thou'st given], Q, HLH, BL, Thou gavest, NLS

        l. 447   [wandering], Q, HLH, walking, BL, NLS

        l. 448   [Some day to wander], Q, HLH, BL, For years of wandering NLS

        l. 454   [o'er], Q, HLH, BL, at, NLS

        l. 458   [subdue . . . and serve], Q, HLH, command . . . to stay, BL, command . . . to obey, NLS

        l. 461   [So], Q, HLH, BL, Then, NLS

        l. 464   [this world below], Q, HLH, this world of woe, BL, a world of woe, NLS

        l. 466   [altered], Q, HLH, BL, brightened, NLS

        l. 468   hardened, darkened, BL

        l. 470   ['neath], Q, HLH, in, BL, NLS

after l. 470   Q omits, HLH crosses out, but BL and NLS insert:

           It rests— mine labours—there the difference lies
           For mine will change but little when it dies

        l. 472   no, not, BL

TEXT l. 475 [Upon the hills of Spain], Q, HLH
On blood-red fields of Spain, BL, NLS
again, even, BL
l. 478 In watch-cloak wrapped, Wrapped in a watchcloak, BL
l. 482 [love], Q, HLH, BL, strive, NLS
l. 483 [But], Q, HLH, BL, Yet, NLS
l. 484 BL concludes here
l. 490 [scenes were], Q, HLH, scene was, NLS
l. 491 [them], Q, HLH, it, NLS
l. 493 [slumbers], Q, HLH, slumber, NLS
l. 495 [but], Q, HLH, as, NLS
l. 497 [a], Q, HLH, one, NLS, room, gloom, NLS†
l. 498 [its], Q, HLH, one, NLS
l. 505 [look . . . sainted], Q, HLH, eyes . . . parted, NLS
l. 508 [form . . . feeling], Q, HLH, *form . . . feeling*, NLS
l. 509 [looks . . . love], Q, HLH, *looks . . . love*, NLS
l. 510 [That o'er life's waters, guiding us from far], Q, HLH, That,
guiding wanderers o'er life's waves afar, NLS
l. 511 [life's], Q, HLH, death's, NLS
glisten, Q, HLH, glitter, NLS

Branwell worked hard on this poem, revising it apparently every two years, and in his last version consulting, it would seem, both his previous versions. G, pp. 154–9 thinks highly of the poem; M, p. 183 more realistically thinks it tedious. Attempts to read this poem in an autobiographical light might seem foolish, as Branwell wrote one version of it at Bradford, another at Broughton, and a third when he had returned home in very different fashion from *Sir Henry Tunstall*. Perhaps one reason for the poem's failure is that it is not autobiographical enough. However, in a draft of a letter to Blackwood's in the Luddenden Foot notebook, dated September 6th, 1842, it might seem that Branwell did see some resemblance between himself and his hero. He says, 'The piece endeavours, I fear feebly enough, to describe the harsh contrast between the mind changed by long absence from home, and the feelings kept flourishing in the hearts of those who have never wandered, and who vainly expect to find the heart returning as fresh as when they had bidden it farewell.'

p. 120   (*Black Comb*)   'Far off, and half revealed, 'mid shade and light'
Manuscript untraceable. First published in L, vol. I, p. 251. G, p. 168. Black Comb is the name of a hill five miles west of Broughton where Branwell was tutor at the house of Mr Posthlethwaite, and thus the date of 1840 would seem to be reasonable.

pp. 120–1   'Oh Thou, whose beams were most withdrawn'
Manuscript in BCL, 2 pp. of Notebook C. At beginning signed PBB and dated August 8th, 1841. In minuscule with little punctuation and some corrections. First published in BST¹, p. 72.

TEXT   l. 4   storms through which 'twould, track its course should, BCL†
        l. 6   storm away, nightlike day, BCL†
        l. 7   sound, light, BCL†
        l. 21   body, frame, BCL†
        l. 24   call Thy wrath to spare, give a humble prayer, BCL†

pp. 122–9   (*The Triumph of Mind over Body*)   'Man thinks too often that the ills of life'
Manuscript in BCH, 9 pp., $9'' \times 7''$, bound in blue morocco. Normal large handwriting, well punctuated and few corrections. Undated, but at end signed Northangerland. There are two other versions of this poem: the first in Notebook B, containing the first 120 lines, pp. 43–7, in small normal handwriting, with good punctuation and few corrections; the second in Notebook C which is partly in BCL, partly in BPM, in minuscule handwriting, some punctuation and corrections. Neither of these versions is signed or dated. The version in Notebook C is entitled *Lord Nelson* and was first published in BST¹, p. 74. The BCH version was published first in SHCBP, p. 374. Variants between this manuscript, the Notebook C manuscript (abbreviated to C below) and the printed version are recorded below. The Notebook B version is printed in full in Section 2, p. 228.

TEXT   l. 2   ceaseless, fruitless, C
        l. 3   With all its train of want, disease and care,
                Its fell disease, grim want and cankering care, C
        l. 5   That when such dark waves round the body roll,
                That faint and feeble proves the struggling soul, C
        l. 6   Feeble and faint will prove the struggling soul,
                Mid the dark waves that ever round it roll, C
        l. 8   that body binds, its body holds, C
        l. 10   Oppressed . . . forehead, Distressed . . . body, C
        l. 11   For none will . . . tell, They will not . . . prove, C
        l. 13   eloquent, long and deep, C
        l. 14   Prove, Are, C
        l. 15   syllable, word, just then, C
        l. 16   That . . . its, The . . . their, C
        l. 17   it, them, C
        l. 25   name, word, C
        l. 28   weary, desolate, C
    ll. 31–2   C omits
        l. 33   Thou hast given thy farewell to thine,
                A farewell given to thy, C
        l. 34   And tears of parting dim, And hot tears dimming all, C
        l. 35   I seem to see thee, Then thou perhaps wert, C
        l. 36   roughly o'er, high above, C
        l. 39   While . . . are straining, And . . . attentive, C
        l. 40   in, 'neath, C
        l. 48   winds whisper, wind whispered, C
        l. 52   storm-worn, wind-worn, C
                C then adds:
                Left him to dare his darts through many a year
                Of storm-tossed life—unbowed by pain or fear.
        l. 54   [on], o'er, BCH
                stern eyes sorrowed on, sailors bore away their, C
        l. 55   Borne, Struck, C
        l. 56   front unblenched, iron front, C
        l. 58   heaven-shaking, death dealing, C
        l. 60   but, and, C
        l. 62   Dyed, Stained, C

TEXT   l. 63   As, When, C
l. 64   first bedimmed, clouds first dimmed, C
l. 65   in, 'neath, C
l. 67   When, Then, C
l. 69   Then—From, But from, C
l. 72   wound ... caused his, blow ... made him, C
l. 74   should be, was, C
l. 78   cares and storms and battles, ocean storm and battle, C
ll. 83–4   lines reversed in C
l. 84   That death was tapping, He heard death tapping, C
l. 85   should, must, C
l. 88   his, the, C
l. 89   should, must, C
l. 90   mourners, watchers, C
l. 92   Should, Must, C
l. 94   A, For, C
l. 96   *to ... with*, to ... on, C
l. 97   would take a glorious, should only take his, C
l. 98   still, soft, C
l. 100   her ... sea, their ... free, C
l. 106   not of vague, not vulgar vain, C
l. 108   with, in, C
l. 109   Yet nought appears, There's nought to see, C
l. 114   They look at, They gaze on, C
after l. 116   C inserts:
         They see the spot where fell a star of glory
         The Finis to one page of England's story.
l. 120   A magic veil ... clouds, A veil ... cloudiness, C
l. 124   a generation's gathered, its shapelessness of mourning, C
l. 125   To shew, And show, C
l. 129   yon swollen torrent, a stream with swollen, C
ll. 133–4   C replaces by:
         He has been absent wandering many an hour
         As wild waves toss a solitary flower
l. 136   darling truant, missing darling, C
l. 143   in, mid, C
l. 144   Mother ... its, Say mother ... his, C
l. 145   Ah oft, since then, he heard the tempests sound,
         Oft since he saw the waters howling round, C

TEXT l. 146 Oft saw far mightier waters surging round,
            Oft heard unmoved, as then, the tempest sound, C

l. 148 Yet saw, But knew, C

l. 149 Be, let, C

l. 150 Sunk far behind the horizon's billowy,
        Be lost amid a distant ocean's, C

l. 151 And Lo! again, Return again, C

l. 156 undoubted sovereigns, mid storm and darkness, C
        Fear, FEAR, C

l. 158 timber, rafters, C

l. 163 its ... its, that ... those, C

l. 164 surely nought to do with, have nought to do with human, C

l. 165 For ... its, Where ... that, C

l. 166 Thine, Thy, C

l. 170 He, HE, C

l. 173 *He* asks, Asks, C

l. 180 As ... vanquished, For ... vanquished humbly, C

l. 181 *soul*, SOUL, C

l. 183 a, the, C

l. 184 Neath, In, C

l. 187 [once o'er, to him], he paid, was cheaply, BCH

l. 188 Honour on earth and happiness, Endless fame on earth and joy, C

l. 189 That, It, C

l. 190 O'er his, On that, C
        [childhood's sunshine], hours of childhood, BCH
        childhood long since, C

l. 191 which, that, C

after l. 192 C adds four lines:

        That spirit cared not that his worn out form
        Was soon to be a comrade of the worm,
        Nor shuddered at the icy hand of death
        So soon—so painfully to stop his breath.

ll. 193-5 C has:

        The guns were thundering fainter on his ear,
        More fading fast from sight that cabin drear,
        The place, the hour become less clearly known.

TEXT l. 199 Oh, But, C
  l. 202 one earthly hope, a hope of aught, C
  l. 204 The farewell beams of the descending,
      The parting glories of God's holy, C
  l. 205 Must . . . the . . . may, And . . . his . . . must, C
  l. 206 Mock my fast freezing, Mocking my wretched, C
  l. 207 Must feel a, Yet feel his, C
  l. 209 my, this, C
  l. 210 narrow, dreary, C
  l. 214 shall, should, C
  l. 217 They'll, They'd, C
  l. 219 *these*, those, C
  l. 220 faded, happy, C
  l. 221 As one who, Who kissed and, C
  l. 223 C omits
  l. 226 NELSON, Nelson, C
  l. 233 who own, beneath, C
  l. 235 frown, threat, C
  ll. 236–7 C has:

      When fate would crush us down—a steadier arm
      A firmer front—as stronger beats the storm.

  l. 240 restlessness, chance and change, C
  l. 242 holy . . . human, humble . . . foolish, C
  l. 249 I lag behind it sad, my own drag heavily, C
  l. 250 void of power to go, grovelling far below, C
  l. 251 hast made, mad'st, C
  l. 252 framed . . . sink in, made . . . bow to, C
  l. 253 which . . . mid, that . . . through, C
  l. 255 earth-born, earthly, C
  l. 257 which seems, to eyes, that seems involved, C
  l. 258 Involved in life's thick, In life's conflicting, C
  l. 259 holy calm, its own heaven, C
  l. 260 fleecy shine, shining fleece, C
  l. 261 mankind its beams so shaded see, so oft eclipsed men pity me, C
  l. 262 on this, at their, C

TEXT   l. 263   find itself, feel myself, C
                  [THEE], Thee, BCH

G, pp. 199–200; M, pp. 127–8. Nelson died in 1805 and, as all three
versions of the poem refer to a period of thirty-six years between
Nelson's death and the time of the poem, it is natural to suppose that
all three were written in 1841, although the sections of the poem in
Notebook C are scattered over a number of pages, some of which
include later material, and other poems in Notebook B would seem
to have been transcribed in 1837. In addition the variations between
the different versions are at least as extensive as those of *Sir Henry
Tunstall* written at two year intervals between 1838 and 1842. Never-
theless it seems probable, if not certain, that Branwell did write all
three versions of this poem in 1841, the Notebook C version being the
first, the Notebook B being an uncompleted fair copy and the BCH
version being the final version, possibly the one that, according to
F. H. Grundy, was sent to various people who thought highly of it.

p. 130   (*Sonnet*)   'Man thinks too often that his earth-born cares'
Manuscript in BPM, p. 2 of Notebook C. At beginning signed PBB
and dated September 3rd, 1841. In minuscule with little punctuation
and some corrections. First published in BST[1], p. 83.

TEXT   l. 1   earth-born cares, earthly life, BPM†
        l. 2   mind, soul, BPM†
        l. 11   lordling's, lordly, BPM*
        l. 14   Mid, From, BPM*

pp. 130–2   'Amid the world's wide din around'
Manuscript in BPM, pp. 4–5 of Notebook C. At beginning signed
PBB and dated September 11th, 1841. In minuscule with some punc-
tuation and corrections. First published in BST[1], p. 83.

TEXT   l. 25   [billow], billow's, BPM, soft wind's, BPM*
        l. 29   known so, remembered, BPM†
        l. 38   prospects, future, BPM*
        l. 42   With, And, BPM*

TEXT   l. 44   withered, darksome, BPM*
        l. 48   gloomy, swelling, BPM*
        l. 49   [he...his], I...my, BPM**
        l. 57   but, then, BPM*
        l. 68   Vincent, Nelson, BPM†

G, pp. 197–9. In this sordid surroundings at Luddenden Foot Bran-
well draws a contrast between his lot and the heroic deeds of others.

pp. 132–3   *On Landseer's Painting 'The Shepherds Chief Mourner'*
'The beams of Fame dry up Affection's tears'
Manuscript in BPM, 1 p., 5½″×6½″. Undated, but signed at end
Northangerland. In normal large handwriting, good punctuation and
corrections. A variant in BCL, part of Notebook C, unsigned and
undated, in normal small handwriting, little punctuation and some
corrections. First published in L, vol. I, p. 299.

TEXT   l. 4   [All that we follow through our chase of years],
                Ambition's pomp and pride devoid of fears, BPM**
                All that man follows through the whirl of years, BCL
        l. 5   our...our, has...his, BCL
                hope, heart, BPM†
        l. 6   Dim or destroy, Dazzle or drown, BCL
                which, that, BCL
        l. 7   form we, forms he, BCL, forms we, L
        l. 8   with Thee—our, so thou—Man's, BCL
                and, or, BCL
        l. 9   We, Man, BCL
        l. 10   [ties yet], ties, yet, L (though as printed in ms)
        l. 11   [form], *form*, BPM
        l. 12   THY, *Thy*, BCL
        l. 13   THEE, thee, BCL
        l. 14   For *him* whom thou, if Love had power, wouldst save,
                For him whom thou if love had strength could save, BCL
                For him—if love had power—thy love would save, BCL*
                For him thy love if love had power could save, BCL†

pp. 133–4   'The man who will not know another'
Manuscript untraceable presumably lost by F. H. Grundy who first
published them in *Pictures of the Past* (London, 1879), p. 78. There are,
however, two fragments in the BCH which clearly represent an earlier
version of the poem that Grundy claimed was especially composed
for a particular incident. These two manuscripts are in minuscule,
unsigned and undated. The first is 2½″ × 4″ with no punctuation and
one correction; the second, 6½″ × 4½″, no punctuation and no correc-
tions. They read as follows:

> The heart which cannot know another
> Which will not learn to sympathize,
> In whom the voice of friend or brother
> Unheard, unechoed, sleeps or dies,
> Between whom and the world around
> Can stretch no life uniting ties.

> The Heart which cannot know another,
> Which owns no lover friend or brother,
> In whom those names without reply
> Unechoed and unheeded die.

pp. 134–7   'The desolate earth, the wintry sky'
Manuscript in BPM, pp. 14, 18, 19 and 20 of Notebook C. At begin-
ning signed PBB and dated December 25 (not 15th) 1841. In a mixture
of minuscule and normal handwriting, with little punctuation and
many corrections, some of them illegible. First published in BST¹,
p. 88.

TEXT   l. 4   drear . . . sad, sad . . . drear, BPM†
       l. 5   bitter, pitiless, BPM†
       l. 12   joy, hope, BPM†
       l. 42   Man's mightiest victory, The souls that cannot die, BPM†
       l. 60   Though poor neglected blind and old,
            With might immortal didst unfold, BPM†
       l. 63   Misery must bow to mind, How misery bows to mind
            BPM*

TEXT l. 79   heart's, soul's, BPM†
      l. 83   wisdom, music, BPM*
      l. 84   his, he, BPM*
      l. 91   o'er despair, over care, BPM*
      l. 92   natural music, Harp of nature, BPM†

Christmas, presumably spent at Haworth, cannot have been very enjoyable for Branwell, as he reflected upon the difference between his lot and that of heroes in the past, even those who, as in this poem, had triumphed over adversity.

pp. 137–8   'O God! while I in pleasure's wiles'
Manuscript in BPM, p. 15 of Notebook C. Unsigned, but dated at beginning, December 19th, 1841. In large normal handwriting with little punctuation and some corrections. First published in BST¹, p. 91.

TEXT l. 5   sustaining, prophetic, BPM†
      l. 7   And see, to see, BPM†
      l. 12   Whom I no more must, For ever lost to, BPM†

G, p. 200; M, pp. 131–2. M compares this poem to a poem of Emily's, written at the same time and with the same hymn book imagery and metre, and argues quite forcefully that, had Branwell received the same intellectual discipline as Emily received with M. Heger his poetry might have developed as Emily's did, to establish and be established by her own personal religion.

pp. 138–40   (*The Afghan War*)   'Winds within our chimney thunder'
Manuscript untraceable. First published in LI, 7 May 1842. This jingoistic jingle was occasioned by the disastrous retreat of the British from Kabul in January 1842 during the first Afghan War. Compare 'When side by side, in twilight, sitting' in Section 3, p. 261.

TEXT l. 14   [We...One], *We...* one, LI
      l. 35   [is], are, LI
      l. 40   [Cruel], Unwept, LI

L, vol. I, pp. 301–5; G, p. 209.

pp. 140–1   (*The Epicurean's Song*)   'The visits of Sorrow'
Manuscript untraceable, but an earlier version is in Notebook B,
printed in Section 2, p. 243. First published in HG, 9 July 1842.

TEXT   l. 10   [awaken], waken, HG
       l. 28   [vanishing], the vanishing, HG
       l. 29   [night], that night, HG

L, vol. I, pp. 22–3.

pp. 141–54   (*Azrael, or Destruction's Eve*)   'Brothers and men! one
moment stay'
Manuscript in BPM, pp. 64–76 of Notebook B, but possibly not really
part of this notebook. Undated and unsigned. The manuscript seems
incomplete. In small normal handwriting with some punctuation and
few corrections. First published in L, vol. I, p. 26, but only the first
48 lines, then in BST², pp. 63–77. Clearly Branwell revised the
manuscript before he sent it to Leyland, but we do not have the
revised manuscript.

TEXT   l. 4   God's blest mercy yet can, Mercy have power to, BPM
       l. 5   Will you compel, Now will you force, BPM
       l. 8   *last*, last, BPM
       l. 12   passed, past, BPM
       l. 15   the, that, BPM
       l. 28   and for its peace alone, beneath its maker's throne, BPM
       l. 30   which... joy, that... joys, BPM
       l. 40   No paragraph in BPM
       l. 41   strife of civil war, coming strife of war, BPM
       l. 42   beams within, brews above, BPM
       l. 46   Piled boding above, Surrounding all heaven's, BPM
       l. 67   Both semi-colons are editorial intrusions
       l. 79   New paragraph, BPM
       l. 82   No gap, new paragraph, BPM
       l. 84   The reading of BPM is that of the footnotes
       l. 131 country-men, countrymen, BPM
       l. 157 No gap, BPM

TEXT   l. 183   pour, pore, BPM
       l. 188   Azrael (*solus loquitur*), Azrael solus loquitur, BPM
       l. 211   shall, should, BPM
       l. 234   Am, I'm, BPM†
       l. 235   Yet, Still, BPM†
       l. 282   frightened, frighted, BPM
       l. 287   THOU, Thou, BPM
       l. 304   *back*, back, BPM
       l. 313   to, on, BPM
       l. 396   seized, took, BPM†
       l. 409   MIDNIGHT, Midnight, BPM
       l. 441   So, But, BPM†

M, pp. 83, 87–8; L, vol. I, pp. 26–8. According to Dearden this was
the manuscript Branwell was going to produce at the Cross Roads
Inn, but instead produced the opening chapters of a novel, claimed by
some to be *Wuthering Heights*. It is impossible to date this incident
accurately, but the presence of *Azrael* in Notebook B would suggest,
but not prove, that *Azrael* was written as early as 1838. The poem
produced in challenge at the Cross Roads Inn was meant to be especi-
ally composed for the occasion, but Branwell may have cheated in
bringing a later revision, and thus the traditional date of the Cross
Roads encounter, namely 1842, may still stand, and even this encoun-
ter hardly proves that *Wuthering Heights* was written as early as 1842.
Branwell's atheism in espousing the cause of Azrael in open revolt
against God and Noah is interesting.

p. 155   (*The Callousness Produced by Care*)   'Why hold young eyes the
fullest fount of tears'
Manuscript in BPM, 1 p., 5½″ × 6¼″. Undated, but signed at end
Northangerland. In normal large handwriting with good punctuation
and no corrections. First published, HG, 7 May, 1842.

TEXT   l. 4   [waken], wake their, HG
       l. 5   [springtide], spring tide, HG
       l. 11   [other's pains—so], comrades dying, and, HG

TEXT   l. 12   [coldly], coldest, HG
       l. 13   [will delight], oft delights, HG
       l. 14   [will make], oft makes, HG

L, vol. I, p. 298; G, p. 209; M, pp. 170–1 (in the context of 1846).

p. 155   (*Peaceful Death and Painful Life*) 'Why dost thou sorrow for the happy dead?'
Manuscript in BPM, 1 p., 5½″ × 6¼″. Undated, but signed at end Northangerland. In normal large handwriting, with some punctuation and one correction. First published in HG, 14 May 1842. There is an earlier variant in BCH, 1 p., 7″ × 4″, unsigned and undated, in minuscule with little punctuation and one correction, which I have printed in Section 3, p. 258.

TEXT   l. 3   [shall], can, HG
      l. 6   [that], the, HG
      l. 9   [Dead alive], *dead alive*, HG
      l. 10   whose life departs, whose spirit flies, BPM†
      l. 13   [HE], *He*, HG
      l. 14   [REAL], *Real*, HG

L, vol. I, p. 300; G, pp. 209–10. L speaks highly of the beauty of this and the preceding sonnet, while G talks about the disillusioned path Branwell was treading.

p. 156   (*The Emigrant. I*) 'When sink from sight the landmarks of our Home'
Manuscript in BPM, 1 p., 9″ × 7¼″. At end signed Northangerland and dated May 6th, 1845. In normal large handwriting with good punctuation and no corrections. First published in L, vol. II, p. 46. Text as printed. G, p. 238. Written just before Branwell's disgrace at Thorp Green it marks the end of a three year period, in which either Branwell wrote very little poetry, or else the poetry he wrote has been lost.

p. 156   (*The Emigrant. II*)   'When, after his long day, consumed in toil'
Manuscript untraceable. First published in L, vol. II, p. 46. G, p. 238.

pp. 157-8   'I saw a picture yesterday'
Manuscript in BCL, 2 pp., 9″ × 7¼″. Unsigned and undated. Written in normal large handwriting with some punctuation and many (some illegible) corrections. First published in SHCBP, p. 409.

TEXT   l. 15   I must believe her feebler still,
                  How little I must prize her power, BCL†
         l. 17   effort. . . picture, picture. . . creature, BCL†
         l. 26   adorn, amend, BCL†
         l. 39   far beyond, worthy of, BCL†

Presumably this belongs to the post-Thorp Green period although Branwell is still fairly optimistic about his love.

pp. 158-62   (*Juan Fernandez*)   'A lonely speck in ocean's waste'
Manuscript in BCH, 6 pp., 9″ × 7¼″. Bound in blue morocco. Unsigned and undated. In large normal handwriting with some punctuation and some corrections. First published in SHCBP, p. 410.

TEXT   l. 6   viewed, saw, BCH†
         l. 12   [hand], head, BCH
         l. 14   Worn out, Outworn, BCH†
         l. 39   whitened, maddening, BCH†
         l. 48   parting, dying, BCH†
         l. 117   Or kindness of affinity, The blood relation or the friend,
                  BCH†

G, pp. 260-2; M, p. 180. The word Lydia in Greek handwriting, this being the name of Mrs Robinson and her eldest daughter, and the note of desperation at the end of the poem suggest a date after the Thorp Green debacle.

pp. 163–5 (*Penmaenmawr*) 'These winds, these clouds, this chill November storm'
Manuscript untraceable. First published in L, vol. II, p. 101 who gives also a letter from Branwell on November 25th, 1845, asking that the poem be forwarded to the *Halifax Guardian*. He had been on a steamer trip to North Wales after his disgrace at Thorp Green, al-thought memories of Thorp Green near the Yorkshire Ouse would seem to have inspired the reference to his angel in line 64. L, vol. II, pp. 99–106; G, pp. 250–1; M, pp. 170–6.

pp. 166–7 (*Real Rest*) 'I see a corpse upon the waters lie'
Manuscript untraceable. First published in L, vol. II, p. 95. L, vol. II, pp. 94–8; M, p. 180. L compares and contrasts poems of Emily and Charlotte.

pp. 168–70 *Epistle from a Father to a Child in her Grave* 'From Earth,—whose life-reviving April showers'
Manuscript untraceable. First published in L, vol. II, p. 128 with the date April 3rd 1846. L, vol. II, pp. 128–30; M, pp. 181–2. M speculates on who the child might be and notes the schizophrenic way Branwell contrives to be outside his body, looking down on his other self.

p. 170 (*Sonnet*) 'When all our cheerful hours seem gone for ever'
Manuscript in BCL, p. 4 of a four-page letter, $6\frac{1}{2}'' \times 4''$, to Leyland signed P. B. Brontë, but undated. In small normal handwriting with good punctuation and no corrections. First published in L, vol. II, p. 134 who gives the date as April 28th, 1846.

TEXT   l. 9 [And if, toward her grave—Death's dreary road—]
              And if—toward her grave—Death's dreary road, BCL

L, vol. II, p. 134; M, p. 186. Though maudlin the sonnet shows a certain technical skill, and could match some of Rossetti's to which it is strangely similar.

pp. 170–1 'While fabled scenes and fancied forms'
Manuscript in BCL, 1 p., 7″ × 4½″. Unsigned and undated. In normal
large handwriting with little punctuation and no corrections. First
published in SHCBP, p. 422. Text as published.

pp. 171–4 *Morley Hall* 'When Life's youth, overcast by gathering
clouds'
Manuscript in BPM, 4 pp., 9¼″ × 7″. Unsigned and undated. In normal
large handwriting with some punctuation and many illegible correc-
tions. First published in L, vol. II, p. 246, where the date of composi-
tion is given as 1846 and 1847.

TEXT   l. 14   [father's], fathers', BPM
        l. 18   flowering, flower bearing, BPM†
                worthless, useless, BPM†
        l. 47   [which once], which—once, BPM
        l. 61   [their], its, BPM**
        l. 71   [antique], ancient, BPM
                [mansion], mansions BPM

L, vol. II, pp. 242–9; G, pp. 265, 270; M, pp. 183–4. M is very rude
about this effort which had occupied Branwell nearly a year. He had
written to Leyland in April 1846 asking for details of the history of
Morley Hall, and in October 1846 said that *Morley Hall* was in the
eighth month of her pregnancy and hoped to be delivered of a fine
thumping boy which he hoped to christen Homer. So clearly Branwell
had intended his poem to be epic, and the result is very feeble. There
is a certain degeneration apparent in the handwriting of the manu-
script we possess, but it is interestingly accompanied by a sketch of
Morley Hall in ruins in 1847, and as it would stand rebuilt in 1947.
This sketch is not without merit, and perhaps has some optimism
about it.

pp. 174–7 *The End of All* 'In that unpitying Winter's night'
Manuscript untraceable. First published in L, vol. II, p. 250, presum-
ably from a late version which Branwell revised and adapted towards

the end of his life to meet his changing circumstance, but there is a much earlier version in Notebook B, written in 1837, published in Section 2, p. 240. L, vol. II, pp. 250–4. There is something deeply pathetic about Branwell revising his earlier manuscripts at this stage in his life.

pp. 177–80 *Percy Hall* 'The westering sunbeams smiled on Percy Hall'
Manuscript untraceable apart from a fragment of the first 14 lines of a different version. First published in L, vol. II, p. 259. The fragment of the alternative version is in BPM, 1 p., $9'' \times 7''$. Undated and unsigned. In normal large handwriting with no punctuation or corrections. It is as follows:

> The westering sunshine smiled on Percy Hall
> And gilt the ivy on its aged wall,
> Where Mary sat to feel the fanning breeze
> And hear its music murmuring 'mid the trees
>
> She had reclined in that secluded bower
> Throughout the afternoon, while hour on hour
> Stole softly past her, shining till the shades
> Stretched—slowly lengthening in the grassy glades—
> Yet she reclined as if she scarce knew how
> The time wore on with heaven-directed brow,
> And closing eyes which only ope'd whene'er
> Her face was fanned by summer's evening air.
>
> She seemed that day a weariness to feel
> As if upon her sleep might almost steal,
> And scarce could rouse her failing thoughts to care
> For day or hour or what she was or where.

L, vol. II, pp. 259–66.

SECTION 2

These poems are all to be found in Notebook B. The words in italics after the title of each poem in these notes represent Branwell's own notes before and after each poem. I have not reproduced a multiplicity of signatures, the place of composition (invariably Haworth) or the number of lines. There are sometimes three dates mentioned, the date on which the events were supposed to occur being added to the dates of transcription and composition. On the first two pages of the notebook Branwell wrote down a list of poems, including the date when they were composed, as opposed to transcribed, and the number of lines, a detail which seemed to obsess him. The last poem so recorded is *Percy's Musings upon the Battle of Edwardston*, p. 222. Several other poems follow; the majority of these would appear to be written in 1837, the year Branwell transcribed the first twenty-five poems. We know this because in some cases Branwell has added the date, and because on the second page of the notebook he wrote down a list of numbers of lines, most of which correspond to the poems. For exceptions to this rule see the note to the poem on p. 228.

In the case of the first twenty-five poems I have recorded the place where the original poem can be found, and where it has been published, but I have not printed the many textual variations, nor been especially thorough in searching through Branwell's scattered prose manuscripts for the original poems. It would seem that the printing of these poems in their original version should take place when and if Branwell's prose juvenilia are properly edited. It is an open question whether this is a worthwhile task; the poems here printed, after revision, are of a very uneven quality, with a strong element of plagiarism in them, nor do we lose a great deal by not knowing the Angrian background for certain.

pp. 183–4   *The Vision of Velino*   'I see through Heaven with raven wings'

Composed by W. H. Warner on the night of battle December 3rd, 1833. Corrected March 9th, 1837.
Originally composed as part of *An Historical Narrative of the War of Encroachment*, recorded by M. Christian in 'A Census of Brontë Manuscripts in the USA', *The Trollopian*, II (1947–8), p. 253 as being in the collection of Mrs P. A. Valentine, Chicago, USA, previously unpublished.

TEXT   l. 26   Together, All festering†

R, p. 76. The War of Encroachment would seem to involve an attack to the southeast of Verdopolis before the foundation of Angria. Warner is, however, an important character in Angrian history, a loyal if unexciting friend of Zamorna, serving him in a number of capacities.

pp. 184–6   *The CXXXVIIth Psalm* 'By the still streams of Babylon'
Composed by Alexander Percy as words to his celebrated meter 'The Captivity'. Written by P. B. B. in 1834. Transcribed March 9, 1837.
Original is untraceable. Based on a similar poem by Cowper according to H. See also Byron's *Hebrew Melodies*. Previously unpublished.

pp. 186–7   *Song* 'I saw Her in the Crowded hall'
Composed by Marseilles, June 26th, 1834. Transcribed and amended, March 9th, 1837.
First version published in SHCBM, vol. I, pp. 410–11 as part of *The Wool is Rising*, manuscript in BL.

TEXT   l. 5   circlet round, ivory of†

R, p. 77 for the best account of *The Wool is Rising*, describing the setting up of the Angrian kingdom.

pp. 187–90   *The Rover* 'Sail fast, sail fast, my gallant ship! Thy Ocean thunders round thee'

Composed by the Earl of Northangerland, May 1834. Transcribed and corrected, March 9th, 1837.
First version published in SHCBM, vol. I, pp. 408–10 as part of *The Wool is Rising*, manuscript in BL.

TEXT   l. 55   light, gloom†

For Percy's exploits as a pirate see M, p. 62.

pp. 190–2   *Augusta*   'Augusta! Though I'm far away'
Written by Alexander Percy in 1812 at the Philosopher's Isle, but by P.B.B. in Spring 1834. Transcribed March 10th, 1837.
Originally composed as part of *The Life of Field Marshal The Right Honourable Alexander Percy, Earl of Northangerland*, manuscript in BCL, shortly to be published by the University of Leeds. Augusta di Segovia, the first wife of Percy, appears briefly in *Harriet II*, living in Jordan Hall. See M, pp. 61–5.

pp. 192–3   *Sound the Loud Trumpet*   'Sound the loud Trumpet o'er Africa's bright sea'
The National Song of Angria. Composed by H. Hastings for the Coronation of Adrian Augustus First King of Angria, Spring 1834. Transcribed March 10th, 1837.
First version published in SHCBM, vol. I, pp. 435–6 as part of *The Coronation of Arthur Augustus King of Angria*, manuscript in BCL. Hastings becomes an important figure in the later and more mature juvenilia of both Charlotte and Branwell. Here he is just mouthing patriotic songs during the founding of the Angrian kingdom. Variant in BPM of lines 14 to end, 1 p., $8\frac{1}{4}'' \times 5''$. Unsigned and undated. In minuscule with little punctuation and some illegible corrections.

TEXT   l. 13   has flown, hath gone, BPM
        l. 14   sunbeams … smile, sunbeam … smiles, BPM
        l. 16   and Adrian, Zamorna, BPM
        l. 18   Hurry their floods toward, Bearest thy streams to, BPM

TEXT   l. 19   our, thy, BPM†
        l. 20   life-giving, glittering, BPM
        l. 21   that shadowing, which high from, BPM
        l. 23   each summit and valley and,
               your torrents and deep shadowed, BPM
        l. 24   Adrian has, Zamorna hath, BPM
        l. 25   tempests and, storms and its, BPM
        l. 27   the West where the suns ever,
               the East in its summer sun, BPM
        l. 33   his, its, BPM
        l. 35   Midnight, darkness, BPM
        l. 37   join hearts, join tongues and hearts, BPM
        l. 38   arising, hath risen, BPM

pp. 193–4   *The Angrian Hymn*   'Shine on us, God of Angria, shine'
Composed by W. H. Warner Esqr, M.P. on the Coronation of Adrian the 1st, Spring 1834. Greatly altered and enlarged by P.B.B–te, March 11th, 1837.
First version published as part of *The Coronation of Arthur Augustus, King of Angria* in SHCBM, vol. I, pp. 436–7, manuscript in BCL.

pp. 194–6   *The Angrian Welcome*   'Welcome, Heroes, to the War'
Composed by Hastings, October 1834. Transcribed by P.B.B., March 11th, 1837.
First version, published as part of *The Opening of the Angrian Parliament* in SHCBM, vol. I, pp. 463–4, manuscript in BCL. Branwell was keenly interested in politics, and, if the politics of Angria seem a little remote from those of today, we must remember that it was in November 1834 that King William IV dismissed the Whig government. See G, p. 87.

pp. 196–7   *Northangerland's Name.*   'History sat by her pillar of fame'
Composed by Hastings, Novr. 1834. Transcribed March 11th, 1837.

First version published as part of *The Opening of the Angrian Parliament* in SHCBM, vol. I, pp. 465–6, manuscript in BCL.

TEXT   l. 1   sat, stood†

pp. 197–8   *Morning*   'Morn comes and with it all the stir of morn'
Written at Gazemba by Hastings, Dec. 6th, 1834. Transcribed March 11th, 1837.
Originally part of a narrative bound together as *Henry Hastings* in HRT, previously unpublished. There is little difference between the two manuscripts in spite of the difference in dates, and even the early version shows a certain amount of maturity with the world-weary Branwell finding it easy to adopt the persona of Hastings.

pp. 198–9   *Lines*   'We leave our bodies in the Tomb'
Composed by Percy and adapted by him to music. Transcribed and corrected, March 11th, 1837.
Originally composed in 1834 as part of *The Life of Field Marshal The Right Honourable Alexander Percy Earl of Northangerland*, manuscript in BCL, shortly to be published by Leeds University.

pp. 199–207   *An Hour's Musings on the Atlantic*   'Blow, ye wild winds, wilder blow'
Composed off Norway by Alexander Percy, 1818. Transcribed and corrected May 2nd, 1837.
First version, dated November 1834, published in SHCBM, vol. II, pp. 55–62, manuscript in BPM.

TEXT   l. 103   [I sought, but found no pleasure then],
                     I paid for peace and purchased pain** (added in normal handwriting)
         l. 129   A note here: 'This whole passage, if as I fear it contradicts in one or two places the rest of the poem, ought at some time to be either cancelled or amended.'

TEXT   l. 170   And, And only†
       l. 171   glimmer, struggle†
       l. 197   shattered, torn and†
       l. 263   Thunder above the whitening sea,
                Whiten above the thundering sea*
       l. 276   o'er, above†

Percy, who has improbably sailed from Africa to Norway, ponders over his past life, in particular the death of his wife Mary, a recurring theme in the SHCBP poems. G, pp. 85–6, strains after an auto-biographical interpretation; M, pp. 61–2, fills in the background to the poem.

pp. 207–9   *Thermopylae*   'Thermopylae's tremendous Height'
Written January 19, 1835. Transcribed May 14th, 1837.
Original is now untraceable. Previous poems on this subject are printed in Sections 1 and 3, pp. 5 and 249, but do not have the topical political stance. Branwell was presumably thinking of the change in government in November 1834.

pp. 209–10   *Song*   'Son of Heaven, in heavenly musing'
Written by Percy in 1813, P. B. Brontë, written Oct. 20th, 1835. Transcribed May 14th, 1837.
Originally composed as part of *The Life of Field Marshal, The Right Honourable Alexander Percy, Earl of Northangerland*, manuscript in BCL, shortly to be published by Leeds University.

pp. 210–11   *The Doubter's Hymn*   'Life is a passing sleep'
Composed by Alexr. Percy, 1813. Written Nov. 1835. Transcribed May 14th, 1837.
Originally composed as part of *The Life of Field Marshal, The Right Honourable Alexander Percy, Earl of Northangerland*, manuscript in BCL, shortly to be published by Leeds University.

p. 211   *Song*   'Thou art gone, but I am here'
Written by Percy in 1814. Written Nov. 17th, 1835. Transcribed May 14th, 1837.
Originally composed as part of *The Life of Field Marshal, The Right Honourable Alexander Percy, Earl of Northangerland,* manuscript in BCL, shortly to be published by Leeds University.

pp. 211–12   *Song*   'Frozen fast is my heart at last'
Written by Percy, 1814. Written Nov. 17th, 1835. Transcribed May 14th, 1837.
Originally composed as part of *The Life of Field Marshal, The Right Honourable Alexander Percy, Earl of Northangerland,* manuscript in BCL, shortly to be published by Leeds University.

p. 212   *Lines*   'Now then I am alone'
Written by Percy on his Departure from Africa, 1818. Written Dec. 17th, 1835. Transcribed May 14th, 1837.
Original is now untraceable. Percy here refers again to exile from Africa, but he would seem, if the confused accounts of the prose narratives in the *History of Angria* can be believed, to have returned in triumph, forcing Zamorna into exile.

TEXT   l. 14   time passed, what hath†

pp. 213–14   *The Spirit of Poetry*   'List to the sound that swells alone'
Written (I believe) in 1835. Altered and amended, May 16th, 1837.
Original is now untraceable. Previously unpublished.

TEXT   l. 26   Loch Maris's, the lonely†

pp. 214–16   *An Angrian Battle Song*   'Storms are waking to inspire us'
Composed by H. Hastings. Written January 1836. Transcribed May 26th, 1837.

Originally composed as part of *History of Angria* II, manuscript in BPM, published in SHCBM, vol. II, p. 117. The history of Angria is extremely confused; this is partly Branwell's fault, partly the fault of T. J. Wise for splitting up the already incoherent saga. But it would appear that Northangerland returning from exile and in alliance with the French and Ashantees defeated Zamorna, forcing him too into exile. The reader's interest in the military and political manoeuvres of this campaign is not very great, and most readers have concentrated on the predicament of Mary, Northangerland's daughter and Zamorna's wife.

pp. 216–18   *The Battle Eve*   'Alone upon Zamorna's plain'
Composed by Lord Richton. Written July 9th, 1836. Transcribed May 26th, 1837.
Original is now untraceable. Previously unpublished.

TEXT   l. 31   lonely, present*
       l. 44   for aye, away*

Viscount Richton is Baron John Flower, another Angrian worthy, narrator of some of Branwell's stories: he had originally been Captain John Flower.

pp. 218–19   *Ashworth's Hymn*   'Before Jehovah's awful Throne'
Composed by Percy. Written May 4th, 1836. Transcribed May 26th, 1837.
Originally composed as part of the *History of Angria* IV, manuscript in BCL, published (in facsimile) in SHCBM, vol. II, p. 172. The first line is taken from a hymn by Isaac Watts.

pp. 219–21   *Lucifer*   'Star of the West, whose beams arise'
Composed by Charles Wentworth. Written June 22nd, 1836. Transcribed May 27th, 1837.
Probably originally composed as part of the *History of Angria*, though bound in HRT as part of *Henry Hastings*. Previously unpublished.

pp. 221–2   *Lines*   'Now heavily in clouds comes on the day'
Composed at daybreak before the Revolution of June 26th, 1836 by Percy.
Written in June, 1836. Transcribed May 27th, 1837.
Original probably part of the *History of Angria*, is untraceable.
Previously unpublished.

pp. 222–7   *Percy's Musings upon the Battle of Edwardston*   'Through
the hoarse howling of the storm'
Written June 22nd, 1836. Transcribed May 30th, 1837.
Original, probably part of the *History of Angria*, is untraceable. Variant
of first 26 lines in BPM, 1 p., $7\frac{1}{4}'' \times 4\frac{3}{4}''$, unsigned and undated, in
minuscule with little punctuation and some illegible corrections.

TEXT   l. 4   was, is, BPM
        l. 5   glimpse, glance, BPM
        l. 13 blast, blasts, BPM
        l. 15 With dying thunder, That heavily are, BPM
        l. 17 And loud and louder peals the cry,
               With whitening clouds which seem to fly, BPM
        l. 18 Sent up with that tremendous,
               Affrighted from that ceaseless, BPM
        l. 19 Where-as, And there, BPM
               broad before, dashed with gore, BPM
        l. 21 roughened, their rough, BPM
        l. 151 did it fall, did he gaze†

pp. 227–8   *Queen Mary's Grave*   'I stand beside Queen Mary's grave
'neath Alnwick's holy dome'
See note on continuation of this poem in Section 3, p. 257. Original
dated December 10th, 1836 in the library of Roger W. Barrett,
Kenilworth, Illinois.

pp. 228–31   'Man thinks too often that the ills of life'
Probably an intrusion into this notebook. On the second page of the
notebook Branwell gives a list of titles, dates and numbers of lines.

To this he has added other figures, presumably the number of lines of additional poems. There is no figure that fits this poem, *Queen Mary's Grave* or *Azrael*. This poem is probably the uncompleted second draft of the poem on Nelson written in 1841, see Section 1, p. 122.

pp. 231–9   *A Fragment*   'The Clouds are rolled away—the light'
Rough draft 1814. Written from May 4th to June 15th, 1837. Transcribed June 16th, 1837.
A prose fragment precedes and follows this. Apparently either an early draft or a revised version of the poem known as *Caroline*, in Section 1, p. 66. This text, previously unpublished, shows considerable differences, and, although one page would appear to be missing, may well represent a final copy.

TEXT   l. 103   Still was her, And her white†
       l. 141   One page would seem to be missing here
       l. 190   midnight, darksome†

p. 239   *Mary's Prayer*   'Remember Me when Death's dark wing'
June 16th, 1837. Previously unpublished.
It is difficult to know whether Mary is here the daughter or the wife of Northangerland.

pp. 240–3   'Upon that dreary winter's night'
December 15th, 1837.
An earlier version of the very late *The End of All* printed in Section 1, p. 174. This manuscript has become detached from Notebook B, but clearly is in place here, both because the torn pages fit the gaps in the notebook, and because Branwell records on page 2 of Notebook B a poem of 112 lines.

pp. 243–4   *Song*   'The Present day's sorrow'
By Henry Hastings. Written December 11th, 1837.
An earlier version of the *Epicurean's Song* in Section 1, p. 140. Previously unpublished.

pp. 244-5   *Sonnet*   'Why hold young eyes the fullest fount of tears'
Composed by Northangerland. Written December 13th, 1837.
An earlier version of a similar sonnet in Section 1, p. 155. Previously
unpublished.

pp. 245-6   *An Analogy*   'Of Earth beneath how small a space'
Composed by Warner H. Warner Esqr.
Previously unpublished. Another ten lines with the date would seem
to be missing, since Branwell records a poem of sixty lines in his notes
on page 2 of Notebook B.

TEXT   l. 10   yon, that†
       l. 49   How truly seems its night our friend,
               How seems their night our only friend*

SECTION 3

p. 249 'When on the thorny bed of death.
(2 versions)
Manuscripts in BPM, each on 1 p., 8½″ × 5½″. Unsigned and undated,
but approximately 1835. In minuscule with little punctuation, and
some illegible corrections. Previously unpublished. Bears some
relation to *Misery, Part I* in Section 1, p. 12.

pp. 249–51 'Now the sweet hour of closing day'
Manuscript in BPM, 1 p., 8½″ × 5½″. Unsigned and undated, but
approximately 1835. In minuscule with little punctuation and some
corrections. Previously unpublished.

TEXT   l. 1   sweet…closing, calm…evening, BPM†
         l. 21   smiling, silent, BPM†
         l. 22   signs of life and, silent signs of, BPM†

See poems on the same subject in Sections 1 and 2, pp. 5 and 207.

p. 251 'He rode across the moor at night'
Manuscript in BPM, p. 1 of Notebook A. Unsigned and undated, but
approximately 1836. In large handwriting, not very similar to Bran-
well's normal hand. No punctuation and many blots. Unpublished.

p. 251 'Our hopes on earth seem wholly gone'
Manuscript in BCH, 1 p., 7⅞″ × 4⅛″. Unsigned and undated, but
approximately 1836. In minuscule with little punctuation and no
corrections. First published in BC, p. 50. The wife of Northangerland
is here referred to. Bears some relation to a number of poems, in
particular *The End of All*, p. 174.

pp. 251–2 'The moon in glory mounts above'
Manuscript in BPM, 1 p., 7″ × 4″. Unsigned and undated, but
approximately 1836. In minuscule with little punctuation and some

corrections. On the same page as part of 'Still and bright, in twilight shining', p. 39, and would appear to be part of that poem. Previously unpublished.

p. 252   'A Breeze embued with rich perfumes'
Manuscript in BCL, 1 p. Unsigned and undated, but approximately 1836. On the same page as six-line variant of 'The heart which cannot know another'. In minuscule with no punctuation and no corrections. First published in BC, p. 52.

pp. 252–7   'Behold the waste of waving sea'
Manuscript in BPM, pp. 25–8 of Notebook A. At beginning signed PBB and dated October 4th, 1836. In minuscule with little punctuation and few corrections. First published in SHCBM, vol. II, pp. 235–9.

TEXT   l. 47   'mid, o'er, BPM†
         l. 81   man to man, hand to hand, BPM†

Percy's early exploits as a pirate seem here recalled.

pp. 257–8   'What seek my eyes? They rest not on the columns arching o'er me'
A continuation of *Queen Mary's Grave* in Section 2, p. 227. The text is taken from H's notes; he says that he has taken it from a transcript supplied by Wise. In M. G. Christian, 'A Census of Brontë Manuscripts in the USA', *The Trollopian*, II (1947–8), p. 256 there is a reference to a poem of 80 lines entitled *Queen Mary's Grave*, at the beginning signed PBB, dated Dec. 10th 1836 and this poem is said to be in the library of Roger W. Barrett, Kenilworth, Illinois.

pp. 258–9   'Cease, mourner, cease thy sorrowing for the dead'
Manuscript in BCH, 1 p., $7\frac{1}{4}'' \times 4\frac{1}{2}''$, bound in morocco by Riviere. Unsigned and undated, but bound with a manuscript signed and

dated Oct. 20, 1837. In minuscule with little punctuation and one correction. Unpublished, though an earlier version of the sonnet published in HG, in June 1842, see p. 155.

TEXT   l. 10   Life, Hope, BCH†

p. 259   'Drink to me only with thine eyes'
This and the following poem I have taken from transcripts by H who says they form part of a short prose narrative, at the beginning signed PBB and dated Feb. 4th, 1839. Manuscript untraceable.

pp. 259–60   'From the thunder of the battle'
See note on previous poem.

p. 260   'Far up in heaven I view the brightest star'
Manuscript in BPM, p. 2 of Notebook C. Unsigned and undated but on same page as a poem dated Sept. 3rd. 1841. In minuscule with no punctuation or corrections. First published in BST¹, p. 83.

p. 260   *Robert Burns*   'He little knows—whose life has smoothly passed'
Manuscript in BPM, p. 11 of Notebook C. Unsigned and undated, but approximately 1842. In minuscule with no punctuation and no corrections. First published in BST¹, p. 86.

p. 261   'When first old Time with me shook hands'
Manuscript in BCL, part of Notebook C. Unsigned and undated, but approximately 1842. In minuscule with no punctuation and one correction. First published in BST¹, p. 87.

TEXT   l. 4   life's, my, BCL†

pp. 261-2 'When side by side, at twilight, sitting'
Manuscript in BPM, pp. 11-13 of Notebook C. At beginning signed
PBB and dated April 25th, 1842. In minuscule with little punctuation
and some corrections. First published in BST¹, p. 92.

TEXT   l. 8   begins, drives on, BPM*
         l. 27   through, o'er, BPM*

Compare *The Afghan War*, p. 138.

pp. 262-3 *Thorp Green* 'I sit, this evening, far away'
Manuscript in BCL, part of Notebook C. At beginning signed PBB
and dated March 30th, 1843. In minuscule with little punctuation and
some corrections. First published in BST¹, p. 95.

TEXT   l. 3   reminds my soul, calls to mind, BCL†
          l. 4   Of happy, The hours gone, BCL†
          l. 5   Unwelcome . . . unthought, Unthought . . . unwelcome,
                  BCL†
      after l. 8   Two erased lines in BCL:
                  I seek for what has smiled one hour
                  And in the next has flown.
          l. 12   thoughts, scenes, BCL†
          l. 14   troubled thoughts, disappointment's frowns, BCL†
          l. 16   scenes, thoughts, BCL†

G, p. 222; M, pp. 151-2, comment on the despondent mood and
dispirited hymn-book jingle. It is difficult to know why no other poem
survives from the period when Branwell was at Thorp Green.

pp. 263-4 'By Babel's waters Israel long ago'
Manuscript in BCH, 2 pp., 9″ × 7½″. Unsigned and undated, but about
1845. In large normal handwriting with some punctuation and some
corrections. Previously unpublished.

TEXT   l. 8   rules, dwells, BCH†
        l. 20   could, would, BCH†
        l. 24   murmured, muttered, BCH†
        l. 39   Sleeping, Resting, BCH†
        l. 40   Waking, Working, BCH†
        l. 47   break, burst, BCH†
        l. 49   vessel, ship, BCH†

The handwriting and subject matter, similar to poems like *Juan Fernandez* and *Morley Hall* suggest a date after 1845. Branwell works over his old heroes; Byron appears in person for the first and last time.

p. 265   'Home thoughts are not with me'
Manuscript in BCL, 1 p. of a four-page letter, $6\frac{1}{2}" \times 4"$, to Leyland. Signed P. B. Brontë and dated by Leyland April 28th, 1846. In normal small handwriting with good punctuation and no corrections. Previously unpublished. Text as printed. One does not know how far to take this poem as an autobiographical confession, and how many times Branwell had indeed pressed Mrs Robinson's breast.

p. 265   'My soul is flown'
Manuscript in BCL, accompanying sketches sent to Leyland in 1846. In normal small handwriting with good punctuation and no corrections. Previously unpublished. Text as printed.

pp. 265–6   'Say Dr Wheelhouse is a jewel'
Manuscript in BCL, pp. 5–7 of a notebook, $7" \times 4\frac{1}{2}"$. The poem is much longer, but several pages have been rubbed so as to be illegible. Unsigned and undated, but approximately 1847. In large normal handwriting with some illegible corrections and punctuation largely consisting of dashes. M, p. 201. Dr Wheelhouse was the doctor in Haworth, and this poem clearly dates to the last year of Branwell's life. Hatfield refused to print it on the grounds that it was drivel.

APPENDIX
PRELIMINARY LIST OF OTHER POEMS BY BRANWELL BRONTË, NOT PUBLISHED IN THIS EDITION

A Collection of Poems by Young Soult the Ryhmer (sic.). September 30th, 1829. In BPM. Unpublished.

Lausanne. A Dramatic Poem by Young Soult the Rhymer. December 1st–23rd, 1829. In BCH. Unpublished.

Caractacus. A Dramatic Poem by Patrick Bramwell Brontë. June 26th, 1830. In BCL. Published in SHCBM, vol. II, pp. 405–22.

The Revenge. A Tradgedy (sic) by Young Soult. November 23rd, 1830. In BPM. Unpublished.

Ode in Praise of the Twelves. In *Letters from an Englishman.* June 11th, 1831. In BCL. Published in SHCBM, vol. I, p. 124.

The Fate of Regina. May 1832. In BPM. Published in SHCBM, vol. I, pp. 159–65.

Ode on the Celebration of the Great African Games. June 26th, 1832. In BPM. Published in SHCBM, vol. I, pp. 165–9.

Poems in *Real Life in Verdopolis.* 1833. In BCL. Shortly to be published by Leeds University.

'Lets drink and be merry'. In unpublished and undated fragment in BCH.

'Round about round about, round about, Jolly Boys'. In unpublished and undated fragment in BCH.

'Sing hey for Cock Robin in regular verse'. In the *History of Angria*, vol. IX. December 11th, 1836. Unpublished.

To the horse black eagle which I rode at the battle of Zamorna. Undated. In BCNY. Published as Charlotte's, though the handwriting is Emily's, and the poem may be by Emily, in *The Complete Poems of Charlotte Brontë* (London, 1923), edited by C. K. Shorter, p. 238.

The Odes of Horace. 1840. In BCL. Published in SHCBM, vol. II, pp. 433–65.

INDEX OF FIRST LINES AND TITLES